John H. Sheffield

Observations on the manufactures, trade and present state of

Ireland

Part the first

John H. Sheffield

Observations on the manufactures, trade and present state of Ireland
Part the first

ISBN/EAN: 9783744735551

Printed in Europe, USA, Canada, Australia, Japan

Cover: Foto ©Suzi / pixelio.de

More available books at **www.hansebooks.com**

OBSERVATIONS

ON THE

MANUFACTURES, TRADE,

AND

PRESENT STATE OF IRELAND.

OBSERVATIONS

ON THE

MANUFACTURES,

TRADE,

AND

PRESENT STATE

OF

IRELAND.

By JOHN LORD SHEFFIELD.

————Non Hostem, inimicaque Castra,
Argivûm, vestras Spes Uritis————

PART THE FIRST.

————

DUBLIN:

Printed by J. Exshaw, for the Company of Booksellers.

MDCCLXXXV.

ADVERTISEMENT.

THE following Obfervations confift principally of materials, which were intended to be employed in another work. Such reputation as might have been acquired by attention to ftyle, ornament, and arrangement, is facrificed for the fake of ftating, while it is not too late, to the People of Great Britain, as well as to thofe of Ireland, fome facts, very interefting to them, and the knowledge of which poffibly may be of fervice with refpect to the queftions that are immediately to come before the Ligiflature.

As it is the management of thefe times to conceal from the Public the meafures that are intended, and as Minifters are fatif-fied with carrying certain queftions through Parliament without troubling themfelves about farther confiderations, the Author can only reafon on the general notoriety of thofe meafures; and he fhall be happy if at leaft part of that, to which it is faid the Govern-ment of the two kingdoms is pledged, may not prove true. A wifh to ferve both countries could alone have induced him to undertake as difagreeable a tafk as has ever fallen to his lot; and when he adds, that he is fenfible how much of what he ftates is likely, till well underftood, to be difpleafing to many in both countries, and unlikely to fuit their prejudices, he, on thofe accounts, hopes he may claim fome fort of merit. The Manufacturers of Britain will not be

fatisfied

fatisfied with all his doctrines; but in this he muft acquiefce for the prefent, as the experience of mankind tells us, that he who does not go every length with thofe who are interefted in a queftion, unavoidably rifks their good opinion.

In refpect to Ireland, it is painful to him in an extreme degree, to feem even to the moft prejudiced and unreafonable, to take a part againft her in the propofed arrangement with Britain, although it be only in the fingle point relative to the alteration of the Navigation Act; (for he cannot confider Protecting Duties as the wifh of that country at large;) but he is convinced that the generality of the People of Ireland are not aware of the whole extent of what has been defired on that head. He thinks them more reafonable than to form fuch a wifh, and is

fure

fure that when the confequences of the propofed alteration are laid before them, that
generofity of character, for which they are
diftinguifhed, muft prevent their continuing
to afk it; and it is only by ftating the cafe
of Britain ftrongly, that they are likely to
fee how unreafonable their claim is. If he
were even to confider the matter merely as
an Irifhman, who only cared for one part of
the empire, without the leaft regard for the
good and advantage of the whole, he would
not wifh the meafure to take place; becaufe,
if Britain fhould be furprifed into it, and the
alteration which is defired fhould ignorantly
and inconfiderately be made, he knows fhe
muft reclaim the conceffion fhe had made.
He moft ardently wifhes that fuch a mortifi-
cation may be fpared to Ireland, and that
the confequences which would refult from
it, may be prevented; and it is from this

wifh

wifh he is induced to take a part in the queftion. If merely from the fear of rifking
the unfavourable opinion of the People of
that Country, he fhould withhold the information which is in his power, or decline to
ftate matters which they ought to know, he
fhould feel himfelf unworthy to belong to
them; and he fhould think it difhoneft, in the
higheft degree, to enter on the fubject, without the refolution to treat it with the utmoft
impartiality. If he had prejudices, they
would probably be in favour of Ireland; and
perhaps their foundation might be traced
to the indignation he has formerly felt on
the treatment of that country. He is, however, equally interefted in the welfare of
both countries; and if he could fufpect himfelf of partiality to either of them, he moft
affuredly would have avoided the fubject.
His fituation in refpect to both, may and

ought

ought to prevent his being prejudiced; at leaft it is fuch as have ferved to give him fome knowledge of the interefts of each. He can have no motive for taking part againft either: his defire was to reprefent the real ftate of Ireland, as far as he could; to prevent mifchievous, idle, or unavailing clamour, and to counteract the defigns of thofe whofe object is to miflead and dupe the people.

It will give him great fatisfaction, if now, or in future, thefe Obfervations fhould lead to cool and difpaffionate examination, and in the end, to the mutual advantage of Great Britain and Ireland. He has ftated many facts; he has freely obferved upon thofe facts; and he hopes what he has remarked will give rife to reflections more ufeful and important.

The

The Tables will give a more correct idea of the state of Manufactures and Trade than could have been formed without them. A greater detail relative to parts of the Fisheries, to particular Manufactures, and to the trade to some countries, which, however, may not at present be of much consequence, should have been given, if there had been more time; but it being declared, that the very business, which is the principal object of these Observations, is immediately to be discussed, the information herein contained, such as it is, if delayed, would have come too late. If there had been leisure for the purpose, the author would have informed himself more fully on some other points, and the whole of what he now offers, might have appeared in a more finished state.

The

The author takes his leave, by wifhing his exertions, in favour of the great points which were the objects of the Navigation Laws, may not be confounded with narrow reftrictions relative to Manufactures and Commerce in general. He is rather difpofed to difcountenance and diffuade all reftraints, except thofe which are neceffary to fupport the Britifh Marine, to make Britain the mart of commerce, and to fecure to her Dominions the only return fhe can reap for the great expence of her foreign fettlements, namely, the monopoly of their fupply.

SHEFFIELD PLACE,
Jan. 25, 1785.

OBSER-

OBSERVATIONS

ON THE

MANUFACTURES, TRADE,

AND

PRESENT STATE OF IRELAND.

THE extenfions given in the courfe of the laſt ſix years to the trade and commerce of Ireland, are ſo recent in the recollection of both kingdoms, that it would be ſuperfluous to ſtate them in detail, notwithſtanding that they form the ground work of the following Obſervations. It would be equally ſuper-fluous to record, as the ſequel of that detail, the expreſſions uſed by a warm-hearted peo-ple, in the firſt flow of their ſentiments, under a change of circumſtances, moſt auſpi-

B   cious,

cious, it may be hoped, not only to them, but to the profperity of the whole Britifh empire, of which they form a confiderable part. Ireland had been placed by the hand of Providence in an advanced fituation between the two Continents, with excellent harbours towards the prevailing winds, and with the blefling of a fertile foil, and temperate climate; but fhe had neverthelefs long laboured in an inefficient and helplefs poverty, under a fyftem of reftraints equally pernicious, unwife, and unjuft.—It is natural, that the minds of her people fhould be elated on the emancipation of their induftry and activity; and perhaps a confiderable period muft elapfe, before they fettle fufficiently, either to afcertain the intrinfic value of their late acquifitions, or to adopt the means of applying thofe acquifitions to the beft effect: the beft habits of exertion are not fuddenly to be expected, though they may gradually be formed by the natural progreffion of a free commerce, and the foftering attention of a wife and fettled government.

From fuch attainments alone can refult that increafe of ftock and capital, which will

will be effentially neceffary, before Ireland
can avail herfelf of half her advantages. In
the mean time, many of her people feem
difpofed rather to feek farther fpeculative and
theoretical claims, than to cultivate the folid
benefits which they actually poffefs; whilft
others are rifquing and prejudicing the principal ftaple of their country, by forcing its
weak capital into too many and new branches.
Thefe unfteady and extravagant attempts
have a tendency not only to check trade,
but to provoke retaliation.

It is now well known among commercial
nations, that manufactures, forced, and fupported by bounties and prohibitions, cannot
long thrive, and are not only a lofs to the
community, in proportion to their expence,
but are farther pernicious, by tempting away
hands from the thriving manufactures. By
aiming at too many things at once, Ireland
will fucceed in none; but by purfuing certain ftaple articles that beft fuit her, fhe may
bring them to that perfection which will
command the markets. A country, of the
extent of Ireland, cannot expect to prevail
in every manufacture; fhe may trifle in many,

but

but she can excel at foreign markets in few;
and thofe, under proper management, may
be amply fufficient to give both employment
and affluence to her people.—It is the abundance of a manufacture, and the general
eftablifhment of it in a country, that makes
it both cheap and good.

The Irifh have been reprefented as being
lazy, and not difpofed to labour: they
are, however, of an active nature, and capable of the greateft exertions; and of as
good a difpofition as any nation, in the fame
ftate of improvement: their Generofity, Hof-
pitality, and Bravery, are proverbial: intelligence and zeal in whatever they undertake
will not be wanting: but it has been the
fafhion to judge of them from their out-
cafts. The Highlanders of Scotland, in
their ftate of nature, are alfo faid to be
indolent. That men who have very little
to do, fhould appear to do little, is not
ftrange; but who thinks them indolent,
when brought into fituations where they
can act? The Highlanders, indeed, have
ftill lefs reafon for indolence than the
Irifh; the country of the former with difficulty

culty can fubfift them, while the plentiful foil of Ireland encourages idlenefs.—Perhaps the cheapnefs of the common food, potatoes, may be juftly deemed a caufe of idlenefs, and confequently detrimental to manufactures; a fmall garden of potatoes will fubfift a family. Few countries have become completely induftrious, till the price of provifions was comparatively high. In how many towns, even of England, where the manufacturers can acquire a fubfiftence, without daily labour, do numbers of them confume the Monday and Tuefday in idlenefs? The common people of Ireland have not had the encouragement they might have had, if an unfortunate difference of religion had not prevailed, and if it had not been thought a neceffary policy, not to bring forward the mafs of the people who differed from the reformed church, but more efpecially becaufe their principles were fuppofed to be hoftile not only to the eftablifhed religion, but to the eftablifhed government. Lately, the fevere laws againft Roman Catholics have been repealed, and many unneceffary reftraints removed ; Reftraints which had fhamefully lafted too long, and can only be accounted for by the

acrimony

acrimony of the times in which they were
impofed. At prefent, perhaps, the improvement of Ireland is as-rapid as any country
ever experienced, nor will any thing check
it, but the weaknefs of human nature, an
ill-founded diffatisfaction, and an extravagant difpofition to innovation and change.

Jealoufies in trade between England, Scotland, and Ireland will ever occur. Such jealoufies in fome refpects ftimulate ufeful competition, and in the end improve manufactures, and promote trade. In the fermen-
tation and progrefs of fuch jealoufies, appeals
will frequently be made to the Legiflature,
and the interference of the Legiflature, when
obtained, will generally prove mifchievous
to the great interefts of commerce, without
giving fatisfaction to any of the contending
parties. In fuch inftances, however, much
good may be done by wife and diligent Mi-
niflers, who think it their duty to watch,
to inquire, and fully to inform themfelves.
Prejudices may be removed, miftakes may
be expofed, and fometimes ufeful regulations
may be introduced. This remark has been
fuggefted by the prefent circumftances of
Ireland :

Ireland: it has been already hinted, that she aims at more than her capital can possibly support, or in which she can possibly succeed: some of her people have been ignorantly eager in professing an unfriendly disposition to British manufactures, and perhaps persuade themselves, that under the term " Protecting Duties *," they can conceal their real meaning — the introduction of a plan of prohibitory duties. Happily, a confiderable proportion of the country thinks differently; and her Parliament, after a full investigation, rejected the measure, by a great majority. Yet, many still retain the disposition to occupy themselves, and disturb others, with attempts to introduce the mischievous system. A war of protecting duties and bounties, would answer to neither country; it would be extremely prejudicial to both; it would be ruinous to Ireland. The duty proposed would be prohibitory. If Ireland prohibits the staple manufacture of Great Britain, measures of a similar tendency would inevitably

---

* The duties proposed were so high as to be prohibitory of British, and therefore protecting Irish woollens.

and

and foon take place, refpecting the ftaple
manufacture of Ireland. Even by doing
much lefs, the great article of trade, on which
Ireland depends, her linen manufacture,
would be ruined; merely the placing Irifh
linens on the fame footing as foreign, would
almoft entirely prevent the ufe of them in
England, and be ten times more prejudicial
to Ireland, than her prohibition of Englifh
woollens would be to Great Britain   Mea-
furcs, too, might be purfued in that line,
which would forward and affift the interefts
of Great Britain, in the north of Europe.

But while prohibitory duties might bring
real evils on Ireland, they would fail of an-
fwering the end intended : they encourage
contraband trade; and no laws could prevent
the fmuggling of Britifh manufactures into
Ireland: the near neighbourhood and great
intercourfc give a facility, which could not
be obviated; nor could non-importation
agreements laft long. Ireland would foon
be tired of the impofitions of her own manufacturers, who would immediately avail
themfelves of the opportunity, and who
have raifed the clamour for the purpofe of
exacting

exacting an additional profit from the conſumer; ſhe would ſoon find ſhe cannot ſupply herſelf, and that efforts which may fall heavily on her in other reſpects, will ſerve her in no reſpect, but would greatly raiſe the price to her people of that eſſentially neceſſary article, cloathing.

Thoſe who examine with a jealous eye the advantages reſulting to Great Britain from her ſupplying Ireland with certain articles, ſhould obſerve the prodigious quantity of linen with which Ireland ſupplies Great Britain; the value of which, in the year ending the 25th of March, 1782, exceeded all the imports into Ireland of the growth, produce, and manufacture of Great Britain: it amounted to 24,692,072 yards, value 1,646,138l. 2s. 8d. Iriſh money * ; beſides

* See the table No. I. The author inadvertently took the year of the greateſt export, but the average of four years, ending the 25th of March, 1778, and previous to the exports of Ireland being hurt by her nonimportation agreements, (which they were) was in value 1,455,990l. 7s. 5½d. In conſequence of thoſe agreements, and other circumſtances, the value of linen exports

fides linen yarn, to the amount of 169,126*l.*
10*s.* In the fame year, all the imports into
Ireland, of the produce and manufacture
of Great Britain, amounted to 1,486,317*l.*
2s. 4d. ; of which the quantity and value
of woollens was as follows, and it happened
to be the year of the greatest import :

	Yards.		£.	*s.*	*d.*
Old drapery, -	362,824	- Value	253,976	0	0
New drapery, -	547,336	- ――	68,417	0	0
			322,393	0	0

And it is farther worthy of notice, that, in
the fame year, when Ireland exported

	Yards.	£.	*s.*	*d.*
To Britain - -	24,692,072 Value	1,646,138	2	8
She exported to all the reft of the world only - -	278,231	―― 18,548	14	8
And coloured linens	113,655¼	―― 5,984	9	9
Total export -	25,083,958¼			

ports fell, in 1781, to 961,455*l.* The next year, 1782,
however, as ufually happens on fuch occafions, it increafed, and to the great amount above mentioned.

Moreover

Moreover it may be obferved, that Ireland does not grow a fufficiency of wool of a proper fort, if fhe fhould manufacture the whole of it, to fupply her own confumption of woollens ; and that fhe could not get the fame articles cheaper from any other country than from Great Britain. At the fame time, a great proportion of the linens which Great Britain takes from Ireland might be got cheaper from the north of Europe : and Ireland fhould remember, that, of all her exports in the fame year, viz. 1782, Britain alone took 2,699,825l. 13s. 8½d. How trifling, comparatively, the remainder of her exports, will appear under the head of her general trade.

The year 1783 was not exactly the period when we fhould have expected the woollen manufacturers of Ireland to be moft clamorous, and that they fhould enter upon the moft violent meafures. Unprejudiced people, at leaft, will think that the complaints were ill timed ; and the following account of the exports of woollens * will prove it. It

* Exclufive of frize, flannels, ftockings, and mixtures of woollens, and hats.

fhould

fhould be remarked, that the export was allowed only during a fmall part of the year 1780.

Old drapery exported from Ireland, year ending the 25th of March,

		Ya ds.
1780	——	494
1781	——	3,740
1782	——	4,633
1783	——	40,589

New drapery exported from Ireland, year ending the 25th of March,

		Yards.
1780	——	8,653
1781	——	286,859
1782	——	336,607
1783	——	538,061

And as a farther proof of the increafe of the woollen manufacture in Ireland, it appears that the export of wool, woollen, and worfted yarn had decreafed above half. The average export of the laft, which is the principal article, for feven years, ending the 25th of March, 1770, was 142,890 ftones. The average of the fame number

of

of years, ending the 25th of March, 1783, was 66,679 ſtones.

It ſhould be remarked, that at the time Ireland, on the opening of her ports for exportation of woollens, made an effort to ſend the above quantity to foreign markets, ſhe increaſed her imports of woollens. This helps to ſhew an advantage in taking away that unreaſonable reſtraint, and ſhould convince us, that the more Ireland exports, the greater her neceſſity will be of import-ing from England. Ireland was enabled to work up her wool in thoſe articles which beſt ſuited it, and to the greateſt advantage, for foreign markets, inſtead of employing it to diſadvantage, and increaſed the impor-tation of ſuch woollen articles as England could furniſh cheaper than ſhe could make them.

On an average of four years, from 1763 to 1767, Ireland imported,

		Yards.
New drapery,	-	281,557
Old drapery,	-	196,047

On

On an average of four years, ending the 25th of March, 1783, Ireland imported,

Yards.

New drapery, - 390,095
Old drapery, - 281,406

But the increafe of the importation of the principal article, new drapery, was only about one-fifth of the increafed manufacture for exportation.

Yards.

Increafed quantity of new drapery
imported, - - - 108,538
New drapery exported, year ending
the 25th of March, 1783, - 538,061
And the export of the latter article, the fame year, exceeded the import near 120,000 yards. And farther it fhould be remarked, that, in the very year when fo large a quantity of Irifh woollens were able to meet Britifh at foreign market, a duty was afked on Britifh to enable Irifh woollens to meet them at the markets of Ireland.

It fhould be obferved, however, that the manufacture of woollens was not fo much increafed as appears from the ftated export of the four laft years: a certain proportion

of

of thofe articles, which now appear in the exports, were fmuggled from Ireland previous to 1778, at which time the prohibition to export was taken off with refpect to the Britifh plantations in America, or the Weft Indies, or any Britifh fettlement on the coaft of Africa. Before that time, woollens could not be mentioned in the Cuftom-houfe ftate of the exports of Ireland; but now that the export is opened to all the world, by the acts of 1780 and 1781, it is found that two-thirds of her woollens go to Portugal, to which place fhe probably fent nearly as much before. The importation, however, of moft of thofe articles into Portugal, both then and now, was, and is, fuppofed to be prohibited by Portugal: and it fhould farther be remarked, that as woollens are not fubject to duties on export, the vanity, and other motives of merchants may have induced them to enter greater quantities for exportation than they have really fent.

But fome of the violent *friends* of Ireland fay, we will have non-importation agreements, protecting duties, prohibitions, &c.

If you don't take our linens, we will not only refuse Britifh, but alfo foreign and colonial commodities from Great Britain, and the two laft amount to near 8co,oool. yearly *.

It will be anfwered, that Great Britain gives to the principal manufacture of Ireland every advantage in every part of her dominions, and may moft reafonably expect that her own principal manufacture fhould, in return, have equal advantages in Ireland, which they have not. The linens Great Britain takes from Ireland are five times the value of

* Some of thefe pretended friends of Ireland, who, whether actuated by an honeft and zealous ignorance, or by worfe motives, are likely to prove her greateft enemies, have been driven, by the abfurdity of their pretenfion, into the moft contradictory mode of reafoning: for, on fome occafions, they treat as a feparate kingdom, not only independent, but utterly unconnected; on others, they claim as a part of the empire, entitled (according to an inaufpicious phrafe) to a reciprocity of equal rights. For the fake of fairnefs in argument, it is to be wifhed they would chufe one predicament or the other. The attempt to blend both characters, is not calculated to promote either candour or perfpicuity.

the

the woollens taken from Britain. Ireland takes nothing from her that fhe can get cheaper or better elfewhere, except the commodities of the Britifh Weft Indies; and in return, fhe has an advantage in her fhare of the monopoly of the Weft India markets, and fhe has no pretenfion to trade with the plantations on any other principle. Whatever elfe fhe takes of colonial or foreign articles, is for her own convenience; and before Ireland cuts off all commercial intercourfe with Great Britain, it may be worth her while to confider the proportion of the exports of Ireland taken by Great Britain, as already mentioned : it will appear that her exports to all other parts did not, in the fame year, much exceed, in value, the twentieth part of her exports to Britain, and in that part are included the exports to the Britifh plantations, which would be found no fmall part, but which would be alfo loft, as fuch proceedings on the part of Ireland, would naturally tend to interrupt all commercial intercourfe with the Britifh colonies and empire. Great Britain has found it poffible to exift, and to maintain, her commercial affluence againft the combinations and inter-

D   ruptions

ruptions of many principal markets in both Continents; but Ireland has not yet made the experiment, how she could exist without the markets of the British dominions: and when Ireland shall be so madly advised, neither fleets nor armies, nor any extraordinary expence, will be neceſſary, on the part of Great Britain, to convince her she is wrong: hurtful it may be for a time; but in the end, and ſoon, Great Britain muſt prevail: Ireland cannot: for it does not appear where she will get what she wants, and that she has credit with other nations to the amount she would require; or where she will diſpoſe of what she has, if she ſhould have no intercourſe with Great Britain or the British colonies. It will be found, that it is the intercourſe with the British dominions that enables Ireland to trade in any conſiderable degree.

This hoſtile mode of argument is, however, very improperly brought on by Ireland. It would ill become either kingdom to encourage even the difcuſſion of ſuch propoſitions; and the ſeat of empire could never adopt the meaſures hinted at, unlefs

unavoidably

unavoidably driven to them. Under the prefent enlarged and free fyftem of commerce, there is demand and trade enough in the world to occupy the utmoft induftry of both countries. This kind of fcrutiny then, fhould not take place; but if Ireland will force it forwards, the inveftigation will not prove either beneficial or flattering to her. She might at leaft be fatisfied until fhe finds herfelf in the fituation of being able to fay to Britain, My ports fhall be open to all your manufactures, free of all duties, on condition that your ports fhall be open to mine in the like manner.—Ireland is hardly in the fituation to agree to that propofal; and the generality of Englifhmen would probably at firft object : but there is nothing in it which fhould alarm them. Great Britain could underfell Ireland in moft manufactures : fuch is the predominancy of fuperior fkill, induftry, and capital, over low-priced labour, and comparatively very few taxes.—Many would object to the extenfion of this idea to raw materials, as well as to manufactures ; but even the permitting Englifh wool and fullers' earth, charged with inland carriage, freight, com-

D 2   miffion.

million, &c. to go to Ireland, need not alarm, on the ground of giving a superiority to the latter *. Let it be remembered, that England underfels other countries even in the manufacture of Spanish wool. The wool grower in England, who submits the monopoly of his wool to the manufac-

turers

* The English woollen manufacturers will say, the export of wool from England to Ireland must greatly reduce the price of wool in the latter country, and, with the low price of labour, enable the Irish manufacturers to underfel them, and of course will urge the same objections as they do, to the export of wool to France. On the other hand, the wool growers of Ireland will oppose the reduction of the price, which is from 3s. to 4s. per stone higher than in England: and it is said, until mutton becomes a more common food in Ireland, and the price consequently rises, it would not answer to keep up the present number of sheep, if not encouraged by the high price of wool. The increase of tillage in that country, it is supposed, will naturally decrease the number of sheep, unless, by a mode of agriculture superior to the present, and a more general introduction of artificial grasses, turneps, &c. she should be enabled to keep a greater stock. Yet the following account of the great fair of Ballinasloe, in Connaught, seems to prove that the number of sheep was increasing in Ireland. Tillage, however, has made, comparatively, very little progress in that part of the kingdom.

ABSTRACT

turers, might receive fome relief. This, however, is a nice point, and does not require any difcuffion at prefent.

ABSTRACT of WOOL fold at the different Fairs of Ballinafloe, from July, 1771, to July, 1778, inclufive.

Date	No. of Bags fold.		No. of do. unfold.		Total.
1771, July, —	1492	—	15	—	1507
1772, ——, —	1286	—	11	—	1297
1773, ——, —	1550	—	33	—	1583
1774, ——, —	1623	—	25	—	1648
1775, ——, —	1574	—	61	—	1635
1776, ——, —	1857	—	64	—	1921
1777, ——, —	2004	—	70	—	2074
1778, ——, —	1359	—	553	—	1912
Total No. —	12745		832		13577
Yearly average	1593		104		1697

N. B. The failure in 1778 arofe from the ftagnation of credit, and a decreafe of the demand for bay yarn from England.

SHEEP fold at the faid Fair.

Date	fold.		unfold.		Total.
1771, Oct. —	51950	—	——	—	51950
1772, ——, —	53632	—	50	—	53682
1773, ——, —	55242	—	6390	—	61682
1774, ——, —	60796	—	5302	—	66633
1775, ——, —	63904	—	1020	—	64924
1776, ——, —	66873	—	639	—	67512
1777, ——, —	63792	—	12743	—	76535
1778, ——, —	44894	—	31588	—	76482

EQUAL

EQUAL DUTIES.

Inftead of protecting or prohibitory duties, which would not anfwer the purpofe of the promoters of them ; or an entire removal cf all duties between the two countries, for which, it has been already obferved, Ireland is not yet ripe ; perhaps to lower the Britifh inoperative duties to the Irifh, would be the leaft exceptionable meafure : it would leave the trade nearly on its prefent footing; and it is the intereft of the Britifh manufacturers that the duties fhould be equalized, rather by lowering them here, than by raifing them in Ireland.

To this many of the Englifh woollen manufacturers would object : but if Great Britain fhould take off the heavy duties on the importation of Irifh woollens into Britain, it would not be of the advantage to Ireland that fhe imagines, nor a material check to the Britifh manufacturers of wool. On the part of England and Scotland, it may be worth while to confider, that lowering high duties to the fcale of the Irifh, while it will take away the arguments, and may

fupprefs

fupprefs the clamours of the difcontented in Ireland, cannot hurt their own manufactures. The heavy duties on the importation of Irifh manufactures into Great Britain are prohibitory: they are in general unneceffary; and only ferve to irritate and keep alive prejudice and falfe notions. For while Great Britain can underfel Ireland, even in the home markets of the latter, in almoft every manufacture, charged with land carriage in Britain, freight, duties on landing, and commiffion; and notwithftanding the bounties given by the Dublin Society, or Parliament; Ireland furely could not fell any quantity of manufactures at Britifh markets, or much more to foreign countries, than fhe does now. She may, indeed, be able to export, in the courfe of trade, and to affort in cargoes, to a certain extent, fome articles which fhe cannot make cheaper than England, but not in quantities to prejudice the latter. Perhaps, one of the ftrongeft objections at prefent to opening the Britifh markets to the Irifh manufactures, is the danger of fmuggling cargoes from the Continent of Europe.

Ireland, it is faid, can afford fome broad ftuffs, durants, fhalloons, and fhags, cheaper than

than Great Britain : her flannels are as good,
if not the beft : her blankets are as cheap :
and in hair plufh and druggets, fhe can rival
France : but if it be true, fhe has not a fufficiency of wool to carry thofe manufactures
to any great extent. The very price of that
article, which is generally 3s. or 4s. at leaft
per ftone of 16 pounds higher than in England, as already mentioned, muft prevent
her ; for it was the low price of labour
alone which enabled Ireland to fend woollen or worfted yarn to Britain *.

It is, therefore, really the fuperior quality and cheapnefs of Britifh manufacture,
that prevents import from Ireland. Mr.
Arthur Young has inquired, why give in
linen what you deny in other fabrics ? Irifh
linen has all the advantages of a freedom
from a great variety of excifes, which the
manufacturers of Englifh linen labour under,
and yet the Englifh manufacture, fo bur-
thened, thrives, from there being a difference
in the fabrics, and as great a difference would
be in other fabrics. The fixed trade, capital,

* It appears from the Table, No. I. that the quantity
of wool fhe fent was trifling.

and

and fkill of England, at prefent at leaft, bid
defiance to the no excifes of Ireland.   If Ireland cannot meet Englifh manufactures in
her own markets, notwithftanding her advantages at home, how can fhe meet England to any great extent at foreign markets,
without thofe advantages.   New fabrics require new capitals, new eftablifhments, and
new exertions.

Taking the year of the greateft export of
woollens from Ireland, viz. 1783, we find,
the quantity of wool, woollen, and worfted
yarn exported, greatly decreafed, and that
the whole quantity of wool exported,
was   -   -   2063 ftones, 10lbs.
and the whole quantity
   of woollen yarn,   -   440 ftones.
    worfted yarn,   -   66677 ftones.
It is clear, that even if thefe quantities had
been of the fort of wool fit for making the
woollens that Ireland imports, it would not
have been fufficient ; for, in the fame year
fhe imported near 800,000 yards, viz.

                   Yards.
   New drapery,   -   420,415$\frac{1}{2}$
   Old drapery,   -   371,871
          E   and

and until Ireland becomes a country of fhep-
herds, and prefers fheep-walks to tillage,
and depopulation to population, fhe cannot
import much lefs. She has grown rich, and
more populous; her demand for woollens
has increafed, and is likely to increafe much
more : Great Britain, therefore, has little to
apprehend; but the confumer in Ireland muft
pay whatever additional expence is thrown
on woollens imported; he muft pay the extraordinary expence of fmuggling, or whatever duty may be laid.

Equal duties muft be low; if high, they
would be protecting or prohibitory duties
againft England. It is obvious, that whatever
they are, they muft fall on the confumer in
Ireland, who muft have thefe articles in
fome fhape.

As to the fyftem of no duties in either
country, if that fhould be propofed, Ireland
will dread the extinction of fome of her
prefent manufactures of woollen. She will
recollect the effect of the Methuen treaty
with Portugal, by which Britifh woollens
were introduced, and the Portuguefe manufactures

factures of wool, which had been eftablifhed above twenty years before, were crufhed; for although that treaty, on the face of it, appears fimple, and the principles of it not reciprocal*, its object was as now ftated; it was underftood fo at the time, and it fuc-ceeded. The conduct, however, of Portugal was not impolitic. It was not poffible for her to carry her woollen manufacture to any great extent, or nearly to fupply her people and colonies. She got a great advantage, as to her wines, by the treaty; and her people were fupplied cheaper with the neceffary article, woollens.

Ireland, perhaps had better be content to remain as fhe is: her duties on her imports, which are 5 per cent. on the cuftom rate, and 5 per cent. more on the rate for import excife, give advantage to her own manu-factures. Her import duties confift of cuf-toms payable like the Britifh, and alfo of an

* Britifh woollens were not to be admitted on better terms than thofe of other countries, although the wines of Portugal were to pay in England lower duties than any other wines.

excife,

excife, called import excife, which is bon-
dable until the goods are taken out for confumption, when it is to be paid, and has
therefore got the name of excife. Draperies,
however, from Britain, do not pay the import excife, only the cuftom.

The manufactures of wool certainly have
increafed, and are increafing; under their
prefent circumftances; and a fufficient quantity is manufactured, to fhew that extraordinary meafures are not neceffary. The clamour on this fubject has been nearly confined
to Dublin, the moft improper place for the
manufacture, and where it is much to be
wifhed it may not flourifh; where a difpofition has appeared rather to riot and infult
the Legiflature, than to cultivate, with induftry, the benefits of an enlarged and free
commerce. The feat of expence and licentioufnefs is not a fit place for the principal
branch of the woollen manufacture, or for
any other, except flight fabrics, which depend upon changable fafhion, and muft be
under the eye of the fhopkeeper.

A good

A good deal has been already said, relative to woollens, which applies to the general requifition from Ireland, that the manufactures of both countries fhall be liable to equal duties, on import into each other. The Britifh duties, when compared with the Irifh, will not, by any means, give to an indifferent perfon the impreffion of fairnefs and equality, or even of utility; they have, however, in truth, little or no effect, except to caufe uneafinefs, to irritate, and feemingly to juftify the idea of protecting duties. Whilft fimilar Britifh commodities command the markets of Ireland, from their fuperior quality and cheapnefs, though charged with the Irifh duties, what chance of fale have the fame articles of Irifh manufacture at Britifh markets, even without a duty? An alteration, therefore, would benefit Ireland, or prejudice Britain, much lefs than is imagined. This argument, perhaps, it will be faid, may anfwer for the year 1785, but may not apply to the probable future ftate of manufactures in Ireland, in 1800— that the progrefs of manufactures in the two countries, one of which pays taxes, to the amount of fourteen millions, and the other

of

of one million only, little or no part of
which can be faid to fall on manufactures,
is not likely to keep an equal pace. To
which it may be replied, that the price of
labour, and expences of all kinds, will undoubtedly increafe with the increafe of manufactures in Ireland; that one million of
taxes is lefs difproportionate to the wealth
of that country, than may appear to thofe
who have not examined their comparative
riches, and that if Great Britain makes no
improper facrifices, fhe will maintain her
prefent fuperiority. It merits, therefore,
the confideration of the Britifh manufacturers, whether the fale of their goods
will not be much more hurt by the diffatisfaction of Ireland, and non-importation agreements, (although the latter will
not be effectual or lafting) than by a
reduction of the duties on the import of
Irifh manufactures. The duty on woollens,
imported into Britain from Ireland, amount
to a prohibition. At the fame time Ireland
has laid duties equal to a prohibition in favour of England, on draperies from all other
countries; they are alfo in favour of her
cwn woollen manufacture.

SCHEDULE.

Schedule of Duties on the under-mentioned Articles in both Countries.

Import Duties payable in Britain.		Import Duties payable in Ireland.	
£. s. d.		£. s. d.	
2 0 $6\frac{4}{20}$	All woollens or old drapery, per yard,	0 0 $5\frac{10}{20}$	
0 5 $11\frac{10}{20}$	Stuffs of all kinds, made or mixed with wool, or new drapery, per yard,	0 0 $1\frac{4}{26}$	
29 15 10	Cotton and linen manufactures, and cotton mixed, for every 100l. value, on oath,	9 18 $5\frac{8}{16}$	
65 10 10	Linen cloth, printed, for every 100l. value, on oath,	9 18 $5\frac{8}{16}$	
65 10 10	Leather manufactures, for every 100l. value, on oath,	9 18 $5\frac{8}{20}$	
0 3 $11\frac{13}{20}$ 35 15 0	Checks, the piece not above 10 yards, besides in Britain, for every 100l. value, on oath,	0 1 $3\frac{17}{16}$	
5 6 $9\frac{10}{20}$	Sugar, refined, per cwt.	1 13 $11\frac{15}{20}$	
4 12 $1\frac{7}{20}$	Starch, per cwt.	0 6 $5\frac{12}{20}$	

Many other inftances might be added, not lefs remarkable : and Ireland does not a little complain of want of reciprocity on the fubjects of malt, beer, &c.

Average

Average of three years, ending Chriſtmas 1777, of the duties ariſing on all goods and merchandize exported from England into Ireland :

	£.	s.	d.
Britiſh goods,	9136	16	8¾
Foreign goods,	719	18	5¼

Average of the ſame years of the duties ariſing on all goods, &c. imported from Ireland into England,   -   £. 6490 11   1½

Average of three years, ending the 5th of January, 1778, of the duties ariſing on all goods, &c. exported from Scotland into Ireland,   -   -   -   £. 602   0   7¼

Average of the ſame years of the duties ariſing on all goods, &c. imported from Ireland into Scotland,   -   £. 585 13   1
It may be obſerved, that the larger ſum is received in that country, where the markets in general are open to the other upon low duties, and that the balance of the general interchange is in favour of Ireland.

BOUNTIES.

BOUNTIES.

As to bounties, Ireland complains of that given by Great Britain on the export of fail cloth to Ireland; fhe finds it extremely hurtful to her fabric, and complains with double force, as it is a branch of her linen manufacture. She will be juftifiable in counteracting, by duties or regulations, all bounties given on export to Ireland, where fhe has fimilar manufactures: but the Britifh act adds to the bounty now given, as much more as at any time Ireland fhall impofe as a duty on the import of Britifh fail cloth into Ireland. The mode of conteft may become ridiculous.

DRAWBACKS.

As to drawbacks, it is defired that Great Britain fhall allow a full drawback on all commodities fhe exports to Ireland, on the principle, that the country which confumes the article, fhould have the ufe of the revenue raifed upon it. Refined fugar and hops are

F   put

put on that footing. It is not unreafonable, and it is encouraging to trade. It fhould always be remembered, that whatever part of a duty is not drawn back, is a tax on the carrying trade.

NAVIGATION ACT,

Colonial and Foreign COMMODITIES, &c.

Exclufive of the feveral difficulties refpecting the interchange of native commodities and manufactures, new pretenfions are brought forward, relative to the commerce refulting from the intercourfe, which has been opened to Ireland, with the Britifh Colonies, Plantations, and Settlements, and alfo relative to the interchange of Afiatic, African, and American produce. Ireland defires that the conftruction of the navigation laws may be altered, fo as to admit Colonial and foreign commodities from her warehoufes into Great Britain, in like manner as they pafs from thence into Ireland.

The

The objections to this, on the part of the people of Great Britain, are numerous and strong. It is said, that the advantage in queftion is the only one fhe has referved to herfelf, as head of the empire, for the vaft expence of fupporting foreign connections, eftablifhing, maintaining, and protecting colonies, which alone belong to her; that when fhe gave the participation of all other advantages, fhe referved this alone; which if fhe yields, there are few other points in which the navigation laws will be of fervice to her, relatively to Ireland. It is the only commercial part of them that is of confequence; it is the fingle privilege, which leaves any gleam of hope to Great Britain, that fhe fhall weather the confequences of the war, to which Ireland contributes nothing. In fact, the very operation in queftion of the navigation laws, is the only barrier remaining againft the migration of her manufacturers and merchants. The preamble of her navigation and other laws, give the reafons, for confining Colonial and foreign trade, viz. " Not only for the fake of employing and " increafing Englifh fhipping and feamen, " and fecuring a vent for woollen and other

" many-

" manufactures; but also to make this king-
" dom a staple of the commodities of those
" plantations, as well as of the commodities
" of other countries for the supplying them;
" (it being the usage of other nations to
" keep their plantation trade to themselves)
" and farther, if Colonial commodities
" should be taken from any part but the
" plantations, that the trade of them would
" thereby in a great measure be diverted
" from hence, and carried elsewhere; His
" Majesty's customs and other revenues
" much lessened, the fair trader prejudiced,
" and this kingdom not continue a staple
" of plantation commodities, nor that vent
" for the future of the victual and other
" native commodities of this kingdom."—
Such was the declared principle of the navigation act *, and such certainly was the principle of those acts † which passed explana-
tory of it; and the act which repeals so much
of the navigation laws, as prevented a direct

---

* 12th Charles II.

† 15th Charles II. and the 22d and 23d Charles II.
confirms the intention of the 15th, to prohibit importation of, &c. from Ireland, and restrain it to Britain.

intercourse

intercourfe between Ireland and the Britifh plantations, does not repeal the 12th Geo. III. chap. 55. * which prohibits the import from Ireland into Britain, of rum, fugar, coffee, and other American and Afiatic goods: nor can it be faid, that it appears from the act, which extended the trade of Ireland, to have been the intention of the Legiflature to make any alteration in that refpect. The cuftom-houfe practice has continued the fame fince, as it was before the paffing the act, and during upwards of a century, viz. not to admit the articles in queftion from Ireland. Nor can it be objected as inequitable, that Britain declines to take from Ireland commodities which that country takes from her. Ireland takes them from the mother country of the colonies; and, ftrictly confidering the matter, fhe has no rightful claim to get them

* Although this act was paffed to bind both countries, and thofe parts which purport to have an internal operation in the levying of forfeitures or penalties, or are directory to the officers of the Irifh revenue, may now be confidered as a dead letter; yet, the fpirit and intention of this act is clear, and that part which was intended to bind Britain, and which prohibits importation of the produce of Afia, Africa, and America, from Ireland, is ftill in force.

in

in any other way from any colonies, except
through the indulgence of the mother country of thofe colonies. Ireland takes little
from Britain of any kind, that fhe can get
cheaper elfewhere : fhe takes as it fuits her,
and fhe cannot object to Britain the price fhe
pays for Weft-India commodities, or the
giving the monopoly of her markets to the
produce of the Britifh plantations, as in return fhe has her fhare of the monopoly of
their markets. It would be an extreme folly
in Great Britain to maintain fettlements at
an immenfe expence of public money, and
to confine herfelf to the purchafe of their
produce at an unreafonable price, and to the
private detriment of individual confumers,
and then to put it in the power of another
country to purchafe, with the manufactures
of that country, the produce of fuch fettlements, and to retail them afterwards in the
Britifh market. The mifchiefs connected
with that point alone are too obvious to
be infifted on. It is farther to be obferved,
that trade is of fo delicate a nature, that it is
almoft impoffible to conjecture, how reftraints
either laid on, or taken off, will operate—
that it is prudent to apprehend every evil, of
which

which there is any probability, however diftant—to fear the effect of a conceffion, the whole extent of which it is at leaft difficult to forefee—and that it is unneceffary to rifk the confequences of the meafure in queftion. The maintainers of thefe objections will add, that Great Britain was greatly benefited by being the depot of American, Afiatic, and African produce; and fhe has reafon to expect, that fhe will ftill be fo in a very confiderable degree. The mere mercantile gain is an inconfiderable object, when compared with the various advantages of the exchange of commodities; with the value and quantity of induftry, which the above fyftem of trade diffufes throughout the community; with the employment given to an incredible number of people; with the various expences incurred from the time of the arrival, until the re-exportation of the commodities, in landing, ftoring, afforting, re-packing, porterage, re-fhipping, &c.; but above all, the increafe of fhipping, and of feamem. The value of trade is beft afcertained by the quantity of employment and maintenance given to the induftrious part of the community. In fhort, it would be entering into a wide field,

field, to enumerate the various advantages which centered in this country, in confequence of the trade in queftion ; befides the great objeƈt of freight, which is juft as much a part of commerce as import and export. It cannot, therefore, be expeƈted, that Great Britain fhould create and eftablifh a dangerous competition for objeƈts of fuch effential importance to her; and in a country, which has peculiar advantages, from fituation and other circumftances, which fhe herfelf has not. It is highly proper, that Great Britain fhould encourage the manufaƈtures and other trade of Ireland : but there is great difference between fuch conduƈt and changing her whole commercial and colonial fyftem; encouraging the migration of men, capitals, and trade, with their mercantile knowledge, their fteadinefs of exertion, their induftry, and talents for commerce, to produce an unequal competition againft herfelf. Ireland has her advantages—let her enjoy them: Great Britain will readily adopt and promote any meafure, by which fhe can benefit Ireland, without materially injuring herfelf: but fhe cannot reafonably be expeƈted to embrace meafures tending to divert the colonial trade, and to tear.

from

from her own merchants, and from her own people, all the beneficial security of an important branch of trade, which so peculiarly belongs to her; of which only she has made any reserve or exception; and on which her continuing to be the staple for colonial and foreign articles depends, and also her naval strength, her population, revenue, and public credit :—She has entirely relaxed all navigation and colonial principles in favour of Ireland, except the point in question. She communicated every other advantage of import and export of colonial articles to the sister kingdom; but wisely abstained from giving the power of importing them from Ireland into her own market. She has given to Ireland the liberty of supplying herself, and any part of the world that will admit Irish vessels, with the produce of the British colonies; and it is surely very unreasonable that she should not be allowed the exclusive right of supplying herself with her own colonial produce. She cannot, therefore, without being regardless of her essential interests, promote still farther the export of colonial articles from Ireland, and encourage the Irish, or rather, the British

G   merchants,

merchants, who would gradually remove
their capitals, to fpcculate largely to her difadvantage : and unlefs Great Britain fhould
yield the advantage in queftion, and thereby
furnifh a new and near market, it will not
anfwer to Ireland to fpeculate confiderably
in articles for which fhe has not ready and
certain cuftomers. She will fear a fuper-
fluity ; and inftead of being a dangerous
competitor with Great Britain in the trade
in queftion, fhe will not very fpcedily import a fufficiency even for her own demand
and confumption. If Ireland could become
the entrepôt, in a confiderable degree, for
Europe, which would naturally happen, if
allowed for Great Britain, fhe would get
poffeffion of thofe articles, and thofe advantages, which would fupply capital :—She
would have the capitals and credit of other
countries to furpafs the mother country ;
and as there would be then no difficulty in
importing into this country from Ireland,
whenever the market fuited, the merchants
of Britain would be encouraged to avail
themfelves of the peculiar fituation of Ireland, to carry on the whole of their re-export trade through that country, and they
would

would find means of supplying three fourths, perhaps, of their cargoes from thence. They would fix houses in Ireland, tranfmit capitals, and by degrees, migrate thither themfelves. The tobacco trade would inevitably fettle in Ireland. The towns that have the re-export trade in Great Britain will loudly complain; and Glafgow, Liverpool, Briftol, &c. will forefee and feel the approaching lofs of their prefent local and other advantages. Such are the fpeculations of Ireland in forming the prefent requifitions! Her object is to become the mart in Europe for the trade of America, for which fhe is fo well fuited by her weftern fituation, immediately open to the ocean, and acceffible almoft with every wind; her veffels often croffing the Atlantic in a fhorter time than the fhipping of London require to clear the Channel. In addition, her fhips can be victualled infinitely cheaper; and every neceffary of life being low, as well as public taxes, the general charge of conducting trade will be proportionably lefs. In confidering this matter, we fhould look forward to the period when Ireland fhall have

attained

attained a much more fignificant commercial
fituation than her prefent, and be able to
trade on as good a footing to the weftern
world as England. She would, from her
fituation and advantages, fupply Great Britain with American produce—The gain of
Ireland, by fuch a meafure, can refult only
from the lofs of Great Britain.

Some farther obfervations, perhaps, are
worthy the attention of the Britifh merchant, the colonial proprietor, and the often-
fible fervants of the Crown. The two firft
claffes, as refpecting themfelves ; the latter,
as having a reference to the Public. The
vaft fums that are due from the Colonies to
the merchants of Great Britain, furely
fhould be confidered. That this extenfive
credit was given on the ftrength of laws
now fubfifting, and which have hitherto
been deemed as part of the colonial conftitution.—That any material deviation may
deftroy that confidence which their immediate and exclufive connection with this
country has infpired, the bafis on which
their credit has hitherto been built, and
the

the beft fecurity to this country for the payment of their debts.

The planters, or colonial proprietors, fhould alfo be induced to reflect on the confequences of any innovation, fhould it appear, that, as Ireland may import many of the articles which are produced in our colonies from other countries, fome of thofe articles may, through that medium, be clandeftinely introduced into Great Britain, and thereby deprive them of the very great advantage they now derive from the exclufive fupply of this country. Befides, it may be fuggefted, that if any regulations take place, which tend to leffen the fecurity of the creditor, that the merchants of Britain will immediately call in their debts, and in future refufe lending fuch fums as they have heretofore done; which is fo effential to the welfare and profperity of the colonies, that it is the event which, of all others, they ought moft to dread. So far the intereft of individuals, or rather of fome particular bodies of men may be affected, fhould the import of colonial and foreign articles be allowed into England from Ireland.

In

In the important article of Revenue, great confequences alfo are to be expected; which, though interefting to every perfon, applies more immediately to thofe fervants of the Crown who have the direction of the public treafure, and whofe duty it is to find equitable and adequate fupplies for the exigencies of the State. Thefe official fervants of the public fhould reflect ferioufly on the confequences which may accrue from the enormous frauds that may be introduced by this means to the detriment of fo interefting a branch of national refource, as the import duties on tobacco, wines, rum, and many other articles. Notwithftanding all the regulations and reftrictions which can be devifed, it may in a great meafure counteract thofe ufeful and beneficial arrangements, which have lately been made for the prevention of fmuggling; and which, we are told from the higheft authority, have fucceeded fo well. Should fuch an alteration take place, it will hold out every encouragement for the revival of that baneful and deftructive mode of traffic. As the duties on the importation of moft articles are much higher in England than in Ireland, it will induce the fraudulent trader

to

to run the rifque of introducing them into this country, more particularly, as the proximity of the two iflands, and the number of ports conftantly open to them, will afford every convenience they can wifh, either as to forming depofits for their goods, or the readieft means of bringing them over hither.

One other circumftance it may likewife be neceffary to mention, as being more favourable to the fmugglers than any thing they have ever yet experienced, namely, the fecurity they will derive from an exemption from feizure, unlefs they happen to be taken in the act of landing their goods ; which is not very probable, on fo wide and extenfive a coaft : for in that cafe, their veffels will be permitted, in the ports of Ireland, to clear out for Great Britain, with thofe articles on board ; and of courfe, being admiffible here, they will be exempt from feizure on their whole paffage, as well as on their approaching the coaft, even in the Thames, protected by clearances; and fhould they be fo clofely watched at any time as not to have an opportunity of landing their goods clandeftinely,

or,

or, in the event of bad weather, being obliged to feek the fhelter of fome Britifh harbour; in either of thefe cafes they will remain fecure, and can always fave their veffels and cargoes by bringing them to an entry, and paying the duty on thofe particular goods; fo that, in the event moft unfavourable to them, they will be on a par with the fair trader.

The conftruction of the Navigation laws now contended for, is, perhaps, the only point in which the interefts of the two countries feem feparate and diftinct; and if Ireland did not expect great benefit, fhe would not fo ftrenuoufly urge the claim; but this given up, England could not pretend to a competition with her in time to come. The matter in queftion indeed feems fo felf evident, that no man of the leaft commercial knowledge, who has talents or abilities to form an accurate idea on the fubject, can hefitate in declaring the meafure a flow, perhaps, but certain poifon, to the commerce, manufactures, and population of Great Britain. In fhort, it is not the bufinefs of Great Britain to encourage the migration

gration of her merchants and people to fituations of greater convenience, where all the articles of trade and manufactures are fo completely unburdened. England in half a century would find herfelf more hurt than fhe has been by all her debts and all her taxes.

The advantage in queftion, is neceffary to counterbalance the advantages of Ireland, and preferve an equality with her. The burdens of the country, and, above all, the taxes on the inland and foreign commerce, fufficiently counterbalance all local advantages which arife from the habits, and the manners of Great Britain. It is effential, that the capitals and trade of the empire fhould not center in that part which does not contribute to the expences of it. The point in queftion would give to Ireland all the advantages of an union, without her taking upon her, any of the difadvantages. Ireland does not at prefent difpute in which of the countries the feat of empire fhall be: but that queftion would be as reafonable, and not of more confequence than the prefent. The affectation of faying that

H   it

it is a point of no confequence, but that it
will quiet Ireland, can only miflead the moft
ignorant or the moft thoughtlefs. We do
not in general obferve, that malecontents,
or people diffatisfied with or without reafon,
are apt to be quieted by unfubftantial favours.
Ireland, indeed, has not been fatisfied with
great conceffions. But if it were in truth
a point of no confequence, thofe who urge
it, are endeavouring to deceive the people
of Ireland, and to prevail upon Great Britain to be acceffary to the deceit. If it
were in truth an unfubftantial favour,
thofe who ftate it as fuch will chearfully
receive the refufal of it. It fhould not
even be admitted, that the point remains to
be fettled—It is fettled—It is a fixed principle, the moft neceffary to fupport Britain—
It is the foundation on which her profperity
depends.

Befides thefe general objections, Great
Britain has another of no fmall confequence.
In the American and Weft-India trade, the
great difficulty has been, and will be, to
obtain payment for merchandize. The
principal mode of payment has been, and
muft

muſt be, by the produce of America and the Iſlands. If that produce ſhould be admitted into this country through Ireland, much of it will go there in payment for proviſions of ſeveral kinds, linen, woollens, and various articles of manufactures and clothing. By ſo much as Ireland ſhall take of that produce to re-export into this country or elſewhere, to that amount will England loſe of the beſt, and, in ſome caſes, only mode of payment from America and the Iſlands; and Ireland, inſtead of paying England as heretofore, will ſend thoſe very articles to her, by which alone ſhe could expect to be paid by America for merchandize ſent there. Others objections to the expectations of Ireland in this point will ariſe in multitudes; thoſe are glaring and obvious. The depreciation of landed eſtates, and the ruin of ſtockholders, and of public credit, would be among the certain and inevitable conſequences of ſuch a conceſſion; and however ſtrong the declaration may appear, it is demonſtrable, that an abſolute and entire ſeparation of the two countries would be leſs pernicious to the intereſts of Britain. If theſe objections appeared even leſs ſolid,

if

if they were but doubtful, or poffibly in fome degree founded on prejudice or jea-loufy, ftill any Minifter would be hardy indeed, who fhould overlook them. On the other hand, it will be falfe patriotifm to difquiet the two countries on a point, which one is not likely to yield, which the other has no rightful claim to prefs or infift on; which is not neceffary to her, having already more ways of employing her capitals and people, and of growing rich, than fhe or any country now, or ever is likely to avail itfelf of; confidering at the fame time, that great conceffions have al-ready been made, and that others are ftill afked which are more reafonable, and more likely to be obtained, and not fo prejudicial to Great Britain.

It is obvious, that the claim in queftion equally relates to Eaft India goods; and it has been faid in the Parliament of Ireland, that as fhe gives a monopoly of her confump-tion to the Eaft-India Company, and takes from her in value to the amount of 350,000l. yearly, which is more than any other coun-try, except Great Britain, fhe fhould be fup-plied

plied in the fame manner, and have equal advantages. The Indiamen fhould have liberty
to land their cargoes in Ireland ; the Company fhould have warehoufes, and attend their
cuftomers there. The India goods imported
into Ireland, fhould be warehoufed without
duty, with a power of exporting to Britain ;
a fixed number of outward-bound Indiamen
fhould vifit Ireland, and there take their
out cargoe, and fuch manufactures for which
there is a demand in Afia, &c. &c. &c.

The anfwer is, that Ireland has no better
claims on the India Company, than fhe has
on any other company of merchants in London ; that fhe has Eaft-India commodities as
cheap, or cheaper, from the Company, than
fhe could have them from any other quarter.
She has no better claim to be waited on, and
her manufactures taken from her door, than
Edinburgh, Glafgow, Liverpool, Briftol,
Quebec, Halifax, &c. The remains of our
Norman dominions have an equal right to the
fame advantages ; and Jerfey and Guernfey
may equally claim to be waited on, and to
fee India fhips in their ports. The charges
of the tranfport of India goods to the diftant
parts

parts of this kindom, are fully as great as to the ports of Ireland ; and the confumers in thofe diftant parts pay heavy duties on thefe very articles, which go towards the expences of the empire, confequently towards the expence of maintaining the India trade, to which Ireland contributes nothing ; for whatever duties are paid by the confumers in Ireland, go to the revenue of that country.

Befides the above, the objections to this claim are generally the fame as to the other, for admiffion of colonial or foreign produce from Ireland : they are not the objections of the Company of Merchants trading to the Eaft Indies, but the objections of the people of Great Britain.—The reftraints are as much againft the Company as againft Ireland ; the Company might victual her fhips cheaper there, and might have feveral advantages, by a direct intercourfe between her factories and Ireland ; but it would be inconfiftent with the intereft of England, and nearly in the fame maner as already fhewn on the fubject of the other claim.

The

The Great *Reciprocal* Commercial arrangement between Britain and Ireland, of which we have heard fo much, confifts, as we have reafon to believe, of all, or moft, of thefe expectations on the part of Ireland : how the reciprocity is likely to arife, does not appear ; or indeed how it is in her power to make an adequate return ; but the American treaty, although not quite fo ftrong a cafe as this may prove, is the precedent on which to found pretenfions. At leaft, thefe are the difficulties ;—the fooner they are determined the better. Great Britain has to lament at this day, that fo many great points have been conceded, without having this material one properly arranged; which, undoubtedly, in the years 1780 and 1782, fhe might have fettled in her own way. We have now only to hope, that minifters will have the wifdom to determine this, and every other point, firmly and decidedly ; fo that Ireland may fettle to induftry, and that no commercial queftion may be again permitted to arife between the countries. Without fuch refolution, any difcuffion of the fubject would be folly. The whole feems ultimately to reft on the expediency.

The

The people of Great Britain think that Ireland is in the habit of making fuccefsful requifitions, and that Great Britain is in the habit of inconfiderate conceffions. The feeble Adminiftrations of England, to avoid the mere difficulty of the day, are fond of expedients. The country has reafon to be tired of them ; it is time fhe fhould fupport herfelf; and there is not only more dignity, but policy, in firmnefs.

END OF PART I.

The Second Part will foon be publifhed.

No. I.

TOTAL VALUE of all Commodities exported from Ireland to Britain for Ten Years, ending the 25th of March, 1783, diftinguifhing each Year, and the feparate Value of Linens, Linen Yarn, Wool, Worfted, and Bay Yarn.

Years	Value of Linen.			Linen Yarn.			Wool.			Worfted and Bay Yarn.			Total of the Foregoing Articles.			Other Articles exported to Britain from Ireland.			Total Exports to Britain.		
	£.	s.	d.	£.	s.	d.	£.	s.	d.	£.	s.	d.	£.	s.	d.	£.	s.	d.	£.	s.	d.
1774	1237121	11	0	175166	0	0	503	11	7¾	95880	16	8	1508671	19	3¾	605177	19	0	2113849	18	3¾
1775	1458543	15	0	183592	15	0	1003	12	11¼	118345	11	8	1761485	14	7¼	615031	18	7½	2376517	13	2¾
1776	1435110	16	4	216915	5	0	529	14	1¾	129790	15	0	1782346	10	5¾	765114	3	5	2547460	13	10¾
1777	1387584	5	5	178190	0	0	867	6	6¾	170054	15	0	1736696	6	11¾	810435	18	1	2547132	5	0¾
1778	1542748	13	1	168653	0	0	832	12	3	184134	0	0	1896368	5	4	816124	0	4¾	2712492	5	8¼
1779	1335043	4	0	214020	10	0	1939	5	5½	151409	3	4	1602412	2	9¼	650564	9	11½	2252976	12	8½
1780	1219921	0	0	254219	15	0	1082	7	5	127321	0	0	1602544	2	5	778690	15	10¼	2381234	18	3¼
1781	961455	13	4	223215	0	0	552	7	11¼	122786	3	4	1308009	4	7¼	872206	3	4½	2180215	7	11¾
1782	1646138	2	8	169126	10	0	1482	8	9	125732	8	0	1942479	9	5	757346	4	3½	2699825	13	8½
1783	1014197	18	0	214877	13	0	1031	10	11¼	100015	15	0	1330122	16	11¼	659167	19	9¾	1989290	16	9

OBSERVATIONS

ON THE

MANUFACTURES,

TRADE,

AND

PRESENT STATE

OF

IRELAND.

BY JOHN LORD SHEFFIELD.

———Non Hoftem, inimicaque Caftra
Argivûm, veftras Spes Uritis———

DUBLIN:

Printed for R. MONCRIEFFE, L. WHITE, and P. BYRNE.

M.DCC.LXXXV.

CONTENTS.

Obſer-

PART THE SECOND.

MANUFACTURES.

TO affift the reader in forming an accurate idea, and in judging of the prefent ftate of Ireland, it may be proper to inquire feparately into her feveral fabrics, and alfo to examine the principal articles of her trade with the different parts of the world. Manufactures being the foundation of commerce, they fhould be previoufly confidered; and the linen manufacture of Ireland, undoubtedly, claims the firft attention.

LINEN MANUFACTURE.

It has fufficiently appeared that the linen is, by far, the firft manufacture of Ireland, and it is reafonable to flatter ourfelves, that there is an opening for a very great extenfion of that trade. The author of the pamphlet, entitled, "Information to the People of Ireland on the "Linen Trade," publifhed by the Linen Board of Ireland, very properly obferves, that Spain and Portugal alone take more linen than any one nation could fupply; and that we

I   fhould

fhould alter and adapt our linens to the demand not only of the Spaniards, but alfo of
the Portuguefe and their refpective colonial
poffeffions. We fhould endeavour to prepare
our linens for the markets of different countries: we have the three induftrious nations of
France, Flanders, and Germany, to contend
with; we fhould obtain patterns, and imitate
the linens of thofe countries which are in greateft demand abroad. If only two or three forts
of our linens could gain credit in Spain, we
might be fatisfied until time fhould give us an
opportunity of imitating others; and to gain
this credit may not be difficult, as our linens in
general are of a more durable quality than the
foreign. When it is confidered that not only
Spain and Portugal, but all America, both
North and South, and the iflands of that continent, the coaft of Africa, and many other
countries, will require an inexhauftible fupply,
it fhould quicken, in particular, the induftry
of Ireland. She has every advantage that France,
Flanders, and Germany have; fhe has more,
a national protection; a parliament forward
to affift with the greateft liberality, and equally

ly eager to give employment and reward to induſtry: and this being the cafe, it is extraordinary that ſhe cannot fell almoſt every article of linen as cheap, or cheaper, than any country. There is not a tax which neceſſarily falls
on her manufactures, unleſs two ſhillings
hearth money on a cottage, and the excife on
beer, can be called ſuch; indeed the remains
of the old fyſtem which did not confider cuftom duties as regulations of trade, but merely
as matter of revenue, ſtill exiſt too much in
Ireland; and fome cuſtoms inwards on raw materials, may, properly, be confidered as a tax on
manufactures. In general, imports into Ireland
pay ten per per cent. and exports five per cent.
duties. ʒ✗

The manufacture of linen cloth is eaſily
learned; it is confined to no one foil or territory,
for where flax will not grow, it may be brought
or imported on reaſonable terms. It is no ob-
ſtacle to agriculture; it is the moſt defirable
manufacture that is known; it does not depend on faſhions; it is the leaſt tranfitory, and
there muſt ever be a great derhand for it. It
ſhould not be confined to one province; it

ſhould

should spread through every country, through
every diftrict, and through every parifh. It is
chiefly carried on in the country, and in fmall
villages, not in great towns or cities. There is
not a county, or fcarce any part of Ireland or
England, where flax may not be raifed, and
fome branch of the linen manufacture carried
on to advantage. Next to agriculture, it is the
beft of all objects; and even in England it
fhould rank with the woollen trade. No meafure can tend more to increafe population, than
the promoting a manufacture which may raife
and fupport fo great a number of induftrious,
fober, and healthful families, in every part of
the kingdom. This manufacture and the fifheries might advance the population of Ireland
to an equality with that of Holland. Tillage
would be greatly increafed, and foreign trade
extended.

It is not a great many years ago fince
linen yarn was fent from the Britifh dominions to be wove in Holland. It was common to fend cloth to be bleached there; and
it is not long fince the better fort of the
people of this ifland wore Dutch Holland for
fhirts: this is now nearly at an end; yet the
value

value of foreign linens, exclufive of Irifh, imported into England, exceeds that of any other foreign manufacture; it ufed to be computed at one million and an half; it is now about one million, and the whole amount of linen annually brought into England formerly, has been computed at three millions fterling. It has been already fhewn, that the exports from Ireland to England of that article, on an average of four years, ending the 25th of March, 1778, amounted to near one million and an half. The amount from Scotland is fuppofed to be near half a million. Of thefe, to the value of about 400,000l. was annually re-exported, one half of which is faid to be foreign. Thirty years ago, the annual import of foreign linens was 32,230,767 yards, but through the bounty of three half-pence per yard on the exportation of coarfe home-made linen, and the fubfidy upon all dry goods imported, which included foreign linen, the quantities made at home were fo much increafed as to reduce, in nine years, the annual foreign importation near feven millions of yards, viz. on a medium of five years, ending Chriftmas, 1765, it was only

25,550,182

25,550,182 yards. It has been computed, that the linen imported into England might employ and maintain upwards of 250,000 people at home, exclufive of thofe employed in raifing and dreffing flax.

It is to be lamented, that the quantity of linen made in England and Ireland for fale, is not afcertained in the fame manner as in Scotland. It would be of fervice in obviating much mifreprefentation. It would point out the progrefs or decline of the manufacture; we fhould know with more precifion the quantity we can furnifh ; at prefent we can only form vague conjectures from import and export.

Notwithftanding we hear fo little of the linen manufacture of England, it is faid to be nearly equal to that of both Ireland and Scotland. It is much, if it is equal in quantity to what is even exported from Ireland. It has been already mentioned that Ireland exported above twenty-five millions of yards in 1782, and laft year, viz. 1783, the total quantity of linen ftampt for fale in Scotland, was

17,074,777

17,074,777 yards, value 866,983l. 10s. ; which is, 1,726,033 yards, value 91,885l. more than the preceding year ; and since the year 1727, she had increased to that amount, from 2,183,975 yards, value 103,312l. 9s. 3d. *. Besides this, the quantity made for private use in Sotland muſt be very considerable. The manufacture, undoubtedly, is capable of being improved to a very great degree ; of being rendered doubly extensive, and the import of flax and linen, it is to be hoped, will gradually diminiſh. Some time may pass before the British dominions can supply themselves fully with linens; yet if the progress of the manufacture should continue equal to what it has been, that period may not be very distant.

* The increase is said to have arisen chiefly from an unusual demand for the coarse fabric called Osnaburgs, which is wholly exported to America and the West Indies.

† The medium value of linen exported from Ireland at the same period, viz. 1727, was 284,721l. which is about one fifth of the late exportation of that article : The produce of cattle then exceeded the produce of linen ; and although it is now so extremely behind, the export has increased one third since that time.

It

It is worthy confideration whether an additional duty on foreign linen might not be
advifeable; it would not only improve the
revenue but alfo operate as a bounty to the
home manufacture.

It has been thought that bounties on the export linens are only neceffary to counteract the
advantages which the high drawback on foreign linens gave them as a branch of export;
and it was faid to be timid policy which prevented the annihilation both of drawbacks and
bounties.   But to refufe the drawback on the
export of foreign linens would be highly mifchievous to our export trade.—We cannot
fupply every fort of linen that our cuftomers
may want, or as cheap, as fome countries, and
we fhould not encourage our cuftomers to fend
directly to thofe countries, if in the affortment
of cargoes they will take them from us.   If,
then, we fhould not be able to command the
more fubftantial advantages of being the manufacturers ourfelves, our next object certainly
ought to be, that of endeavouring to fecure
the fupply of the foreign markets with thefe
articles, whereby our own merchants will draw
                                        the

the commercial profits arifing from being the importers and exporters; we fhould then partake of the carriage, and American and other fhipping would have lefs occafion for going to other countries.

The aid that has been given to labour in the cotton manufacture by machinery is not likely to be applied to the linen manufacture in any great degree. The fly-fhuttle and the flax-mill are the principal aids lately acquired by the latter. The ingenuity of Mr. Arkwright and others has done much for manufactures, but the nature of flax makes it difficult to apply to it the cotton machinery, even to the degree that has been introduced into the woollen manufacture within three or four years, efpecially in fpinning and fcribbling.

The following is the account of linens for three years exported from Ireland into England previous to the laft war with France.

	Irifh linen, plain.	Do. checked, or ftriped.	Do. Sil cloth.
	Yards.	Yards.	Yards.
From Chriftmas 1774, to Chriftmas 1775,	21,376,822.	53.	12072.
1776,	20,989,371.	124.	5,3674.
1777.	2.,151,065.		2,708¼.

K

An

An Account of the total Quantities of British and Irish Linen; exported from that Part of Great Britain called England, shewing the Bounties paid on each Species, from the 5th of January, 1776, to the 5th of January, 1778, distinguishing each Year.

			From 5th January 1776, to 5th January 1777.				From 5th January 1777, to 5th January 1778.			
			Quantities.	Bounties paid or payable thereon.			Quantities.	Bounties paid or payable thereon.		
			Yards.	£.	s.	d.	Yards.	£.	s.	d.
British	Plain,	5 to 6d. per yard,	670	2	15	10	4347	18	2	3
	Ditto,	6 to 18d. per yard,	2875905	17974	8	8	329610	20122	11	3
	Checked,	7 to 18d. per yard,	1671928	3483	3	8	1802402	3755	0	1
	Diaper,	6 to 18d. per square yard,	6123	38	5	4	9038	56	9	9
	Sheeting,	6 to 18d. per square yard,	4050	25	6	3	5458	34	2	3
Irish	Plain,	5 to 6d. per yard,		0	0	0	126	0	0	3
	Ditto,	6 to 18d. per yard,	1324397	8277	9	7	2234940	13968	7	4
	Diaper,	6 to 18d. per square yard,	70	0	8	9	955	5	19	4
	Sheeting,	6 to 18d. per square yard,	6381	39	17	7	3818	23	17	3
		Total	5889052	29841	15	1	7280644	37984	14	9

An Account of the Quantity of British and Irish Linens exported from England, without Bounty, from the 5th of January, 1776, to the 5th of January, 1778, distinguishing each Year.

	British Linens.			Irish Linen. Plain.
	Plain.		Checked.	
Pieces.	Ells.		Ells.	Yards.
From the 5th of January, 1776, to the 5th of January, 1777,	38379 and 25978		44167	76412
From the 5th of January, 1777, to the 5th of January, 1778,	43840 and 3333		41589	141642

JOHN TOMKYNS, Assistant Inspector General.

Custom House,
London, June 2, 1778.

K 2

The quantity of linen exported from Ireland to every country, exclusive of Great Britain, distinguishing each country, for the year ending 25th March, 1781.

		Yards.
East Country	-	29,612
Holland	- -	67,826
Spain and Portugal	-	108,215
America	- -	288,973
West Indies	- -	142,099

The quantity of linen yarn exported the same year to Great Britain, was 37,202 Cwt. value 223,215l.

The quantity of linen exported from Ireland to Great Britain, and the value.

	Linen cloth, plain.	value.		
	Yards.	£.	s.	d.
Years ending ⎱ 1782	24,692,072	1646138	2	8
25th March. ⎰ 1783	15,212,968	1014197	18	0

	Linen coloured.	Value.		
	Yards.	£.	s.	d.
Years ending ⎱ 1782	767	62	6	4½
25th March. ⎰ 1783	——	— 0	0	

The

The quantity of linen exported from Ireland to every other country, (exclufive of Great Britain) and the value.

	Linen cloth, plain. Yards.	Value. £. s. d.
Years ending ⎱ 1782	278,231	18,548 14 8
25th March. ⎰ 1783	826,737	55,115 16 0

	Linen, coloured. Yards.	Value. £. s. d.
Years ending ⎱ 1782	73,655½	5984 9 9
25th March. ⎰ 1783	166,127¼	13,151 15 1½

The extraordinary decreafe of exportation of linens to Great Britain, in the year ending 25th March, 1783, muft principally have arifen from the unfettled ftate of the country, from the increafed exportation to other countries, and from the checks occafioned by the viciffitudes of war; perhaps partly from the market being glutted by the great export of the preceding year; but the next year the quantity increafed again. The author has not the Irifh account of exports for that year; but the Englifh, which it has been already remarked is not made up to the fame period, is as follows:

An

An account of the linen and linen yarn imported into England from Ireland, from the 5th of January, 1782, to 5th January, 1783.

Yard's.

Linen   -   16,194,189

Lbs.

Linen yarn   -   3,937,726

Irifh linen entitled to bounty, exported from England in the above   Yards.

year   -   -   -   1,087,561

Irifh linen not entitled to bounty   150,266

Total   1,237,827

The above quantity exported with and without bounty is nearly the average for feveral years paft.

Linen imported from Ireland into England, from the 5th January, 1783, to 5th January, 1784—20,687,528 yards.

The Table, No. 2, fhews the demand for linens in America previous to the war, and gives the quantity of Britifh, Irifh, and foreign linens,

CALLICOES.				CANV	
Various.	Printed.	Excife.	Cambricks. Demy.	Heffian.	
Pieces.	Sq. Yds.	Pieces.	Pieces.	C. Qrs. Ells.	C
43214	270151	4800	22135	999 2 10	4.

An Account of the BRITISH and IRISH LINENS and COTTONS imported into NORTH AMERICA, from GREAT BRITAIN, in the Year 1771; the several Sorts and Quantities distinguished.

L I N E N S.

	BRITISH			Cwt.	COTTONS								IRISH						
	Stamp.	Fine			British ... Scotch		Printed	Coarse & Scotch	Checkd	Bark	Handkerchiefs	Sheeting	Fine	Linen & Scotch	Napkins	Printed	Red Check	Thread Checks	
	Yards	Pieces	Yards	Cwts.	Yards	Pieces	Yards	Pieces	Yds	Pr	Pr	Red	Yds	Doz	Yards	Pieces	Yards	Pr	No.	Yd	Ells	Doz
n.	1313711	18190	177833	743	.0002.	188	33779	6028	45947	48	3	1	888	2788	1807981	2582	80594	99	12	61783	310408	28

AN ACCOUNT of the FOREIGN LINENS and CALLICOES imported from BRITAIN into NORTH AMERICA in 1771; the several Sorts and Quantities distinguished.

L I N E N S.

CALLICOES				CANVASS			DAMASK.		DIAPER.					DUCK		GERMANY.			HOLLAND	LAWNS, ELLIES.			RUSSIA.			
									BRITTY	foreign.	German.															
Servat	Printed	Each	Cambric, Clouts	Hollan.	Brown	Ells	Cafed	Table, Toiling	Tabl.	Yds.	Yds.	Tabl. Napk.	Yds.	Yds.	Pr.	Yds.	Roven	Bowl	Out of Time		Varnished	Whited	Agned, Lace	Broad	Drilling	Narrow	Printd
Pieces	Sq Yds	Pieces	Plain	C. Qrs. Ells	C. Qrs. Ells	Yds.	Pa.	Yds.	Pa.	Yds.	Yds.	Yds.	Pa.	Yds.	Pa.	Yds.	C. Qrs. Lbs	C. Qrs. Ells	C. Qrs. Lbs	Pa.	Pa.	Pa.	Yds.	No. C. Qrs. Ells	C. Qrs. Ells	C. Qrs. Ells	Sq Yds
13812	130431	3800	21733	579 1 10	4988 1 12	1300	1183	8833	66	147	113	8434	3881	13313	7003 lent.	181937	10688 3 11	38 0 17	38 1 7	38	1043	34688	52688	15859 281	2388 3 28	153 2 6	130 1 16	19300 3

linens, cottons, and callicoes, imported there from Great Britain in 1771, diftinguiſhing the quantities and forts.

The following Report of the late Board of Trade is ably drawn up, and conveys much Information relative to the Linen Manufacture :

To the Right Honourable the Lords of the Committee of Council appointed to confider the Iriſh Bills.

MY LORDS,

YOUR Lordſhips having been pleaſed, by your order of the 6th inſtant, to refer to us a bill, lately tranſmitted from Ireland, intitled, " An Act for granting Bounties on " the Export of the Linen and Hempen Ma-" nufactures of this Kingdom, therein enu-" merated ; and for repealing the Bounties " on Flax Seed imported, and for encourag-" ing the Growth thereof in this Kingdom ;" and having required us to report, how far the proviſions of the ſaid bill may affect the

linen

linen trade of this kingdom, we forthwith proceeded to take the fame into our confideration accordingly.

Finding, however, that it would be neceffary to feek for much information, not contained in any papers tranfmitted to us, we defired the attendance of feveral refpectable merchants interefted in the general export trade, and in the linen manufactures of Manchefter and Scotland, as alfo of fome principal factors concerned in the imports and exports of Irifh linens, and of other perfons converfant in the extenfive fubject before us. In the refult, we now beg leave to report to your Lordfhips,

That thofe claufes in the bill which repeal certain bounties now payable on imported flax feed or linfeed, and apply the average annual amount thereof to encourage the growth of flax feed and hemp feed in Ireland, cannot affect the interefts of the linen trade of this kingdom, and are, fo far as bounties may in any cafe be expedient, wifely and providently applied by thefe new provifions, to promote the intereft of the Irifh linen trade.

The

The value of flax feed annually imported into Ireland was in 1773 eftimated at from 60,000l. to 80,000l. exclufive of this great expence, it is the evident intereft of that kingdom to give every reafonable encouragement to the internal produce of materials on which her ftaple manufacture depends, and to which her foil and climate are peculiarly fuitable; and the trufting to her foreign importation for the fupply of flax feed is more efpecially ineligible, as the feed fo imported is faid not to be fo good and fo certain, as that which is raifed by the Irifh culture.

It is confiftent with the fame reafoning, and equally unconnected with any fpecial interefts of our linen trade, that the bill impofes a duty of fix pence per gallon on imported linfeed oil, which is chiefly imported from Holland, and applies the produce in aid of the new bounty above mentioned. And here we fhall take occafion to obferve, that fuch farther duties as are impofed by the bill for the farther purpofes therein fpecified, cannot come within the import of your Lordfhips' general queftion refpecting our linen trade; for they confift in an

L   additional

additional charge of five per cent. on the produce of all impoft, excife, and cuftoms inwards,
except on tobacco, fugar, hops, and the produce of the Britifh colonies in America, the
Weft Indies, or the fettlements in Africa,
whereon any duties may be impofed, or altered,
during the prefent feſlion of parliament, and
except alfo on any Britifh hops or fugars.

We prefume, then, that we have done right
in confining our attention and inquiries to the
remaining provifions of the bill, by which
bounties are given to certain fpecies of Irifh
linens exported to Africa, America, Spain,
Portugal, Gibraltar, and Minorca; and alfo
to Irifh-made fail cloth exported to any place
except Great Britain.

In examining thefe bounties, we found them
in moft refpects fimilar to the bounties granted
in Great Britain upon the exportation of Britifh or Irifh linens. There is fome fmall difference with regard to linens of 5d. per yard,
which are fo ftated in the Irifh bill, in order
to anfwer ours of 5d. Englifh money, inftead
of being put at 5d. $\frac{5}{12}$, the proportion in
Irifh money; in confequence of which, the
bounty

bounty given in Ireland is, in a flight degree, higher than it is in Great Britain. There is, however, a difference much more material in the bounty on fail cloth, which, in the Irifh bill, at 6d. $\frac{1}{2}$, upon every three ells, although in England it is only 1d. per ell. In other particulars we do not obferve any difference, except in the denomination of money, for the purpofe of equalizing the feveral bounties, refpectively, to the proportions of what are given in this kingdom.

In taking a review of the laft-mentioned bounties, which, on the average, are about 12 per cent. in favour of low-priced linens exported, it may not be immaterial to ftate to your Lordfhips the manner in which the British bounties have operated in favour of the Irifh manufacture. The firft bounties on linen exported took place in 1743, and the export from England, of Irifh linen, intitled to bounty, was, in

Yards.

1743 — —		40,907
1753 — —		1,039,967
1763 — —		2,588,564
1773 — —		2,832,246

L 2   This

This increafe has been aided alfo by accumu-
lated duties on the import of foreign linens into
this kingdom, notwithftanding that fuch duties are faid to have operated to the prejudice
of our own woollen trade, by inducing
foreign powers to lay reciprocal burdens and
reftrictions on our woollen manufactures.
The confequence, however, has been, with
refpect to the Irifh ftaple, that the general import of Irifh linens has alfo been increafed very
greatly; for, the Irifh linens imported into
London, and the out-ports, were,

			Yards.
In 1743	—	—	6,418,375
1773	—	—	17,876,617
		Increafe,	11,458,242

That this may be attributed to the fyftem
of bounties and duties, rather than to the general increafe of our trade, will fufficiently
appear from the proportionable decreafe in the
import and export of foreign linens, compared
at the fame periods.

Foreign linens imported into London and
the out ports, were,

In

Ells.

In 1743   ⊥   —   18,584,503

1773   —   —   8,954,649

Decreafe, 9,629,854

Foreign linens exported from London and the out-ports, were,

Ells.

In 1743   —   —   9,894,837

1773   —   —   4,385,276

Decreafe, 5,509,561

In order to fhew farther the importance of this confideration b tween the two kingdoms, it deferves remark, that the total value of linen cloth exported from Ireland, was,

Ells.

In 1741   —   —   480,516

1751   —   —   751,993

1761   —   —   803,258

1771   —   —   1,691,787;

and it is eftimated, that bout 7-8ths of that whole export is fent to Great Britain.

Having obferved, that our fyftem of linen bounties and linen dutics, the poff.bility, in many cafes, unexceptionable in the great fcale

of

of commercial policy, has proved an effential encouragement to the Irifh ftaple, we think it right to add, that it has alfo been the means of forcing forwards an extenfive linen manufacture in this kingdom, though ftruggling under a great difadvantage as to the growth and fupply of the raw material.

The export of Britifh linen, intitled to bounty, was,

Yards.

In 1743	— —	52,779
1753	— —	641,510
1763	— —	2,308,310
1773	— —	5,235,266

The increafe in the exports of Britifh and Irifh linens, not intitled to bounty, has, during the periods above mentioned, been nearly as great in value, though not in quantity; and has been much promoted by the duties on foreign linens, which, when exported, leave behind a certain part of the duties paid on importation, and are fubject to other cuftom-houfe charges; fo that, before they can be refhipped, there is a difadvantage againft the foreign manufacturer, equivalent from 5 to 6 per cent.

On

On thefe facts your Lordfhips will obferve, that England is the principal market for Irifh linens, to the annual amount in value of more than one million fterling; and that fo large a fum is paid by this kingdom, not fo much for export, as for her own internal confumption, at leaft 4-5ths of the whole quantity of imported Irifh linens, and thofe of the higheft price, being confumed in England. The other 1-5th only is exported; your Lordfhips will fee, then, that Ireland has a folid and permanent market for her linen at prefent, whence fhe draws fpeedy and certain payments, and is thereby enabled to make large returns. And, confequently, the export of the 1-5th to the places fpecified in the bill, and the refulting advantages of that export, in a general extenfion of trade, muft be the object of the prefent bill. The tracing how this may operate in Ireland, will beft lead us to the probable effects of the meafure on the linen trade of this kingdom, and thereby enable us to throw fome light on your Lordfhips' inquiry.

From a comparifon of what has been ftated to us by different gentlemen, whofe evidence we have taken, it does not appear, that the

average

average expence of freight, commiffion, ware-
houfing, wharfage, and other incidents at-
tending the import of Irifh linen into Britifh
ports, in order to its export from thence,
ought to be eftimated at lefs than 5 ½ per cent.
The bounties, therefore, being equalized in the
two kingdoms, Ireland will be able to export
this article, under the new opening given to her
trade, to an advantage over the Englifh exporter, equal to 5 ½ per cent.

This advantage will, for a certain period,
be much counterbalanced by the long credits
which will be neceffary in the markets to which
fhe muft go; by the uncertain returns from
thofe markets; by the difficulties of fuddenly
diverting any trade from its accuftomed channel; and alfo by the inability of the Irifh merchants to fend full and well-afforted cargoes,
fuch as are fent from England, and which include India goods, foreign lirens, and the various articles of manufacture to be collected from
Manchefter, Birmingham, Sheffield, Norwich,
and elfewhere. All thefe embarraffments are
likely to bear hard on the firft adventurers;
but means of palliating thefe will gradually be
found; and it muft be expected, that an exift-
ing

ing operative advantage, in favour of any branch of trade, will ultimately effectuate its establishment.

Under these considerations we see, with some regret, an experiment tending to interrupt and hazard a great branch of commercial intercourse between the two countries, which has been highly and reciprocally advantageous. We are convinced, too, that this new speculation, so far as it succeeds, will operate to the diminution of our export trade, to the diminution also, of the returns for that trade; and consequently to the prejudice of our navigation, and of the commercial interests in general; but we cannot think that such mischiefs are suddenly to be expected to any considerable extent.

If, however, contrary to these reasonings, such a revulsion of trade should take place, it may be well to have foreseen and considered how far Great Britain would have some remedy within her own reach. The foreign manufacturers, notwithstanding the disadvantages under which they labour by the operation of our bounties and duties, which amount,

M   in

in their average effect, to near 15 per cent. have
been able to preferve fome degree of competition, efpecially in the fine linens; a fmall reduction therefore in thofe duties would, in the
event fuppofed, enable this kingdom to fupply herfelf with linens as cheap as ever, and
with advantage to the revenue. It might
probably, too, obtain in return a larger confumption of woollen manufactures and other
goods upon the continent of Europe.

If, however, the firft effect of the bill in
queftion fhould tend to raife the price of the
Irifh linen, which it probably may, and which
we are affured has already happened in fome
degree, it may be expected, that a larger importation of foreign linens will at once take
place without any lowering the duties; and
this will more particularly happen in the inftance of foreign linens imported for home
confumption, if, by the direct export of low-
priced linens from Ireland, the Irifh drapers
fhould no longer be able to make fuitable af-
fortments for the Englifh market.

The confequence would be, that the import
of Irifh linens in general would be confiderably
dimi-

diminifhed, and thofe concerned in the fine branch of the manufacture would fuffer in their bufinefs. Another confequence would be, if it fhould be thought expedient to continue the bounties, as at prefent, that the demand from the Britifh manufactures increafing much, their produce would alfo increafe in proportion; for it deferves remark, that, though this kingdom carries on her linen trade, fubject to great and irremovable difadvantages, fhe is fuppofed at prefent to manufacture more linens than are exported from Ireland, and is therefore in that improved ftate of the bufinefs, which can furnifh a quick fupply to any fudden deficiency or increafed demand.

Upon the whole view of the meafure before us, we are not called upon to form an opinion, how far its fudden adoption, though favourable to the interefts of the Dublin factors, and calculated to accelerate and extend the benefits of the North-America and Weft-India commerce now open to Ireland, is likely to promote the increafe and fecurity of the Irifh ftaple manufacture. With refpect to the operations of that meafure on the linen trade of

this

this kingdom, it is neceffary to advert to the
ftate both of our exports and of our manufactures; and, with regard to the firft, we fubmit
to your Lordfhips, that, as far as the direct export of linen from Ireland may take place in
confequence of the bounty now propofed by Ireland, in fo much will our exports be affected,
and the detriment refulting to our general trade
from that circumftance, will be increafed by
the returns made for fuch exports, and by all
the collateral confequences of a proportionable
transfer of our navigation and general commerce to the ports of Ireland.   With refpect
however to the operation on our linen manufactures, we think them much more likely to be
promoted than injured by it; and we truft, for
the reafons which we have already detailed to
your Lordfhips, that the latter effect may be expected from this bill, and that the former will not
fpeedily take place to any confiderable extent.

We ought, before we clofe this Report, to
take notice of that part of the bill which extends the bounty to the exported checked linens, of which our annual exportation from
London, and the out-ports, is at prefent to the
amount

amount of 120,000l. This valuable branch of trade, which is chiefly fupplied at prefent by Manchefter, is certainly liable to be affected by the bounty now propofed in Ireland—it has hitherto been fupported by the vigor and enterprifing fpirit of our manufacturers, though under the difadvantage of either purchafing the raw material from Ireland, where it is fubject to a duty upon exportation, or from Embden, Hamburgh, and other places, where it is fold at a high price. It is eafy however to forefee, that Ireland, having the material and the export, muft gradually and ultimately have gained ground in this branch of trade, even without the bounty; and yet with that advantage it may be doubted whether fhe will fuddenly furmount the various embarraffments, which fhe has to encounter, and which we have already defcribed to your Lordfhips.

We are, My Lords,
Your Lordfhips
Moft obedient and
Moft humble fervants,

CARLISLE.

Whitehall } C. F. GREVILLE.
July 17, 1780. } Wm. EDEN.
ANDW. STUART.
E. GIBBON.

PRO-

PRODUCE OF CATTLE.

This, undoubtedly, fhould be rated as the fecond great article of Irifh commerce, and unlefs improper advantages are given to the American States, Ireland muft profit very much, particularly by the articles beef and butter.

The prefent relaxation of the navigation laws by the proclamations, is likely to prove extremely prejudicial to Ireland, efpecially a the continuance of it may, at length, form a precedent, which afterwards will be confidered as a principle. The colonial fyftem of navigation laws, very properly gives the fupply of the plantations and colonies to the Britifh dominions alone. The fuffering the produce of the American States to go to our fettlements, has already prejudiced Ireland, and encouraged the provifion trade of the American States: the latter has exceeded expectation as to quality, and unlefs that juftice fhall be done to the Britifh dominions, to which the navigation laws entitle them, they will almoft entirely lofe the provifion trade in a fhort time. Not only that right fhould be affured to them, but immediate

mediate attention fhould be paid to the falt
iflands, which, fince the feparation of the colonies, are become objeds of importance, although hitherto little noticed. Proper attention and regulations relative to them may give
great advantage to the fifheries, as well as to
the provifion trade. The American States take
an immenfe quantity of falt from thofe iflands,
and employ a great number of veffels in the
trade; the falt of Turk's Ifland, Saltatudas,
and Bahamas, is faid to be ftronger* and fuperior to Lifbon, Spanifh, or any European falt;
and that it cures not only fifh, but pork and
butter, and all fubftances that are of an oily
nature, more perfedly. It would anfwer to
the American States to pay two pence or three
pence per bufhel duty, rather than to go elfewhere; the duty would amply pay the expence
of the frigates or floops that it might be neceffary to ftation at thofe iflands, it would give
an important advantage to the Britifh dominions, an advantage *now* eafily to be eftablifhed.

---

* Salt made by the heat of the fun is faid to be
ftronger than that made by fire, and in proportion to
the heat and drynefs of the climate.

At

At this moment a plan is in agitation, to admit the flour, live provifions, &c. of the American States into Newfoundland, and to give the fupply of our fifheries to them. The apparent object in this cafe is not of fo much confequence as the precedent to be eftablifhed by it; and if the new ftate of things made it neceffary to declare the law, inftead of this dangerous indulgence, the opportunity fhould have been taken of eftablifhing a general principle. It is aftonifhing that the propofition fhould be liftened to; it is moft ftrongly againft the fpirit of the trade laws; it proves that there is neither fyftem nor principle on which men act. Minifters will take liberties with the people of England; but it is certain that the people of Ireland will refufe the monopoly of their markets to the Britifh plantations, if they are deprived of their fhare of the monopoly of the plantation markets. Ireland has lately increaf-ed her trade to Newfoundland, and it is likely to increafe to a great extent; but this new fyftem tends to undo her there, and eftab-lifh fmuggling moft compleatly, which flou-rifhes by far too much already.

Water-

Waterford and Youghall will be essentially hurt; but it is not Britain and Ireland only that will suffer, the province of Quebec will be ruined if the system should continue. When the American States fulfill the treaty, and the posts on the lakes are given up, that province will lose three fourths, or at least two thirds, of the fur trade, and her recourse must be to the corn and provision trade. Her export of corn, previous to the disturbances in America, considering she had exported little before 1771, was immense, and proves how capable she alone may become to supply not only the British fisheries, but also the British West Indies. In 1774, she exported nearly equal to the consumption of the latter. It is to be observed, the river St. Laurence is open in the month of May before the fishery begins.

The hopes and expectations of the provinces of Nova Scotia and New Brunswick, will also be blasted; they must principally depend hereafter on the fisheries and provision trade. The system, if carried to any extent, would deprive the remaining colonies of those

N   advan-

advantages which alone can make it their intereſt to adhere to the Britiſh empire.   An
accidental ſcarcity of corn or proviſions ſo
immediately after a deſtructive war, and before the provinces could poſſibly recover their
calamities, or ſettle, or in conſequence of a
very unfavourable ſeaſon, is ſurely an inſuf-
ficient pretext for the propoſition alluded to;
but when a good ſyſtem is formed, and the
merchants know on what they may depend,
the ſupply of the colonies will be regular and
certain.   The exportation of corn from Quebec, during the war, was prohibited by the
government of that province.   The war, the
public ſervices, the corvees, and in ſome
degree the apprehenſion that there would not
be a ſufficient demand at home, prevented the
cultivation of the land.   The addition of 15,000
troops, Loyaliſts and Indians, to the people
of Quebec, however, increaſed the demand
at home; and it muſt not now be brought as
an argument, that the Newfoundland fiſheries did not receive their full ſupply of flour
or proviſions from the province of Quebec.
Even circumſtanced as ſhe was, ſhe latterly
ſent ſome flour and biſcuit to Newfoundland,

St.

St. John's, and Nova Scotia. A very extraordinary rainy feafon, and early froft, after a
great part of the crop was cut down in 1783,
eccafioned the fcarcity in 1784; but all accounts agree, that the crop of 1784 is very
abundant, equal to any that has been known
in that country, and fully fufficient to fupply
not only the fifheries, but alfo the remaining
colonies, efpecially when we confider the
quantity of land cultivated by new fettlers at
Cataraqui, and other parts of the St. Laurence,
at Chaleur bay, and the neighbourhood of
Lake Chaplain, through which, and the river
St. Laurence, the produce of the Vermontefe
State muft pafs.

It is obvious that other plantations will
think themfelves better entitled to the indulgence in queftion, and will affert their claim.
To talk of the admiffion of flour and live
ftock from the American States into Newfoundland, as an encouragement to the fifheries, is ridiculous. The five or fix hundred
veffels, from one hundred to two hundred
and fifty tons that go to that fifhery, generally carry out as much or more provifions

N 2   than

than they confume. The fifhermen live on
fifh and fat pork, of which, with hard bifcuit,
they make a difh that is preferred by them to
frefh provifions; neither the bank fifhing, nor
the in-fhore, or boat fifhing, will admit of any
other but falt provifions. We fhould not,
then, take fteps to encourage permanent fettlements at Newfoundland. It is farther to be
obferved, that the whole annual confumption
of flour by our people on that ifland, does not,
in value, exceed eight or nine thoufand pounds
prime coft at the moft which the bill fuppofes
Britain, Ireland and the remaining colonies, cannot fupply. As to frefh provifions, there is
little demand, except for officers and a few
others; and in the profperous year 1770, the
whole import from all America of live cattle,
was one hundred and fifteen; carcaffes twenty
four; fheep one thoufand and twenty; poul-
try, fifteen dozen; and of flour and bifcuit,
fix hundred and feventy-feven tons, value thirteen fhillings per cwt. Moft affuredly more
New-England rum, and contraband articles,
will be fmuggled, by means of this indulgence, from the American States to Newfoundland.

foundland, than live provifions and flour, will be imported. This mifchievous precedent fhould not be allowed to Newfoundland in particular. The fhipping that go there are not half laden; they fhould carry with them what is wanted for themfelves and the ifland, by which fome money will be faved to the country; at leaft it fhould have no competitors in that fupply except the remaining colonies; and thofe employed in the fifheries, fhould be well content to give the advantage to that country, which, by great bounties and encouragements, enables them to carry on their bufinefs. In addition to the above, the general objections to the promoting intercourfe between our colonies and the American States will occur; that it is contrary to the true fpirit of all colonial regulations, for the advantage of the mother country and the appertaining dominions; that it infallibly promotes the fmuggling of New-England rum; and that a great lofs of feamen, on our part, will be a certain confequence.

The excellent fyftem which was eftablifhed in King William's reign, and which was fo

well

well underftood by fome who have commanded on the Newfoundland ftation, fhould not
be forgotten or neglected. The mafters of veffels were obliged, under penalties, to bring
back the men, or as many as they carried out
with them, and every ftep was taken to prevent their fettling there. The paffing the Atlantic twice every year; at the fame time that
hardy and excellent feamen were raifed, gave
this country an opportunity of availing itfelf
of their fervices in cafes of neceffity, on their
going out in fpring, and return in autumn.

But, to refume; the provifion trade is infinitely more advantageous to Ireland than feems
generally to be imagined; and there cannot be
worfe policy than her exportation of live cattle. On the contrary, fhe fhould flaughter her
own cattle, and cure the beef for exportation:
it is as much a manufacture as linens; although the management of the beef, the hides,
the tallow, &c. may not, perhaps, employ,
proportionably, quite fo many hands as flax.
The turning too much land to the raifing of
cattle, under a bad fyftem of hufbandry,
might tend to depopulate, but there is no danger

ger of that kind in the prefent thriving ftate of Ireland. The provifion trade is faid to be in fome degree, uncertain ; but that affertion requires examination; and it would furely be imprudent for Ireland, on mere furmife, to decreafe her quantity of cattle, when butter, cheefe, &c. &c. have yielded fuch large returns *. Agriculture is concerned in raifing and feeding cattle, and tillage is not prevented in the degree that is often imagined by maintaining thofe neceffary animals. One thoufand acres, of which a due proportion is tilled, will maintain, under good management, by artificial graffes, turnips, &c. more cattle than an equal quantity of pafture land. Provifions are a natural ftaple article of commerce for Ireland; her climate is better adapted to it than any other ; her cattle can remain longer in the field, and her beef can be cured a greater part of the year than elfewhere, from the temperature of her feafons ; neither froft nor heat interrupting that bufinefs for a long continuance.

---

* The gateage, or one penny per head on all cattle entering the gates of Cork, amounts to 600l. yearly, that is, on 144,000 head.

That

That the provifion trade has been particularly unequal, does not appear from the imports and exports, its fluctuations have been
imputed to peace and war, and it is fuppofed
that it declines in peace: on the contrary, from
the following average of the export, for five
years of peace, and alfo for five years of war,
it appears that the peace export of beef, butter, cheefe, &c. exceeds the war export.   It
fhould be obferved, that the provifions taken
on board fhips of war and tranfports in Ireland, are not included.   In 1778, the export
of beef from thence, on account of the troops,
was,   —   —   13,206 barrels,
Butter   8,701 cwt.
which is not half fufficient to make up the
difference.   The great increafe in the exportation of pork did not arife merely from the
war.   The quantity of hogs raifed of late years
in Ireland, has been much greater than formerly and the import of pork from Ireland
into England alone, in the year ending 5th Jan.
1783, was 45,995 barrels, which exceeds the
whole export of pork from Ireland twenty
years ago.   Confidering that Ireland is fo great
a dairy country, it is extraordinary there was
not

not a greater abundance of fwine fooner. It may however be remarked, that the buttermilk of Ireland is much better than that of England, and is there the food of man.

The average of five years, ending 25 March, 1774, of the following articles exported from Ireland:

Beef	{ barrrels	—	202,559		
	carcafes	—	68		
Butter, cwt.		—	266,481	3	22
Cheefe, cwt.		—	2,179	1	0
Candles, cwt.		—	2,107	3	19
Tallow, cwt.		—	44,270	3	27
Hides	{ tanned, No.	—	46,795		
	untanned, No.		84,227		
Bullocks and cows		—	1,088		
Bacon, flitches, No.		—	14,354		
Hogs, No.		—	319		
Hogs lard, cwt.		—	2,105	1	25
Pork, barrels,		—	46,924		

The average of five years, ending 25th March, 1782:

Beef	{ barrels	—	172,690		
	carcafes	—	21		
Butter, cwt.		—	245,683	1	21

O   Cheefe,

Cheefe, cwt. —	1,374	3	15
Candles, cwt. —	4,524	3	12
Tallow, cwt. —	42,476	1	16
Hides { tanned, No. —	11,973		
ditto, cwt. —	35	3	24
untanned, No.	63,547		
Bullocks and cows, No.	2,993		
Hams, cwt. —	317	1	21
Bacon, flitches, No. —	5,983		
Hogs, No. —	280		
Hogs lard, cwt. -	3,392	2	26½
Pork, barrels —	87,085		

Twenty years ago, and immediately following the former war, the export of beef and alfo
of butter, was nearly the fame as the above
peace average : and about fixty years ago the
average export of beef was nearly two thirds
of the late exportation, viz. 135,270 barrels ;
and of butter the fame, viz. 161,123 cwt.
which proves that tillage and population have
not decreafed the quantity of cattle in Ireland.

The late arret concerning the commercial intercourfe allowed to foreigners with the French
Weft-Indies, appears to give the fame advantages to the Britifh European and American

can dominions, as it does to the American
ftates. Although dated the 30th Auguſt, 1784,
it was not publiſhed till the 30th November
following. It ſeems to grant greater advantages and to open the French iſlands more to
ſtrangers than any former arret; but it per-
mits in faƈt little more than was allowed,
though not always publicly, before the war,
except, that certain European articles may now
go direƈtly there, without paſſing through the
medium of the ports of France. All the ſea-
ports of that kingdom are remonſtrating moſt
vigorouſly againſt it; and when the court of
Verſailles perceives the prejudice that will be
done to the marine of France, attention will
be paid to the complaints of the merchants.
However a conſiderable preference is reſerved
to the French ſhipping and fiſheries. The advantages given to the American ftates by
France have been ſo much miſrepreſented and
exaggerated that the principal articles of the
arret will be inſerted in a note*, eſpecially as
the

* ARRET du Conſeil d'Etat du ROI, concernant
le Commerce étranger dans les iſles Françoiſes de l' Ameri-
que, du 30 Août, 1784.

the fame advantages are given by it to the Britiſh dominions.

This

ARTICLE PREMIER.

L'ENTREPOT ci-devant aſſigné au Carénage de Sainte-Lucie, ſera maintenu pour ladite iſle ſeulement, & il en ſera établi trois nouveaux aux Iſles du Vent ; ſavoir, un à Saint-Pierre pour la Martinique, un á la Pointe-á-Pitre pour la Guadeloupe & dépendances, un á Scarboroug pour Tabago. Il en ſera pareillement ouvert trois pour Saint-Domingue, ſavoir, un au Cap Franç̧ois, un au Port-au-Prince, un aux Cayes Saint Louis : celui qui exiſle au Mole Saint-Nicholas dans la même colonie, ſera & demeurera ſupprimé.

II.

Permet ſa Majeſté, per proviſion & juſqu'à ce qu'il lui plaiſe d'en ordonner autrement, aux navires étrangers, du port de ſoixante tonneaux au moins, uniquement chargés de bois de toute eſpèce, même de bois de teinture, de charbon de terre, d'animaux beſtiaux vivans de toute nature, de ſalaiſons de bœufs & non de porcs, de morue & poiſſon ſalés, de riz, mais, légumes, de cuirs verds en poil ou tannés, de pelleteries, de réſines & goudron, d'aller dans les ſeuls ports d'entrepôt déſignés par l'article précédent, & d'y décharger & commercer leſdites marchandiſes.

III.

Il ſera permis aux navires étrangers qui iront dans les ports d'entrepôt, ſoit pour y porter les marchandiſes permiſes par l'article II, ſoit à vide, d'y charger pour l'étranger, uniquement des ſirops & taffias, & des marchandiſes venues de France.

TOUTES

This fubject brings to recollection a curious publication of laft fummer, entitled, " A
" State

IV.

To u t es les marchandifes dont l'importation & l'exportation font permifes à l'étranger dans lefdits ports d'entrepôt,
feront foumifes aux droits locaux, établis ou a établir dans
chaque colonie, & payeront en outre un pour cent de leur
valeur.

V.

Independamment du droit d'un pour cent, porté en
l'article ci-deffus, les bœufs falès, la morue & le poiffon falés, payeront trois livres par quintal ; & fera le produit dudit
droit de trois livres, converti en primes d'encouragement
pour l'introduction de la morue & du poiffon falés, prove-
nans de la pêche Françoife.

VI.

Les chairs falés étrangères qui feront introduites dans
les colonies par des bâtimens François, expédiés directe-
ment des ports de royaume, ne feront point affujetties au
payement des droits mentionnés dans les deux articles
précédens.

VII.

Il fera établi dans chaque port d'entrepôt un nombre
fuffifant de commis, pour veiller à ce qu'il ne foit introduit
ni exporté d'autres marchandifes que celles que font fpéci-
fiées dans les articles II. & III. du prefent arrêt ; & afin
qu'il ne refte aucun foupçon d'inexactitude dans cette fur-
veillance, autorife fa Majefté les négocians François réfidans

dans

" State of the Allegations and Evidence pro-
" duced, and Opinions of Merchants and
" Others, given to the Committee of Council."
The prefumption with which the report of
that very refpectable Committee has been
treated, was referved for thefe times; that
Committee was not to be tampered with. A
great defire was expreffed not only by the
Public, but in Parliament, for the publication
of that Report. After it had been agreed,
that it fhould be printed for the members, the
Houfe was told, that it would be improper, on

dans chacun defdits ports d'entrepôt, ainfi que les Capi-
taines de navires qui pourront s'y trouver, à nommer re-
fpectivement entr'eux des Commiffaires, lefquels feront
chargés de dénoncer les négligences ou abus qu'ils pourroient
reconnoître, & affifteront, lorfqu'ils l'eftimeront convenable,
à toutes les vifites qui auront lieu, foit à l'arrivée, foit au
départ des navires étrangers,

Thefe articles do not feem calculated by any means to
encourage foreign veffels to go to the French free ports in
the Weft-Indies; and the laft of the above articles feems to
put foreigners in the power of the French merchants and
French mafters of fhips.

There are twelve other articles which regulate the entry
of the foreign veffels, &c.

account

account of individuals, to give more than extracts; undoubtedly, in fome inftances, it was proper to withhold names, and that would have been fufficient, or all the names might have been withheld; but at the end of two months, the above extraordinary performance appeared. It is little worth while now to analife, or mark what it is, but the French arret reminds us of the following affertion contained in that publication, which could not be accidentally inferted; it was intended to have great weight, viz. *that permiffion is given to the veffels of the American States, to load with the produce of the French iflands without any limitation*; this moft certainly is not true. It is not difficult to difcover for what purpofe it was calculated; but, neverthelefs, the publication fabricated, and in the occult manner that it has been, fufficiently proves, that to open the Britifh Weft Indies to the American States, not only is unneceffary, but would be extremely mifchievous.

Not merely the provifion trade is greatly prejudiced, but the commerce and marine of the Britifh dominions are likely to be effentially

tially impaired, through the encouragement
which is given to infractions and fufpenfions
of the navigation laws by the unprincipled or
unfyftematic proceedings of Adminiftration.
It would require a volume to ftate to the public the abufes communicated to the writer of
thefe Obfervations, relative to the regiftering
of fhipping, not only in the Weft Indies,
where there is fcarce an attempt at conceal-
ment, and in Ireland, but alfo in Great Britain.   A few pieces of money will immediately convert an American into a Britifh-built
fhip ; and a certificate may be got in Britain,
in Ireland, and the Britifh Weft Indies, for a
fhip now building at Philadelphia.   It is ab-
folutely neceffary to the falvation of the moft
effential of all manufactures, namely, fhip-
building, that the abufe be ftopt; and furely
it is time that our Minifters fhould underftand the neceffity of it.   The greatnefs of the
abufe leads us to inquire into the neceffity of
permitting other certificates or regifters to be
given in the diftant fettlements, at leaft to
veffels trading with the Britifh European dominions, except fuch as may be fometimes neceffary to bring a veffel home.   Without pre-
fuming

fuming to propofe the proper checks to the evil, it is greatly to be wifned fome meafures may be adopted for that purpofe.

The late infraction of the navigation laws, by the opening the ports of Jamaica for four months to all the fhipping of the American States*, and in effect, to every good or bad manufacture or produce of Europe and America, and juft at the time that the legiflature of Great Britain had refufed to adopt fuch a ruinous principle, furely deferves a public inquiry.

It was by no means neceffary to open the ports; the hurricane which had happened was by no means general over the ifland; nor had it fpread far into the country; or if it had, was the ftep which was taken proper. It was to be expected that advantage would be taken of the calamity for the moment; but that could not laft long, neither did it, there was Britifh fhipping abundantly employed in the trade, and fully fufficient to fupply every thing that might be wanting.

The commerce and marine of Great Britain muft not depend on the wifdom or intereft of

* It has been extended to fix weeks longer.

P   plantation

plantation governors, or, rather, of thofe that furround them. Our merchants do not know how to act; they do not know, they cannot guefs, what it is now worth while to fend: common prudence will direct them to fend nothing. The Britifh merchants meet fufficient checks and difficulties, without this additional fporting with their profeffion and fortunes; if there is to be no commercial fyftem, it muft be their refource to retire to fome village, where they will only fuffer equally with the reft of the inhabitants.

The provifion trade, which is now the fubject of inquiry, muft have received a fevere blow. It was apprehended that the provifions which were preparing, if fent, would go to an overftocked, at leaft to an unfteady or uncertain, market; but it apppears that the meafure of a partial, or temporary and occafional, opening of the ports to the American States, has, in reality, produced a fcarcity; and that the fame effect may be expected in Newfoundland. The merchants in thefe kingdoms keep back the export of provifions, becaufe they fuppofe that the market will be overftocked from the
American

American continent, and thofe of the American States are equally apprehenfive, becaufe they fuppofe it may be glutted from hence. Many of the moft refpectable planters reprobate the meafure; they forefaw the confequences; and letters from Jamaica mention, that fhortly after the hurricane, a great number of Britifh veffels arrived with provifions, and articles of all kinds, which were fold as cheap as at any time. Shortly after, lumber was fold there very confiderably below the price at Philadelphia. The Britifh veffels finding the trade was laid open, gave it up. The lumber was bought up at a low price; it was foon raifed, and was retailed at a high price; and the Americans have now raifed lumber and other articles very much. The manufacturers of thefe kingdoms will obferve, that, with lumber and provifions, all forts of manufactures will be introduced in the fhipping of the American States; and as the Americans do not pay for them, they may be, afforded very cheap indeed. This digreffion may be excufed, becaufe the fubject is highly interefting.

Befides

Befides beef and butter, there is other very valuable produce from cattle, fuch as tallow, hides, &c.; and when Ireland thinks proper to quit her unprofitable purfuits, fhe will, if fhe is wife, greatly extend her trade in the manufactures of leather, efpecially to America and the Weft Indies. At the time that the minds of her people are employed in unavailing or hurtful fpeculations, fhe is fuffering an exportation that is extremely prejudicial. The quantity of live cattle fhe has fent to Britain within feven or eight months is prodigious. Perhaps when a temporary fcarcity of cattle fhall have raifed the price greatly, and they cannot be got for the better purpofe of barrelling for exportation, and hides alfo fhall be fcarce, thefe circumftances will ferve for additional declamation on ruined trade and in favour of non-importation agreements and reform. It is not only bad policy to fend out live cattle, but alfo hides tanned or untanned. It is obvious that the manufacture of all materials fhould be carried as many ftages as poffible. Hitherto Ireland has exported an inconfiderable quantity of wrought leather.

leather. Her exports of fhoes to all parts, in the year ending the 25th of March, 1783, was only 14,803lb.* all of which went to America and the Weft Indies, except 224 lbs. to Denmark and Norway, 1436 lbs. to Portugal, and 448 lbs to the Straits. And of fadlers' ware fhe exported only to the value of 98l. 6s. The tanned hides exported to all parts the fame year was 10,488 in number, and 73 cwt. of which nine tenths went to Italy and the Straits. Untanned hides to all parts, 58,079 in number, of which 50,204 went to England, and 4585 to Scotland. Calves fkins 22,510 dozen, almoft the whole of them to England and Scotland. It is known that great frauds are committed in the entry of hides, and efpecially of calves' fkins outwards; there is a duty on the export; and it is certain that the quantity exported exceeds greatly the quantity entered in the Cuftom-houfe books. It is remarkable that in the

---

* And in 1773 fhe exported only 48 lbs. to all parts, and in 1777 fhe exported none. England exported, on an average of years ending with 1774, 443,899 lbs. of wrought leather.

fame

fame year, Ireland imported 284 cwt. of fheep ſkins entirely from Britain, except 72 cwt. from France, and 25 cwt. from Flanders.

The fcarcity of bark in Ireland gives England an advantage over her in the tanning buſineſs. She imported in the year ending 25th March, 1783, 90,836 barrels, all from Britain, except 1406 barrels from Germany, and 10 barrels from Denmark and Norway.

Abſtract of bullocks ſold at Ballinaſloe fair in the following years, which ſeems to prove an increaſe of cattle.

BULLOCKS.

	Sold.	Unſold.	Total.
1771 Oct.	10,876	——	10,876
1772 —	12,346	257	12,603
1773 —	9,764	469	10,233
1774 —	9,328	263	9591
1775 —	10,201	113	10,314
1776 —	9,635	4475	14,110
1777 —	9,646	1815	11,461
1778 —	7,920	4448	12,368

N. B. The failure in 1778 aroſe from the ſtagnation of credit.

FISH-

F I S H E R I E S.

Notwithftanding the prefent infignificant
ftate of the Irifh fifheries, it may reafonably
be expected that in due time they will, among
articles of trade, rank, at leaft, third in
point of national profit, and immediately
follow the linen and provifion trade. In
point of general advantage, they might, perhaps, rank firft, by the great extenfion they
may caufe of the navigation of Ireland.

At prefent Ireland comparatively with her
neighbours, and confidering her fituation and
advantages, has very little fhipping: part at
leaft of her anxious care for the woollen manufactures might be well transferred to this branch
of trade, which has never yet been made an
object of her attention; and the opinion that
fhe can never build as cheap as her neighbours
was as ill founded as the other vulgar errors
which we daily hear. In moft places of England and Holland, where the bufinefs of fhip-
building is carried on to great advantage, the
timber is imported, and alfo the naval ftores
and fhip chandlery. When once embarked, it
is of little moment whether thofe articles are

carried

carried coaſt ways or a few leagues farther
acroſs the ſea. Oak timber, naval ſtores, and
ſhip chandlery, on an average, ought to be as
cheap in Ireland as in Britain or Holland ; and
the injudicious and much higher duties on fir
timber imported into Britain, of which vaſt
quantities are uſed in ſhip building muſt give
ſome advantages to Ireland, where the duties
are ſo much lower.*

The

* As Ireland does not produce at preſent, and is not
likely, for a long time, to afford a quantity worth notice
of any kind of timber for ſhip building, the policy of
laying duties on ſuch timber does not appear; but as
England produces a large quantity of the beſt oak timber, it may be expedient to maintain the duties on that
article coming from foreign countries, leſt the growth
ſhould be diſcouraged at home. Even while the duties
exiſt, the growth is much diſcouraged by the diſtance of
the profit. The advantage to be derived at the end of
almoſt a century, is not very inviting. In the mean
time, ſome expence is incurred in maintaining the
woods; in many parts, however, the underwood yields
a conſiderable profit where the timber is not thick.
Scattered trees, or thoſe that grow in hedge rows, are
by no means clear gains, for they are detrimental to
agriculture; yet, in the end, oak timber is very profita-
ble, eſpecially in good land. It may be anſwered, where-
ever

The eftablifhment of the fifheries of Ireland will, of courfe, promote fhip building, and greatly extend navigation, which will open new' markets. Her manufactures will be carried cheaper, and in a manner forced into countries where they now either do not go, or go under difadvantages; for nothing can be more certain than that thofe nations which have much of the carrying trade, derive ma♦ny benefits from it, more than the profit of freight *, which, however it is very confider-able.

ever it grows well, other things will alfo grow well, pro-ducing a prefent profit ; where, however, an immediate in-come is not wanted, it pays better in the end then any other produce. The no fmall recommendation of a timbered country, is, that it in a manner imperceptibly enriches the owner, and often faves an eftate from fale. On the whole, it may be doubted whether it would be expedient to admit' without duties, fuch timber as we can grow, left, in the end, we fhould become entirely dependent on foreign countries for fhip timber, and be reduced to a mode of fupply both precarious and expenfive. If it fhould be eafy, on the importation of other kinds of timber, to difcriminate be-tween that which is ufed for fhip buiding, or for other ufes, it might be advifable to remove the duties entirely from the former, or at leaft to reduce them.

* Even thofe that are jealous of Irifh manufactures, fhould not be equally fo of the increafe of Irifh fhipping.

Q To

able. It is needlefs to ftate the number of artificers employed in fhip building, and the many trades dependent on it; but the fifheries are the firft and beft foundation of a marine. It is the firft ftage; and if the country does not furnifh freight for a quantity of fhipping, the fifheries will help to provide it for them.

Ireland has advantages in the feveral fifheries which no other country in Europe has, particularly in fituation. Her numerous creeks and harbours give other natural advantages. The almoft lavifh difpofition of her Parliament to promote every feeming intereft of the country, and the eagernefs of individuals to inform themfelves, and to encourage fuch undertakings, appear likely to infure fuccefs.

To the empire at large, it is indifferent to which of the iflands fhipping belongs; there is full room for both to extend themfelves. The furnifhing of feamen and marines are the means by which Ireland can beft contribute her quota to the fupport of the empire; and judging from the well-known fpirit and temper of her people, there can be no doubt of her liberal compliance, on emergency, with requifitions for that purpofe from this country.

Thefe

These are great and leading advantages; but the moſt neceſſary of all requiſites, the habits of the trade, correſpondencies and private capitals, which can ſtand in competition with the eſtabliſhed fiſheries of the north of Europe, are ſtill wanting. Much is ſtill to be done before Ireland can take a lead in any one branch of the fiſheries : in the mean time her attention is divided, and her capitals dwindled into trifles, which can never enable her to rival Holland. It is adviſable that ſhe ſhould confine herſelf to one branch, in which ſhe muſt endeavour to become perfect; and until ſhe excels, and by a great extenſion of her exertions can afford to ſell cheap, there is no probability of her commanding foreign markets.

HERRING FISHERY.

It is in the herring fiſhery ſhe is moſt likely to excel, and it is that, principally, which ſhe ſhould, at leaſt for a time, purſue. She ſhould not ſuffer herſelf to be diſtracted by uncertain attempts at other fiſheries until ſhe is well founded in this; England, by being in

poſſeſſion

poffeffion of the whale fifhery, has great and almoft unfurmountable advantages over her in that branch; and the difference of diftance is not, perhaps, fo great an object as at firft appears.

Notwithftanding the herrings have, in great meafure, during the laft fifteen years, deferted the coaft of Scotland, except, perhaps, the north-weftern, and almoft unexplored parts, yet the fuperior frugality, fobriety, and fteadinefs of her people, their induftry in taking the fifh, and greater cleanlinefs in curing them, will enable her to rival Ireland, although the latter has the fifh at her very door, where the Scotch now come to look for them. For on the north-weftern coaft of Ireland the herrings are caught in vaft quantities clofe to the fhore.

It is the north-weft wind which throws the herrings towards this coaft. There is confiderable uncertainty as to the bay or creek where they may firft be found. They fometimes firft appear in Sligo bay; but the beft fifhery is at the Roffes and near Killebegs. The north-weft wind, which prevails on this
coaft,

coaft, is terrible, and produces a great fea, that is no fmall interruption to the fifhery. This part of the coaft is very bold, the creeks and harbours not fo frequent as elfewhere, nor always to be approached. It is difficult for the veffels to run into fhelter, when they can no longer keep the fea. A huge fwell dafhes againft the roots of the mountains which form this coaft, and this feems to give an advantage to the Scotch fifhery which is carried on in the loughs or branches of the fea which run into the land, and between the main land and the Hebrides. The laft muft afford great fhelter; but, on the other hand, it is faid, that the fifhery fucceeds beft in ftormy weather; but if fifh is not wanting, we cannot doubt a fufficiency of ftorm amidft the Hebrides. Herring nets can be handed only in fmall boats, and the fifhery is never hurt by any weather in which the boats can live; a little wind is even neceffary for them, as they always drift before it, when fifhing, or with the tide, which ever prevails. The veffels on the bounty, as well as thofe from Liverpool and the Ifle of Man, come into the harbours and remain there. The fifhery is

entirely

entirely carried on by the boats (and within the bays, fometimes to the head of the fmalleft and narroweft creeks) and thofe moftly of the country, as the veffels feldom look out for any fifh, but buy of the fifhermen of the place. The Scotch, indeed, come over in buffes, and bring boats, falt, nets, buoys, &c. and take their own fifh, and royals, packs, or barrels, on board their buffes.

In 1780, one hundred and thirty bounty veffels were at the fifhery in Lough Swilly: they expended, in the cure of fifh, 1708 tons of falt, which falt cured in bulk (allowing 30 maize, or 15,000 fifh to one ton of falt) 51,240 maize. A maize is 500 herrings.

In 1781, the bounty veffels in the fame lough were 147 : falt expended, 1914 tons: maize or barrels cured, 57,420.

In 1780, feventy-one veffels from Liverpool and the Ifle of Man, purchafed cargoes in Lough Swilly for their red-herring houfes. They brought, per cocket, for curing fifh at fea, 650 tons of falt, (on which the duty, if demanded, 335l. 16s. 8d.) and with the falt they
bought

bought, and royaled, 39,000 maize, for which they paid 8,125l. at 10d. per hundred.

In 1781, one hundred and seventeen vessels, from the same places, bought cargoes there, for the same purpose. They purchased, and royaled, with the salt they brought, 49,950 maize or barrels, and paid 12,487l. 10s. so that the above vessels in those two years purchased in Lough Swilly 88,950 maize or barrels, for which they paid cash, and left in Lough Swilly 20,612l.

Total of herrings taken in two years, by the bounty and red-herring men, out of Lough Swilly, 197,610 maize or barrels.

In the Summer, 1784, the herrings came upon the north-west coast about the last week in June, and continued until about the last week in September. At first they were of a small size, but increased considerably; and latterly they were large, but, by no means, the size of the winter herrings. It is almost impossible to give even a satisfactory guess at the numbers that were taken. There was, for a considerable part of that time, no other demand

demand than from the country about thirty
miles around, and the take was fo very great,
and the demand fo fmall, that incredible
numbers were thrown away; and, upon an
average price for a month, they did not
exceed 1od. per thoufand. The number was
fo great, that 4d. 5d. or 6d. was the price of
an horfe load, and there was no reftriction as
to the load. They were boiled for oil, the
price of which was 1od. per gallon, and was
very good for lamps. The guts of 500 of the
fmalleft harveft herrings, when boiled, produce about a gallon of very good lamp oil,
which is moftly loft at prefent. This kind
of oil is much ufed by curriers.

The number of boats that were employed in the herring fifhery, was from 70
to 100; and during the height of the feafon,
each boat could have taken at leaft as many
more as they did, feldom having occafion to
fhoot their nets more than once for the boat
load. As to the fum each boat made, it is
faid to be about 54l. and computing the
price of herrings to be 20d. per thoufand,
each boat took 648.000. which multiplied

by

by 70, the number of boats employed, gives 45,360 000, the number of herrings fold, exclufive of what were boiled for oil, or were thrown away.

The herrings taken in July, Auguſt, and September, have hitherto been fuppofed incapable of being properly cured, on account of their very extraordinary richnefs; but this is found to be otherwife; for fome of them in their richeſt ſtate have been cured, (and finer there cannot be) and it appears that if a fufficient quantity of falt is ufed, they may be preferved as well as the winter herring: but, by not taking proper care, and by a trifling faving, the commodity has been brought into difrepute. It has been fuggeſted, that fome regulation in the curing the harveſt herring is neceffary. The quantity of falt ufed for the winter fifh, will preferve the harveſt herrings for a fhort, but not for a long time.

Sir Lucius O'Brien and Mr. Groffett have collected and given to the public much ufeful information relative to the fifheries; and fome very intelligent gentlemen of Ireland having interested themfelves in this

R   bufinefs,

bufinefs, there is no doubt that it will have all the affiftance that can be given to it.

Our prepoffeffion in favour of the fifheries, founded on the patriotic wifh to affift the navigation and marine of the empire, is highly laudable. It however, perhaps, leads us willingly to credit golden dreams of inexhauftible markets, without much examination. We read of the fifheries having produced to Holland nine millions fterling yearly, and a revenue of one million. Almoft all the writers on this fubject copy Vice Admiral Sir William Monfon, or thofe that copied him; of courfe there feems to be a good mafs of evidence to the fame point. The number of buffes, and people employed, and lafts of herrings, and other fifh caught, is prodigious. One writer, however, Meynert Semyens, who publifhed *A Brief Defcription of the Herring Fifhery*, in Dutch, printed at Enchuyfen in 1639, and who lived in the time of Monfon, does not make the number of buffes employed half fo many as the other writers, who fay 1800 buffes, and 9000 veffels of all forts

were

were employed in that fifhery, Meynert Semyens mentions 700 buffes only : this is a great number. It is now reduced to 200; but it fhould be obferved, that the tonnage of the buffes in thofe days was about 16 tons, and now that they are, on an average, 26 tons.

Sir William Monfon had diftinguifhed himfelf as a fea officer in the reigns of Elizabeth and James I. He feems a refpeétable writer, and to have been a man of refearch and obfervation; he had the beft opportunities of information, and had explored the feas he mentions, particularly the coaft of Ireland and north weft of Scotland; he had commanded in thofe feas, and his defcription generally agrees with the beft accounts that can now be had. As to the prodigious quantity of fifh taken by the Dutch, he mentions, that the account was obtained from the cuftom-houfe books of Holland. He gives us the feveral markets, and the quantity of fifh taken by each place, and the whole feems to be authentic; but we fhould have had more fatisfaétion in believing him, if he had not believed that in

R 2   Spain

Spain a mermaid came out of the fea, " en-
" gendered with a woman on fhore, and be-
" gat on her a child."

At all events, we know that the advantage
of the herring fifhery to the Dutch has been
very great, that it is diminifhed, but ftill is
very confiderable; that the Swedes and Eaft-
landers have got a confiderable fhare of it.
That the French have little of it, nor are they
likely to have much more, the herrings in the
feas which are convenient to them, being
fmall and bad, as they are on the fouth coaft
of England and fouth of Norfolk. It is obferved, that coming from the north, they become comparatively a bad fifh when they arrive
fo far fouth as Orfordnefs, and that as they
return to the north again, they improve; and
when they arrive near the Weftern Ifles, they
become once more a fine fat fifh.

And here the unfriendly difpofition of the
two nations of Ireland and Scotland, on
the fubject of the fifheries, fhould be noticed. It is injurious to each, as the utmoft and united exertions of both countries
will,

will, with great difficulty, gain upon the Dutch, and enable them to obtain and supply the foreign demand. While the herrings were on the coaſt of Scotland, the complaints were againſt the Scotch; but they are now turned againſt the Iriſh. It ſhould rather be the buſineſs of Ireland to learn the art of fiſhery and curing fiſh from the fiſhermen of Campbeltown ; they ſhould court their aſſiſtance; and it would be ſtill better if a colony of Dutchmen could be ſettled at the Roſſes. Neatneſs, in which the Dutch excel, is not the quality for which the lower ranks of Scotland or of Ireland are moſt diſtinguiſhed ; yet it is the neatneſs of the Dutch, and care in curing, that acquired, for their fiſh, a high reputation, and gained for it ſo extraordinary a market.

The legiſlatures of the two iſlands ſhould form the neceſſary regulations, which might be enforced by ſloops or cutters. It is ſaid, that beſides other ill treatment complained of when the Scotch veſſels come upon the Iriſh coaſt, advantage is taken of the hovering act to oblige them to enter, (though not to land,) and pay the Iriſh duty for ſalt. The Britiſh

duties

duties are drawn back on the falt used in the fifheries, but the Irifh are not; the latter are not confiderable, being only 12s. per ton on falt imported; yet the Irifh think it hard the Britifh veffels fhould have this advantage of them on their own coaft. Perhaps it may be advifeable for Ireland to allow a drawback of the duty on all falt used in the fifheries : this may give an opening to fome fraud, and the revenue may fuffer a little; but even lefs than four pence per barrel (each barrel takes a bufhel of falt) is a confiderable and unneceffary weight to fall on the fifhery in its infancy, and this would remove one difficulty between the Scotch and Irifh fifheries. The Irifh fifher, at prefent, is obliged to land the falt which is brought from Britain ; for when he enters it outwards from thence, he engages in a bond for 6s. 8d. per cwt. defeafible, upon producing a certificate of its being landed in Ireland ; and in order to get fuch certificate, he is obliged to unload all his falt, and refhip it for the fifhery ; but the Scotch having entered theirs to be expended upon the curing of fifh at fea, on their return to Great Britain,

tain, have an allowance of fo much as they have wet, duty free, and have, therefore, no occafion for the Irifh certificate. Ireland farther complains, that Britifh herrings come into their home markets at 2s. and 8d. bounty on export from Britain, and only 1s. duty in Ireland, the Britifh falt alfo being without duty. It fhould be obferved, that a nominal drawback of the whole duties in Scotland does not remove all expence; the bufinefs of bonds and certificates caufes trouble and delay; fome gratuities muft be given; attendance and time are expence, which is not drawn back, and probably amount to no fmall part of the Irifh duty on falt *.

The north-weftern fifhery of Ireland although fo promifing, is yet in a very mean

---

* Ireland is allowed to export from Great Britain Rock Salt, duty free, to be boiled down and refined there; that privilege is denied to all Great Britain except to the Ports Swanfey, Hollyhead, and Lawn Marfh, and within ten computed miles of the Salt Pitts. By which reftriction it is faid Ireland is enabled to fupply the weft coaft of Great Britain with fmuggled falt, at a reafonable rate, to the great prejudice of the Revenue.

ftate;

ftate; there is little to mention, except what
nature has done ; and furely, all things confidered, fhe has done as much for Ireland as
for any part of Europe. We learn that in
other parts the herring is an uncertain fifh,
but we have not heard that it ever entirely
failed on this coaft. Unfavourable winds prevented the herrings from embaying fufficiently early the laft feafon, to enable Ireland to
furnifh the ufual quantity for the Weft Indies,
confequently the price rofe to 4l. per barrel in
thofe iflands. It is probable the fifhermen
too foon defpond of finding fifh; and fometimes the difappointment happens through
want of fufficiency of buoy rope : an incident
of laft year feemed to confirm it. The three
firft nets or dippings were proved twice, and
only ftraggling herrings found in them ; on
proving them a third time, there was the fame
appearance, but on taking in the nets to
change ground, it was found the buoy of the
center net was burft, by which it funk five
feet of the line; upon drawing it into the
boat it was full of herrings. From this circumftance it is conjectured, that a want of a
fufficiency

fufficiency of buoy rope is the reafon country fifhermen are fo often unfuccefsful, although immediately above the herrings.

Perhaps if the hint given by Mr. Pennant was followed on the coaft of Ireland as well as of Scotland, it would be as ufeful a kind of bounty as could be offered by government, viz. each year to fend out fmall veffels to make a thorough trial in every branch of the fea; they would undoubtedly find fhoals in fome of them, which, together with founding the banks and examining the coaft might be performed by the floops or cutters appointed to enforce the neceffary regulations of the fifheries.

The deftruction of the Scotch fifhery has been in part attributed to the largenefs of their nets : they were often fo loaded with herrings that the nets could not be taken out of the water till the following day. This was the opinion of an intelligent perfon who had been engaged in the Scotch fifhery thirty years.

If the Dublin fociety fhould think proper to print the beft rules and obfervations on

S   the

the fubject that can be collected, and difperfe
them among thofe concerned, and the fifhermen, poffibly a better mode will be fooner
introduced in the place of bad habits and
ignorant prejudice, and the fifhery may
fooner arrive at perfection. At prefent the
Irifh method of curing fifh is extremely
flovenly. Herrings caught and cured by the
Scots in the fame feas, are much preferred
and fell at a confiderably higher price in the
Irifh market. No fmall part of the herrings
exported from Cork are imported from Scotland, although they are not intitled to any
bounty on re-export, but the great bounties
on export from Scotland enables them to go
to Cork to be fent abroad notwithftanding
that difadvantage. The fuperiority of the
Scotch herrings over the Irifh, arifes principally from the latter being carried in bulk to
Cork there to be barrelled. They are much
hurt by the preffure in the package and by
their not being gutted till they arrive. They
fhould barrel at or near the fifhery.

There are not at prefent the neceffary
buildings and conveniences on the coaft,

Holes

Holes are dug in the earth, in which the fifh is falted, then covered with earth, and the people are furprifed to find that fnow and rain hurt them in that ftate. The want of proper eftablifhments and ftores has fubjeded the fifheries of Ireland to great inconveniences; in particular it has been feverely felt in the enormous price of falt occafionally when the take of fifh was great. In 1771 falt was at 10l. 10s. per ton. The ordinary price is about 3l. 10s. Several perfons have now fet up falt works on the coaft. The falt is weaker than the Englifh becaufe it is not fo much boiled. This is among many articles in which Britain muft always have an advantage through her greater abundance of coal.

Befides ftores on the coaft, infpedors are wanted, to fee the herrings properly cured and made up; and there fhould be regulated packers as in Holland.

The principal herring fifhery of Ireland is from Lough Swilly to Broad Haven. It has been recommended to eftablifh a ftore at Kil-

leybeggs,

leybeggs, on account of its being the moſt commodious harbour for the early fiſhery : certain intelligence of the ſoutherly fiſhery, viz. Ballywell, Sligo bay, Killalla, Black Rock and Broad Haven, is to be got there, or at Donegal. Beſides there are about that harbour a number of ſmall creeks and bays, viz. M'Swine's bay, Portnacroſs and Tillon, into which the herrings generally ſet and where boats can run in eaſy weather. However the Roſſes ſeem beſt calculated to be the head quarters or chief ſtore ; and in caſe red-herring houſes ſhould be erected, the fiſh there is larger and of courſe better adapted for that purpoſe *. They have likewiſe the advantage of an eaſier communication with Britain for the importation of ſalt and wood. The ſituation too is convenient for the Dernfernachy and Lough-Swilly fiſheries. In every reſpect the Roſſes muſt anſwer beſt for a general ſtore to collect all the fiſh got on either ſide.

The making of oil from the ſummer fiſh ſhould be encouraged, and alſo from the guts

---

* There is only one red herring houſe in the kingdom, which was built laſt ſummer.

of herrings as well as from feals, dog-fifh, fun-fifh, &c. &c.

The herring fifhery was at its height before the Newfoundland fifhery became confiderable. The former has fince decreafed, but we are told thofe fifheries have not in the leaft interfered with each other, and that the herring fifhery has not been prejudiced by that of Newfoundland. The affertion is contrary to reafon. The great relaxation as to lent-keeping in Europe muft alfo have diminifhed the demand for herrings; and, perhaps, every country, to a certain degree, fupplies itfelf with more fifh than formerly. From thefe circumftances it may be thought the foreign markets for herrings can never be raifed to what they were, or to what the Dutch enjoyed. No new market has occurred fince the high profperity of that fifhery, except the Weft Indian, for which, in the year ending 25th March, 1783, Ireland exported 35,960 barrels.

This kind of examination is neceffary for the purpofe of difcovering to what extent markets can be expected, and of avoiding the

lofs

lofs and difappointment of fpeculating too far in this fifhery. However, Ireland having the advantage of all other countries in the herring branch of the fifheries, with proper exertions, might furpafs them in it; and then fhe need not fear the want of a fufficient market.

The increafe of the fifhery appears from the following account:

Average annual quantity of herrings exported from Ireland for four years, ending 25 March, 1767, 4672 barrels.

Average annual quantity of herrings imported into Ireland, for the fame years, 52,824 barrels.

Average annual quantity of herrings exported from Ireland, for four years, ending 25 March, 1783, 24,273 barrels.

Average annual quantity of herrings imported into Ireland, for the fame years, 12,277 barrels.

As the latter were years of war, the increafe of exportation is more extraordinary.

It

It is remarkable, that the imports and exports of the two periods, colle&ively taken,
and compared, are nearly equal.

WHALE FISHERY.

There are, undoubtedly, whales off the
porth and north weft coaft of Ireland, which
come clofe in fhore. The fpermaceti whale
may be found at fome diftance from the coaft.
The bone whale follows the herrings into
the bays, and one of the *figns* of fifh, as the
fifhermen phrafe it, is the whale. Some
years ago 1000l. was given by the parliament of Ireland, for the purpofe of carrying
on this fifhery. The perfon to whom it was
granted killed feven whales, but has not fince
purfued that fifhery. Its practicability on
that coaft is, however, firmly afferted, and
that Ireland, at leaft, might fupply her own
demand with the produce of the whale, and
thereby keep a confiderable fum of money at
home. Ireland certainly has fome advanta-
gess in this fifhery; and fince the act of the
15th of the prefent reign, which opens the
ports of Great Britain for whale fins and
blubber,

blubber, and oil alfo of all creatures living in the fea, to all the fubjects of his Majefty's European dominions, there can now be no doubt of a market, and her own confumption of oil is greatly increafed. But if the attempt to lower the duties on oil from the American States fhould fucceed, the intereft of the empire at large will be extremely prejudiced : a propofal more mifchievous to our fifheries, and confequently to the Britifh marine, cannot be made.

The WHITE or COD FISHERY.

The abundance of cod, ling, and hake, on the coaft of Ireland, is well known ; there are banks conftantly frequented by white fifh, which is faid to be as good, and even larger than what is taken at Newfoundland*. But it has been faid there are other banks off the north weft of Ireland and Scotland, mentioned alfo by Sir William Monfon, and fup-

---

* A Company of merchants engaged in the White fifhery a few years ago: after two or three years they relinquifhed the purfuit, having loft a confiderable proportion of their capital.

pofed

pofed by fome to be a part of a chain which extends to thofe at Newfoundland; others think they extend towards Cape Farewell, off Greenland. In 1783, Captain Ellifon, in the Ariadne, went in fearch of thefe banks. The moft accurate foundings were taken to afcertain the extent, but no traces of them were found, perhaps the fearch was not extended far enough. But as the examination was made under the direction of the Lord Lieutenant, it is probable that all the information that could be obtained was given, to guide and affift the undertaking.

FISH

FISH imported into Ireland.

		Year 1711	Year 1734	Year 1738	Year 1740	An average of 7 years ending 25th March, 1762.
Anchovies	Barrels.	309	776	619	$401\frac{1}{2}$	564
Cod	C. q. No.	$\frac{1}{2}$	$300\frac{1}{2}$	$112\frac{3}{4}$	678	427 2 24
Cod	Barrels.	14	15	—	22	33
Hake	C. q. No.	—	—	—	—	36 3
Herrings	Barrels.	$1702\frac{1}{2}$	$764\frac{1}{4}$	7418	4081	25603
Ling	C. q. No.	—	$39\frac{1}{2}$	$\frac{1}{2}$	$43\frac{3}{4}$	214
Mackerel	Barrels.	—	—	—	—	18
Pilchards	Hogſheads	—	—	—	—	69
Salmon	Tons.	$13\frac{2}{3}$	$1\frac{1}{2}$	1	$6\frac{1}{6}$	21
Stock	C. q. No.	—	—	—	$3\frac{1}{2}$	55 1 18
Sturgeon	Kegs.	49	355	188	179	192

FISH exported from Ireland.

		Year 1711	Year 1734	Year 1738.	Year 1740	An average of 7 years ending 25 March, 1762.
Cod	Barrels.	141	2	—	—	32
Cod	C. q. No.	—	—	—	—	6
Hake	Ditto.	1859 2	470 2	1532	1245	1163
Herrings	Barrels.	6674	21057	$7743\frac{3}{4}$	$258\frac{1}{2}$	5838
Ling	C. q. No.	27	—	1	—	77 7
Mackerel	Barrels.	—	20	110	293	671
Pilchards	Hogſheads	—	$2594\frac{3}{4}$	2754	366	$\frac{1}{2}$
Salmon	Tons.	920	545	$513\frac{1}{3}$	$383\frac{2}{3}$	489
Dried	C. q. No.	59 16	—	—	—	1 0 14

Total of Fiſh exported from Ireland to all Parts, the year ending the 25th March, 1783.			Ditto imported into Ireland for the ſame Year.		
Cod	Barrels.	272	Anchovies	Barrels.	294
Cod	C. q. No.	5	Cod	C. q. No.	531 5
Eels	Barrels.	$1\frac{1}{3}$	Herrings	Barrels.	4324
Hake	C. q. No.	1367 3 10	Ling	C. q. No.	281 1 5
Herrings	Barrels.	$48481\frac{1}{2}$	Oyſters	Gallons.	5
Ling	C. q. No.	170	Salmon *	Tons trs.	47 4
Salmon	Tons trs.	$253\frac{21}{60}$	Sturgeon	Kegs.	33

* The importation of ſalmon was probably accidental.

OIL exported from Ireland in the year, ending 25th March, 1783.

	Hogſheads.	Gallons.
Train oil, - -	1 -	7

OIL imported into Ireland the ſame year.

	Gallons.
Linſeed, - -	$25,311\frac{1}{2}$
Seville, - - -	$29,475\frac{1}{2}$
Sweet, - -	$97,95\frac{23}{30}$
Train, - - -	$76,595\frac{33}{60}$

WOOLLEN MANUFACTURE.

The woollen manufacture of Ireland is undoubtedly very conſiderable, and now produces more than her fiſheries ; but it will not be carried to an extent much greater than at preſent, as has been already remarked on the ſubject of protecting duties. By ſacrificing greater advantages than could be attained through a forced increaſe of the manufacture, more wool might be raiſed, and more cloth might be made, but the woollen is not likely to be the principal manufacture of Ireland for export.

It

It is curious to obferve the illiberal arts and injudicious exertions of oppreffion, employed by one country to deprefs and prevent the exportation of the woollen manufacture of the other; and the equally ignorant difpofition of Ireland, almoft conftantly during this century, to impute her poverty and inability of growing rich, to the want of a woollen export trade, while it is probable that fince the revolution fhe barely grew wool enough to cloath her own inhabitants. This has been partly fhewn by comparing, under the article of protecting duties, the late import of woollens with the export of wool and yarn; for we know that if wool is now fmuggled from Ireland, the quantity is trifling. The home market is, and has been fo high for a confiderable time, that no foreign market can afford to pay the additional expence of fmuggling; which has been computed at 6d. per lb: and it is generally underftood that when wool is above 10s. per ftone in that country, it will not anfwer to fmuggle it.

Some manufactures of wool exifted in Ireland previous to the reign of James the Firft,
but

but they were not confiderable. They then made fome progrefs, and in the fucceeding reign, although Lord Strafford difcouraged them*. The civil war which followed, al- moft

---

* An EXTRACT from Lord Deputy STRAFFORD's LETTER to CHRISTOPHER WANDERFORD, giving an Account of the Report he made to the KING and COUNCIL, dated London, July the 25th, 1636.

'That there was little or no manufacture amongft them, but fome fmall beginnings towards a clothing trade, which I had, and fo fhould ftill difcourage all I could, unlefs otherwife directed by his Majefty and their Lordfhips; in regard it would trench not only upon the clothings of England, being our ftaple commodity, fo as if they fhould manufacture their own wools, which grew to very great quantities. We fhould not only lofe the profit we made now by in-draping their wools, but his Majefty lofe extremely by his cuftoms; and in conclufion it might be feared, they would beat us out of the trade itfelf, by underfelling us, which they were well able to do. Yet have I endeavoured another way to fet them on work, and that is by bringing in the making and trade of linen cloth; the rather in regard the women are all naturally bred to fpinning; that the Irifh earth is apt for bearing of flax; and that this manufacture would be in conclufion rather a benefit than other to this kingdom: I have, therefore, fent for the flax feed into Holland, being of a better fort than we have, and

moſt annihilated every manufacture in Ireland, and that country which had ſo abound-
ed in cattle and proviſions, was after Cromwell's *ſettlement* of it, obliged to import proviſions from Wales *. However it was ſufficiently recovered ſoon after the Reſtoration
to alarm the grazing counties of England, and
in the year 1666, the importation of live cattle, ſheep, ſwine, &c. from Ireland was prohibited. The principle of the bill was bad in
every reſpect, but it proved an excellent law
for her. It was repreſented that the rents of
England had fallen one fifth through the public *nuiſance*, as it was termed, of importing cat-

and ſown this year a thouſand pounds of it (finding by
ſome I ſowed the laſt year, that it takes there very well.)
I have ſent for workmen out of the Low Countries and
South of France, and ſet up already 6 or 7 looms; which,
if pleaſe God to bleſs us this year, I truſt ſo to invite them
to follow it, when they ſee the great profit ariſing thereby
as that they ſhall generally take and employ themſelves
that way, which if they do, I am confident it will prove a
mighty buſineſs.

* Sir William Petty, ſtates the cattle and ſtock of Ireland to be worth above four millions in 1641, and that the
whole cattle in Ireland was not worth 500,000l. in 1652.

tle

tle from Ireland, although the value of thofe imported the years previous to the law was not above 132,000l. The hides, tallow, and freight whereof, were worth half that fum. Obferve how it anfwered the narrow views of England. Before that time great numbers of young cattle were fent to England : little butter, fcarce any beef, hides, or tallow, were exported ; and the money received for the cattle was paid for Englifh commodities. Ireland turned to fheep, to the dairy, and fattening of cattle, and to tillage, and fhe fhortly exported much beef and butter, and has fince fupplanted England in thofe beneficial branches of trade. She was forced to feek a foreign market ; and England had no more than a fourth of her trade, although before that time fhe had almoft the whole of it. The woollen manufacture of Ireland * towards the end of that

* A report of the board of trade made in the year 1697 gives the following account of the Irifh woollen manufactures.

	New Draperies.	Old Draperies.	Frize.
Years.	Pieces.	Pieces.	Yards.
1665	224	32	444,581
1687	11,360	103	1,129,716
1696	4,413	$34\frac{1}{2}$	104,167

century,

century, began to recover, and England (not content with her extraordinary experiment in refpect to cattle) immediately fuppofed her own manufacture ruined, and a narrow fpirit which was more excufable in the manufactures, becaufe they feemed in a degree interefted, induced the legiflature to pafs an act in 1699 prohibiting the exportation of woollen manufactures from Ireland to any other places but the few wool ports in England, where they were liable to duties which amounted to a prohibition.

And, obferve again, the miftake of England. The woollen manufacturers of Ireland, who, or their anceftors, came chiefly from England *, now emigrated from Ireland; certainly, however, in fmaller numbers than were at the time reprefented. In their refentment and neceffities many of the Proteftants

* About the year 1664, fome clothiers from the Weft of England fettled in Dublin, and eftablifhed the manufacture, which ftill continues there. It is faid, nearly at the fame time, fixty Dutch families of clothiers fettled at Limerick. Some Englifh clothiers fettled alfo at Cork and Kinfale. Some French introduced the Drugget manufacture at Waterford; and, in 1675, fome London merchants fet up a woollen manufacture at Clonmell.

moved

moved to Germany, many of the Roman Catholics to Spain, and others of each defcription to France, where they received encouragement, and fhewed the way how our wool might be fmuggled from both iflands. The foundation of manufactures were laid, or they were promoted, highly to the prejudice of England; and thus fome return was made for the manufactures eftablifhed in the Britifh dominions by the equally wife edict of Nantz.

But the account of the woollen manufactures exported from Ireland, in 1698, the year preceding the prohibition, will beft fhew the wantonnefs of that oppreffive meafure.

		England	Scotland	Elfewhere.
Apparel	Value	102 3 4	—	517 19
Drapery	New Pieces	601	2128	20556½
	Old Pieces	1¼	29¼	250½
Frize	Yards	127601	1355	537945
Hats	Number	479	1125	2866
Rugs	Number	30	10	418
Stockings	Wol. doz. pair	745	5	7002
	Wor. doz. pair	16 9	—	158 8

For the better underftanding of this account, it is neceffary to know, that the only article in it, of which the amount is confiderable, namely frizes, was not made in England*.

U   That

* It is extraordinary how much the export of frize from Ireland is reduced. The quantity lately exported from Ireland is trifling.   1781

That the frizes and ſtockings exported the preceding year, 1697, together, amounted to 14,625l. 12s*. and the old and new drapery, which alone interfered with the Engliſh manufacture, amounted only to 8988 l. 17s. 6d†. In 1698, 13,480 ſtones of yarn and 217,678 ſtones of wool were ſent to England, which was 9,812 ſtones of yarn more than in 1687, the year of greateſt export; and 38,913 ſtones of wool leſs ‡. In the above-mentioned year of the greateſt export, viz. 1687, the value of all the woollen manufactures exported, did not exceed 70,521 l. 14 s. and of that ſum the

1781, 1779 yards, moſtly to America.

1782, 800 ditto, all to America.

1783, 784 ditto: 84 to America, 700 to Flanders, but the conſumption of the inhabitants is probably increaſed. It is remarkable, that it was the principal woollen manufacture of Ireland, when her wool was much finer than it is now. The large part of the frizes that came to England were dreſſed, and receiving a great degree of manufacture, afforded a conſiderable profit to this country.

* This calculation is taken from J. Smith on Wool: it appears very low.

† Total of woollen manufactures exported that year, 23614l. 9s. 6d. accounting the wool whereof to be one fourth, the value of the labour was about 18,000l.

‡ J. Smith on Wool.

frizes

frizes amounted to 56,485 l. 16 s. coarfe ftockings, 2520 l. 18s. Old and new draperies did
not exceed 11,514 l. 10s. It feems, from the
cuftom-houfe accounts, that Ireland had not
recovered above one third of the woollen trade
fhe had before the war of the Revolution,
and it is remarkable, that in the above year,
1687, fhe fent more wool and yarn to England than in any of the preceding years, viz.
of yarn, at 18lbs. to the ftone, 3668 ftones,
of wool, 256,592 ftones.

England feems to have been blind as to a
very obvious confequence of prohibiting the
exportation of woollens from Ireland, namely,
that it would lead her to manufacture her
wool into a great variety of articles for her
own confumption, which fhe then took from
England, and reduce her import of Englifh
manufactures; whereas the frizes, the then
principal manufacture of Ireland, did not
interfere with any branch of her woollens.

It had the confequence of leffening the import from England, although not for the
years immediately following. In 1700, were
imported from Britain,

Yards,

	Yards.	Value.
Old drapery,	12,119½	9,014l. 12s. 6d.
New drapery,	24,522	2,043l. 10s. 0d.

But, in 1706*, we find the quantity imported from England reduced to lefs than half of the broad cloth, and to about two thirds of the narrow.

	Yards.	Value.
Old drapery,	5514½	4,135l. 17s. 6d.
New drapery,	15,308½	1,913l. 11s. 3d.

The quantity of wool imported into England from Ireland, in 1700, was 336,292 ftones, at 18lbs. Yarn, the fame year, 26,617 ftones. But the prohibition having promoted the fmuggling of wool, the peace of

* Some years after, the quantity imported gradually increafed with the population and riches of the country, and in 1714 it exceeded the importations previous to the prohibition. About that time alfo, it fhould be obferved, the fmuggling of wool increafed, in confequence of the low price of wool at home. One mode of fmuggling was by preffing the wool very clofe in barrels or cafks with fcrews; and placing a little butter or beef at top, it was fent abroad as either of the laft : and as it was the intereft of the country to export it, although the cuftom-houfe officer knew the deceit, he did not dare to detect it. Tobacco has been fmuggled in the fame manner.

Utrecht

Utrecht rendered that bufinefs more eafy, the intercourfe with France was greater, and in the year 1714, the quantity of wool imported into England from Ireland, was diminifhed to 147,153 ftones*, and it has fince continued to decreafe to the fmall quantity now exported; which will be mentioned hereafter.

The quantity of woollen yarn imported into England from Ireland, had increafed from 26,617 ftones in 1700, to 91,854 ftones, in 1729, the year previous to the alteration of the duty on export from Ireland. Since that time the duties were entirely taken off, in England, by the 12 and 26 Geo. 2. from

* The quantity of yarn exported from Ireland to England, in 1714, was 58,147 ftones, at 18lbs.

+ But this was not propofed in favour of Ireland. It was not much better than a job in favour of the Englifh manufacturers, whofe intereft it was not to diminifh the quantity of Irifh wool, though their wifh was totally to deftroy the Irifh manufacture, and (notwithftanding the monopoly that was already given to them of Englifh wool) it was thought reafonable that the wool-growers of England fhould fubmit to this additional depreciation of that article. This law, however, tended to leffen the fmuggling of wool from Ireland to foreign countries, at the fame time that it lowered the price, (which was, perhaps, already too low) in England.

woollen

woollen and worfted yarn imported from Ireland. To which, and the increafed demand
for worfted yarn from Manchefter, and the
circumftance that fpinning is much cheaper
in Ireland than in England* being added,
the increafed export of yarn which took place,
may be imputed. The value of wool was
raifed very confiderably above the price in
England, by the demands of the merchant,
who was enabled to give an extraordinary
price, being reimburfed through the low price
of fpinning. Smuggling of wool, of courfe,
decreafed, and has for many years almoft
ceafed; and here it may be remarked, that the
depreciation of wool in any country, below
its natural value, by prohibitions or mono-
polies, encourages fmuggling more than the
particular want of it in other countries.

On an average of five years, ending 1768,
the quantity of woollen and worfted yarn
exported was 160,295 ftones, and of wool
25,284 ftones. But latterly the quantity has

* Viz. in Ireland, two pence-halfpenny and three pence.
In England, at five pence and fix pence. Other eftimates
fay at nine pence per lb, for fpinning in England; five
pence in Ireland.

decreafed

decreafed very much; principally from the increafe of the woollen manufacture in Ireland, the increafe of the people, and confequently increafed home confumption; and fome add that the corn bounties and increafe of tillage has diminifhed the number of fheep. Export of woollen and worfted yarn on an average of five years ending 25th March 1783, 84,255 ftones, and of wool 2435 ftones.

The quantity of wool exported from Ireland to England at different periods has been mentioned down to 1714, and of woollen and worfted yarn down to 1729. The quantity of wool exported from Ireland to England that year was 38,667 ftones at 18lb. and the quantity imported the fame year of

Old drapery from England,
23,399½ yards, value 18,299l. 8s. od.

Old drapery from Scotland,
13 yards, value 9l. 15s. od.

New drapery from England,
35,521 yards, value 3,552l. 2s. od.

New drapery from Scotland,
384 yards, value 38l. 8s. od.

From

From that year the importation of draperies decreafed very confiderably, and in the
year 1737 it was lefs than half, viz.

Old drapery from Great Britain,
9626½ yards, value 6497l. 17s. 9d.

New drapery from Great Britain,
17569½ yards, value 2635l. 8s. od.

For which the writer of thefe obfervations
cannot account, unlefs by the impoverifhment
and diftrefs arifing from the fcarcity of corn
in the years 1728 and 1729. It appeared in
the latter year, that corn had been imported
in eighteen months to the amount of 274,000l.
a vaft fum at that time, confidering the ftate
of the country. Yet in 1740 and 1741, years
alfo of fcarcity, the importation of draperies
had increafed, viz.

Old drapery, in

1740	1741	1742 and 1743	
Yards.	Yards.	Yards.	Yards.
16,714.	12,918.	22,971.	14,582.

New

New drapery,

39,064. 42,504. 53,364. 65,880 *.

But from that time the importation began to increafe, and foon very rapidly and progreffively till the greateft import took place in 1777, viz.

Old drapery,
381,330 yards, value 266,931l.

New drapery,
731, 819½ yards, value 91,477l. 8s. 4d.

But the average of five years ending 1777 was only,

Old drapery,
289,053¼ yards, value 202,337l. 6s. 10½d.

New drapery,
544,493½ yards, value 68,061l. 13s. 1½d.

In confequence of non-importation agreements, and other circumftances, the importation fuddenly and greatly fell.

---

* Average export of woollen yarn for five years ending 1743, 14799 ftones. Ditto of worfted or bay yarn 64,983 ftones.

X   Old

Old drapery imported in

1779	1780
176,196 yards.	64,346 yards.

New drapery,

| 270,839 yards. | 159,428 yards. |

But in the following years the importation of old drapery rofe above the average of former years, and amends were made for non-importations, as was the cafe in America on like occafions. The new draperies did not rife to the quantities imported in 1774, 1775, 1776, 1777, and 1778; but it may be accounted for by the increafe of that manufacture in Ireland.

Old drapery imported from Great Britain in

1781,	1782, and	1783.
326,578 yds.	362,824 yds.	371,871 yds.

New drapery,

| 433,198 yds. | 547,336 yds. | 420,415 yds. |

It is rather to be wifhed than expected, that the reflections which arc naturally fuggefted by fuch a detail, may tend to the fuppreffion of narrow and abfurd notions in the legiflative regulations of trade; but it was principally
intended,

intended, with the details given on the fubject of protecting duties, to evince the fmall probability that Ireland, under a great increafe of inhabitants, an increafed tillage, and probable decreafe of fheep, is likely to prejudice the Britifh manufacture by diminifhing her demand for Englifh woollens, or by carrying her woollen manufacture to a much greater extent, or exporting much greater quantities than fhe has already done. It will require great improvements in the whole fyftem of agriculture, and the labour and experience of many years, before fhe can confiderably increafe her fheep without decreafing her tillage, which is of much more confequence to her. If fhe extends her manufacture much farther, it muft be done by an entire revolution in the fmuggling line, and the cheap wools of England muft be introduced into Ireland; but the expence of fmuggling, or even of a qualified importation from England, with all the charges attendant on it, would make the article fo dear, that Ireland could not vie with the Englifh manufacture, efpecially in the coarfer fabrics, where the raw material bears a greater proportion of the value than in the finer.

As to the quality of Irifh wool, it is certainly much decreafed in finenefs; but the increafed quantity more than compenfates *. Sir William Petty mentions the fleece to weigh about two pounds, and he fuppofes that there were then in Ireland four millions of fheep, and this was probably about the time of the act againft the importation of Irifh

---

* The writer of thefe obfervations can fay, from experience, that increafed quantity more than compenfates for quality. His flock confifting of above 1000 fheep, was originally from the fouth downs of Suffex. It was croffed ten years ago with one of Mr. Bakewell's rams, whofe wool was by no means of the coarfeft or longeft kind. The fleeces of the flock were increafed from an average of 2¼lb. which fold for 9d. per lb. to full 5lb. which fold for 8d. at the time wool was cheapeft. The fleeces have returned towards their former weight; they average about 2¾lb. It fold in the year 1784, at ten pence per lb. only, although the price of fine wool is higher than it was a few years ago, and although fome of the fleeces were fo fine as to weigh only one pound five ounces. It is clear, then, that five pounds of coarfe wool at 8d. anfwers better than 2¾lbs. at 10d.; and in general, what is moft beneficial to the individual in matters of this kind, is beft for the country.

cattle.

cattle. It is faid Ireland produced excellent clothing wool the laft century; but there are only three counties in that kingdom that now furnifh any quantity of that kind, or even coarfe, proper for clothing; (Clare furnifhes the beft) and the quantity produced, bears no proportion to the quantity of coarfe cloth confumed in Ireland: there muft, therefore, be a balance againft one of the woollen manufactures of that country.

The Irifh fleeces, inftead of 2lb. are now double, or near treble that weight. Mr. Young's examination of that point is very fatisfactory; and he, from the minutes made on his Tour of Ireland, ftates the average weight of the fleece to be 5lb.

As to the price of wool being too high, it may be remarked, that notwithftanding this fuppofed extraordinary value, the quantity of fheep is faid to decreafe in Ireland, and, undoubtedly, would decreafe much more if the price was as low as in England. A prohibition of the export of wool and yarn for the fake of lowering the price of wool to affift

the

the manufacturer, would, probably, diminifh
the price, and much diminifh the number of
fheep; but, in the end, from the depreciation of
the price, would rife again in confequence of
the decreafe of fheep; and confidering the higher price of wool in Ireland than in Englnd, it
is probable there is a redundancy of the kind *
that goes to the latter, that it is of a fort for
which there is not as yet a full demand ; but
as foon as the manufacture arifes or increafes,
a demand will flop the exportation. Until
the manufacturers are more induftrious, and
confequently can afford to live better and
confume more meat, fheep, when wool is
low, will not anfwer as well as in England,
where the price of mutton is much higher, and
makes it anfwer to the farmer to raife fheep
when the price of wool would not. But it
does not appear that wool is at an unnatural
price in Ireland ; it is dearer than it was when
there was little demand from fpinners, and
when the low price made it an object to

* The inconfiderable quantity exported appears in the
table, No. 1, and that, on an average, it does not exceed in
value 1000l. yearly.

fmuggle.

fmuggle. It is dearer than the wool of England, of which a monopoly is given to the manufacturers; but comparatively with the wool
of other countries, it is cheap.

Barely to ftate the price of wool at different
periods, only mifleads; and thofe who wifh to
acquire ufeful information on that fubject,
muft examine into the circumftances of each
time, when the price is mentioned.

We are told that the wool of Belton, in Lin-
colnfhire, was 24s. per todd in 1642; that
Englifh wool in general was 15l. the pack, of
240lb., in 1647, when the exportation was firft
prohibited; and ordinary wool 12d. per lb. in
1651; that the fame fort of wool which was
bought for 15l. in 1647, was, in 1677, fold for.
12l. It is neceffary to recollect, that in 1647,
the devaftation of the civil war had grealy diminifhed the quantity of fheep in England.
In 1677, wool which fold for 16d. and 18d.
per lb. during the war, was bought at 12d.
and other accounts fay, even fo low as 4d.
or 5d. per lb. and 3l. 10s. per pack; in 1680,
it was faid, wool had fallen from 30s.
and

and 40s. to 12 and 13s. the todd; in
1697, wool fell from 12, 14, and 16l. per
pack to 11l.; in 1702, to 7l. 10s.; and in
1703, rofe to 12 and 14l.; in 1709, it was
at 9l.; in 1711, it was at 18s. per todd; in
1717 and 1718, wool bore a higher price than
for near thirty years; and foon after, it is to be
regretted, that the Englifh woollen manufacture did not derive its great profperity from
any other caufe than the deftructive plague at
Marfeilles. In 1737, long wool was lefs than
6d. per lb. and in 1739 at 4l. 10s. per pack;
in 1743*, it advanced from 12s. to 28s. per
todd, fuppofed to be owing to a great demand
from France; in 1750, it rofe ftill higher, and
fell again on the import of Irifh wool and yarn
into all the ports. Englifh wool, which fold
at Amfterdam in 1751 at 37s. fell, in two
years to 1l. 1s. and 1l. 5s. viz. 1753. In

---

* Price of wool per todd from the fame farm. Smith's
Memoirs of Wool.

				£.	s.	d.
1718,	—	—	—	1	1	0
1719,	—	—	—	1	0	6
1738,	—	—	—	0	13	6
1739,	—	—	—	0	13	0
1743,	—	—	—	0	19	6

1758,

1758, it rofe again; in 1768 it fell; it was
ftill lower in 1770, and has fince rifen, but
the price of long or combing wool fell from
18s. and 6d. in 1776, to 9s. in 1781. In fhort,
that the price has often been below what it
ought to be, will be generally allowed, and
the caufes of the variations are, in general,
clearly imputable to war, prohibitions, demands from abroad, and admiffions of wool
and yarn from Ireland, rather than to the ftate
of the woollen trade. Thofe who wifh for a
greater detail on this fubject, previous to 1750,
will confult Smith's Memoirs of Wool. The
quality of wool varies fo much in England,
that it is extremely difficult to give a comparative view or average price. The following account is the beft that offers at prefent, the
computation was made in 1779:

Prices of Wool in different Parts of
England, per lb. weight.

						s.	d.
Norfolk, at	-	-	-	-		0	6½

Sussex.

South Down wool weighs about 2lb. and ½ the		
fleece on an average	- - -	0 9

N. B. The fineft fells, fome years, at near 15d. per lb.

Y   Kent

K E N T.

In West Kent, South Down sheep's wool   -   o 7

The horned west country sheep brought into

     West Kent, weighs about 3½ lb. the fleece   -   o 6

In East Kent, South Down sheep's wool   -   -   o 5½

Romney Marsh (large)   -   -   -   -   o 5

West-country sheep   -   -   -   -   o 4½

L I N C O L N S H I R E.

Long Lincolnshire weighs about 9½ lb. the fleece   o 6

Lincoln Heath wool weighs about 5½ lb. ditto   -   o 5

N O T T I N G H A M S H I R E.

Fallow Field weighs about 4 lb. the fleece   -   o 5

Forest weighs about 2 lb. the fleece   -   -   o 7¼

Y O R K S H I R E.

At Halifax, as sold by Wool Staplers (little Wool is grow
in that Part of Yorkshire.) The second column is the
Price in 1779; the first is the Value about a Year before.

	s.	d.			s.	d.
Low-price combing wool	-	o	5½	- -	o	3½
Hog and weather wool mixed	o	9¼	- -	o	7
Superfine clothing	- - -	1	7	- -	1	6
Second ditto	- -	1	2	- - -	1	0½
Third ditto	- - -	o	8	- - -	o	6¼
Fourth ditto	- -	o	6	- - -	o	4

Inclosures and artificial grasses have introduced
large sheep, and have, in some parts of England, diminished the quantity of fine wool;
this

this is the cafe in parts of Shropſhire. The
fineſt wool of that country is at Morf near
Bridgnorth, and at the Wrekin ; the fleece is
about 1lb. and an half. This year, 1784, it
fold at 24s. per ſtone of 14lb. fometimes it is
as low as 18s. a guinea, or 1s. and 6d. per lb.
is the average. It is ſaid to be as good as any
in England, except that of Rofs in Hereford-
ſhire, which rifes as high as 2s. 6d. per lb.
The wool ſtaplers at Shrewſbury ſort their wool
into nine parts, from 6d. to 2s. 2d. per lb. all
for clothing, the 6d. per lb. for lifting or edg-
ing ; but the introduction of artificial graſſes
has not diminiſhed the fine flocks on the
South Downs of Suffex, notwithſtanding more
of the Downs are plowed than were formerly.
Artificial graſſes, rape, turneps, and other
improvements in huſbandry, enable the farmers to keep larger flocks. The ſtaple, perhaps,
is not quite ſo fine as it was, in confequence
of the ſhcep's living on coarfer food, but the
beſt wools fell fome years as high as 40s. per
tod of 32lb.

As to the price of wool in Ireland, we
are told, that the medium price from 1703 to

Y 2   1729,

1729, was 6s. 6d. per ſtone; alſo that Iriſh wool and yarn, on a medium of eight years, ending 1782, was worth 10s. and 4d. per ſtone; and that fine wools in Ireland, in the year 1743, ſold for 16s per. ſtone, the medium 12s. which was above the medium of Engliſh.

Middle price of Wool, in the Fleece, in Ireland.

		Iriſh, per ſtone of 16ib.			
		s.	d.	s.	d.
1770,	from	14	0	to	15	0
1771,	——	14	6	——	15	6
1772,	——	15	0	——	16	0
1773,	——	15	0	——	16	0
1774,	——	14	0	——	16	0
1775,	——	16	0	——	17	0
1776,	——	17	0	——	18	0
1777,	——	17	6	——	18	6
1778,	——	10	6	——	11	6
1779,	——	10	0	——	11	0
1780,	——	10	6	——	11	6
1781,	——	11	0	——	12	0
1782,	——	10	0	——	11	0
1783,	——	11	6	——	12	6
1784,	——	11	6	——	12	6

The fall in 1778 was owing to the ſtagnation of credit, and to the demand of bay yarn from England being decreaſed.

But

But the friends of the woollen fabrics of Ireland, inftead of inflaming and difturbing the manufacturers with extravagant notions and mifchievous expectations of protecting duties, would do more fervice by fhewing the advantage of carrying their art to higher perfection. Improvements in the feveral manufactures might do much for them, but prohibitions of Britifh would debafe Irifh manufacture; the prefent imperfect modes would be confirmed, the progrefs towards Englifh perfection would be checked, the manufacturer would be carelefs of his work-manfhip, thinking he had a monopoly of the market, ftrength would be given to combi-nation. Yet thofe who can afford to wear fine and good cloth, would have it at any rate, nor will they be forced to wear imper-fect manufactures; and, to prevent a contra-band introduction, in fome fhape or other, of what is good, would be impoffible. The only means of recommending the Irifh ma-nufacture, and of obtaining a fure market, at leaft at home, will be, by a greater atten-tion to its excellence; the only certain and proper way of excluding Englifh manufac-

tures

tures from the Irifh market will be by attain-
ing an equality of perfection. It would infure, at leaft the home market, as far as the
quality and quantity of wool would enable
it to go. For the Irifh manufacture is, in
general, more hurt by the flovenlinefs of the
work than by the price of the wool. Suppofing the price of labour the fame in both
countries, the carriage of woollens through
England, the freight, duties, and commiffion, furely are more than equal to the difference of price of wool; but as to the fine
manufactures, in which Spanifh wool alone,
or chiefly, is ufed, they might have every
advantage in Ireland as elfewhere. Indeed,
at prefent, Ireland finds it convenient to
import her Spanifh wool through London,
paying double freight and double commiffion; but that is no reafon for laying prohibitory duties, as thofe propofed on every fpecies of Britifh clothes would prove; nor is
it fair ground for non-importation agreements. In fhort, to lofe time and exertions
for any other extent of the manufacture than
what is now pointed at, at leaft until there

is

is more of the material, does not appear very wife.

But the firft ftep towards amendment fhould be by tempting the principal woollen manufacturers from the metropolis, the feat of licentioufnefs, drunkennefs, diforder and expence, where the manufacturers are always liable to be made the idle tools of turbulent and interefted men. No manufactures fhould be there, but thofe that immediately depend on varying tafte, and fhould be under the eye of the fhopkeepers. There is no change of fafhion in the woollen manufactures that might not be attended to at a diftance. By removing the manufacture of fine woollens from Dublin, it will be lightened of the extraordinary expence, diffipation, and irregularity of the capital, and of the bad effects of combinations, and the manufacturers will be faved the time and trouble of controuling the commercial interefts of the kingdom. Why fhould they not be invited by advantages to the new city that has been deferted by the Genevans? The fituation is good for trade, and it would not there

interfere

interfere with the linen manufacture; but there are many situations that would be good; any would be better than the present. It is defirable that it should not be in large cities, but in towns or large villages, not very far diftant from each other. When the whole of a manufacture is brought together, combination is fure to be the confequence; and generally extraordinary numbers collected together raife the price of provifions beyond their level or natural price, and the country is not fo generally benefited as when the people are more difperfed. The ftile of the Yorkfhire manufactures feems beft for Ireland. They are moftly of wool the growth of the kingdom, and they are of that fort of fabric beft adapted to the Irifh trade.

It is very extraordinary that there fhould not be wool ftaplers in Ireland: and in this there appears a capital defect in the outfet of the manufacture.

There are perfons called wool merchants, who purchafe from the grower; but, in general, they fell the wool again without forting it. It is the wifh and practice of the clo-

thier

thier to buy in the fleece. He gains thereby, as he thinks the profit of the wool merchant and the opulent manufacturer oppreffes the poorer clothier, by being able to purchafe large quantities from the grower. He fells to him what is left, after taking what he wants for himfelf; but his oppreffion does not always anfwer to him. He is often embarraffed to get rid of the part he cannot ufe, which is not properly forted for the poorer man, who, when he buys it, finds a variety of forts not fit for his line of bufinefs, which become an incumbrance to him, and, in failure of fale, he is obliged to work it up himfelf, which throws him out of his line of bufinefs, or forces him to a mixture of wools, to the injury of his manufacture. It is a defect, that the fame perfon fhould go through the whole procefs, from purchafing the wool from the grower to the finifhing of the piece; the manufacture confifting of fuch variety of branches, all of which requiring great fkill and attention, is more than the fame perfon fhould undertake.

It appears from the Report of the Committee of the Irifh Parliament, appointed

Z   laft

laſt ſpring, to inquire into the ſtate of manufactures, that ſorted wool is nearly as
dear again in Ireland as in England, and
that there is not ſuch diſproportion in the
prices of fleece wool. It appears from hence
how much wool ſtaplers in the ſame ſtile as in
England are wanted in Ireland, who purchaſe
the wool from the grower, and ſort it into
different parts or degrees of finenefs to ſuit
the different manufactures. The advantage
of this is obvious, that the wool ſtaplers can
afford to ſell it cheaper, and that the wool
will be better prepared for the purpoſe wanted,
and all of a ſort. The poor manufacturer
buys his ſmall quantity on the ſame terms as
the rich, and ſupplies his immediate want,
without being incumbered with more than he
has preſent occaſion for. It is very eſſential
that there ſhould be well-regulated cloth halls
for the ſale of the goods, near which wool
ſtaplers generally reſide, and the manufacturers are accommodated with wool without
additional expence or loſs of time, when they
attend the cloth market.

Cloth halls in England are markets as well
as repoſitories for cloth ; and, indeed, for almoſt
all

all forts of woollens, and are regulated as well for the advantage and difpatch of the feller as of the buyer, where the goods are fold by wholefale. If the manufacturer refides at a diftance too great to attend the fale of his goods, he configns them to one of the factors (of which there are many) who belong to the hall. They are perfons of fuch property as to be able to advance to the manufacturer, if required, a fum of money at intereft, upon the fecurity of the goods depofited, which, when fold, they repay themfelves, with the proper and ftated charges and commiffion. Thus the poorer manufacturer is enabled to proceed with his bufinefs upon a very fmall capital; but fuch of the manufacturers as can wait the return of the fales, are fubject only to the commiffion for felling. This is the cafe at Blackwell Hall in London, where few, if any, attend the fale of their own goods, the diftance being too great for any manufacturing county; but at the Cloth halls of the towns in the manufacturing counties, as at Leeds, the manufacturers have the opportunity, and do always attend themfelves; and there are ftated days

and

and hours of fale, which are on the ufual days of markets for provifions, &c. The halls in the country are moftly for the fale of rough cloth ; the buyers or merchants are the dreffers or finifhers of thofe cloths; they receive commiffions, and at the halls can get the affortment they want in a very fhort time. The goods are paid for in money or bills, after having undergone a clofe infpection (called perking) by hanging them up againft the light; if too thin in any part, if there are defects of any kind, they are immediately feen, and ftoppages are made from the manufacturer. The cloth becomes the property of the merchant, who, undoubtedly, finifhes well for his own emolument.

How very advantageous fuch halls would be to the manufacturer, and to the rendering more perfect the manufacture of Ireland, is obvious. It feems effentially neceffary to encourage the makers of rough cloth * to fettle in proper places, and to oblige them,

* Rough-cloth markets in England are clothiers in the firft ftages of the bufinefs; they buy their wool from the ftapler, manufacture it at their dwellings, and fell it at the

them, or make it their intereſt, to ſell their cloth rough from the mill in the proper market,

the cloth halls when milled. They for the moſt part hold ſufficient land to afford them mantainance for a cow and horſe, and a garden for vegetables, which they till themſelves. The whole family is engaged, and if they are not ſufficient themſelves, they hire ſervants to card, ſpin and weave. The uſe of a horſe is to take their cloth to the mill, thence to the hall, and return with wool and marketing. As a ſmall capital will ſet up a rough maker, ſo they are very numerous, and are diſperſed through the country.

As every Rough maker has within his own family and under his own eye, the ſeveral operations of ſcribbling, ſpinning and weaving, and his return of profit depending upon the quality of his cloth when finiſhed, it is to be preſumed that he endeavours to bring it to the ſtage in which he ſells it as perfect as he is able; as he lays him-ſelf out to make but one ſort of cloth, in which his people are practiſed, he is more likely to ſucceed in making a good manufacture. And another inducement to enſure good work, is that his cloth muſt undergo a cloſe in-ſpection before it is paid for, and large deductions made for defects, or be returned upon his hands.

In thoſe branches the children even of the family can find employment; the are initiated and kept to induſtry from their infancy; and as by this mode of doing buſineſs,

all

ket, or cloth hall, which ſhould be built in
ſome conſiderable place, and certain privi-
leges

all advantages which the manufacturers can afford cen-
tering within themſelves, together with the helps from
their piece of land ; they work cheap, and find comforts
which others are unacquainted with.   And being thus dif-
perſed throughout the country, they have not the ſame
opportunity of aſſembling as thoſe in towns or cities, to
form combinations or regulations of their own, which are
ever found to be the great bane to manufactures.

But in Ireland there are very few Rough-cloth makers
profeſſedly, a few in the country do occaſionally ſend rough
cloths to Dublin ; but as the attendance of the ſale is ex-
penſive and uncertain, the practice is diſcouraging.   Clothiers in Dublin for the moſt part go through the whole
proceſs ; they give out the wool, after they have prepared
it, to a maſter or undertaking ſpinner, to whom he pays
per ſkain for ſpinning.   This perſon employs hands to
work under him and undertakes for every one who will
employ him ; he receives a variety of work, ſome coarſe
ſome fine, upon which his hands being occaſionally chang-
ed from one to another, cauſes an unevenneſs which is prejudicial to the manufacture, and as the undertaker's employment depends upon the quantity he gets done for little
money, the ſcribbling branch (which is extremely material)
is for the moſt part ſlighted.   The clothier gets home the
ſpinning, and then gives it out to an undertaking weaver,
who is paid per yard according to the fineneſs.   Thoſe operation

leges might be granted, at leaft for a time. The Rough-cloth makers will fettle in the neighbourhood, and that the manufacturers may not be difcouraged from going to diftant fituations, as Ireland is fond of bounties on inland carriage, a fmall premium might be allowed on the carriage of all goods received at the hall according to the diftance; fomething, perhaps, might be fpared from the bounty on the inland carriage of corn. No mode appears fo likely to extend the manufacture into the country, and prevent combination, as to induce perfons who are fkil-

rations being done out of the clothier's fight, and the undertakers not being perfons of any property, and generally in ftrong combination, no recovery can be had for neglect or bad work in any of thofe branches, and the mafter clothier muft receive it in whatever ftate they pleafe to bring it home.

From this practice it may be conceived that neither cheap nor good manufacture can be obtained in the firft ftages of ground work of the bufinefs: nor will the work people in general admit of either machine or method to facilitate labour or amend the fabric. For twenty pounds a rough-cloth maker may fet up with one loom, fcribbling frame and cards, four or five fpinning wheels and other neceffary articles.

led

led in the firft ftages of the bufinefs, and
will practife the moft improved methods to
carry on the manufacture, as in England,
from the wool to the mill, and difpofe of it
in that ftate, to which a fafe repofitory for
their goods, and a certain and fpeedy return
muft be their inducement.   This mode is
alfo preferable, becaufe a very fmall capital,
viz. 20l. will fet up a rough-cloth maker,
and not lefs than 300l. will fet up a clothier
to go through the whole procefs, and that in
a confined way : there is a certainty that one
will become more general than the other, and
alfo a certainty that the manufacture, by fuch
means, would be better, becaufe the emolument of the maker will depend on its quality,
which muft be better known in its rough
ftate, than when difguifed by dreffing, fine
drawing, and preffing.   The perfons who
are the moft numerous and moft refpective
are employed in the fcribbling, the fpinning, and the weaving.   By difperfing them
throughout the country the knot will be
broke, and in a fhort time, they would be
brought to better practices.   If rough-cloth
halls were eftablifhed, the merchants of Ireland

land would be enabled, in a fhort time, to compleat their orders, which they cannot do at prefent either with convenience or with certainty of giving fatisfaction. After they have received their orders, the goods are to be befpoke and waited for; which, when finifhed, may not be well manufactured; yet they are fent abroad; and even if they did not go out of the ifland, the manufacture is difcredited.

Nothing can point out more clearly the advantage of regular ftated places of fale than the Kilkenny fair for the frize trade, which, though diftant from both buyer and feller, and attended with inconvenience to each, yet being a certain place of meeting for them, feldom fails to anfwer the expectations of both.

Machines of the beft conftruction might be iffued from thefe halls, and fold to the manufacturers, making the payment eafy to them through the means of their factors.

As to the imperfection of the manufacture of Spanifh or fine wool, Ireland can

A a   only

only blame herſelf. Till ſhe could make ſufficient for her own people, and ſuch as th·y would wear, ſhe had no pretenſions to ſucceſs at a foreign market. With proper management, ſhe might make it as cheap and as perfect as England, as both countries import the raw material; but ſhe does neither at preſent, and particularly in the important branch of finiſhing, ſhe is very deficient. She has much to do before ſhe will rival her neighbours in this branch; ſhe muſt not depend too much on her advantages as to the price of proviſions or price of labour, they are of much leſs conſequence than habits of induſtry and intelligence in trade, and character, and correſpondence, when foreign trade is in queſtion.*

Her importations of Spaniſh wool have been unequal.

* It is ſuppoſed that the conſumption of fine woollens has in part decreaſed in Ireland, from the ſame cauſe as in England, namely, the introduction of Mancheſter manufactures of cotton, which are worn as cloathing, and ſo generally for waiſtcoats and breeches.

Year

Year ending 25th March:
Cwt.

1774 — 210 — 48 of which only was imported from Spain, the
reſt from Britain.

1775 — 96 — 41 of which only was imported from Spain, the
reſt from Britain.

1776 — 328 — 155 of which only was imported from Spain, the
reſt from Britain.

And,

1783 — 261 *, none from Spain, 5 from
Flanders, the reſt from
Britain.

But the woollen manufacture of Ireland
feems to be taking the moſt natural and beſt
turn. The new drapery branch advances rapidly. It confumes the wool of the country.
It is lefs difficult in many branches, and requires lefs ſkill than the fuperfine broad
cloths. It has been already ſhewn that the
importation of new drapery decreaſes, and

---

* 261 cwt. at 2¼lb. to the yard, would make 12,992
yards. That is about the quantity ufed in a yard of Englifh
fuperfine, but it is a full allowance where only Spanifh
wool is ufed.

that

that the exportation is become very confiderable †.

The amount of the confumption of woollens in Ireland we cannot know, but it is very great; and, perhaps, no country whatever, in proportion to its number of inhabitants, confumes fo much. The lower ranks are covered with the clumfieft woollen drapery, and although the material may not be fine, there is abundance of it. Befides coat and waiftcoat, the lower claffes wear a great

† When a parcel of wool is not fit for broad cloth, it is applied to the manufacture of worfteds, the fineft part to hofe, and to worfteds for mixing with filk, viz. poplins and tabinets, from 1s. 3d. to 6s. 6d. per yard. crapes from 1s. 2d. to 4s. per yard. The greater part of the combing wool is confumed in worfted for making

Per yard.

Shaloon, —	6d. to 2s. 8d.	
Callimanco, ——	9d. to 2s. 2d.	
Everlafting, ——	1s. 3d. to 4s.	
Satinet, ——	2s. to 4s.	Called new dra-
Camblet, ——	10d. to 1s. 8d.	pery in the
Stuffs, broad and narrow, fingle and double,	6d. to 1s 6d.	book of rates.
Plufh, ——	8d. to 3s. 6d.	
Worfted Crapes, —	7d. to 9d.	

In many of thefe branches Ireland excels; her poplins and tabinets are beautiful, efpecially as to colour; but as they have the appearance of filk, and in great part are made of it, they fhould more properly be ranked under that article.

coat,

coat, both fummer and winter, if it can poffibly be got. Not only their clothing but their ftockings feem to contain a double quantity of wool, and the women among the peafantry feem to depend on other charms than elegance or ornament; they alfo wear the clumfieft woollens. There is no intention of infinuating that they always wear ftockings, but that which covers their perfons, and their petticoats, and alfo their cloke, if they have one, contain much wool, and all of the moft gloomy colours; linen or cotton gowns are feldom to be feen among the common peafantry of Ireland.

There feems little doubt of there being at leaft three millions of inhabitants in Ireland. Perhaps, we have not a better mode of judge-ing of their number than from the hearth-money tax, which fome years amounts to above 60,500l. of which about 36,000l. are paid by houfes of one hearth, which, at two fhillings each hearth, make 360,000 houfes. The well-known difpofition of the Irifh to in-creafe, and their eftablifhed character in that refpect, caufes it to be generally allowed, that

at

at leaft fix may be reckoned to each cottage.
Mr. Young's minutes make it near 6½. The
above number of houfes with one hearth,
multiplied by fix, makes 2,160,000. If we
allow for the remaining 25,500l. or 255,000
hearths, only 840,000 inhabitants, we have
three millions; and if that is thought too
many, we muft mention the inhabitants of
the houfes which are excufed the tax on account of their poverty.

But if we knew the number of inhabitants,
there would be difficulty in fettling the quantity they wear of woollens *; and it can only
be afferted that they confume a great quantity,
and more in proportion than their neighbours.
The lower ranks of men in the fouthern parts
of England ufe little; a coat or great coat
they feldom wear; but inftead of them a frock
or rather fhirt of brown or white linen, which
covers all. It keeps out more rain and weather than could be expected, but, when wet,

---

* Four or five pounds of wool for cloths, flockings
and hat, confidering how coarfe and heavy the common
woollens are, might not be too much, and it would
amount to a large quantity.

it

it muft be worfe than woollen. It is fome objection alfo, that the material comes from Ruffia.

More attention has been given to the woollens, as an article extremely interefting, and concerning which both Ireland and England are apt to be alarmed: moft of the late difcontents were among this branch of the manufacturers in Ireland, but they were nearly confined to thofe of the woollen branch in Dublin. In general, the apprehenfions for the woollen manufacture in this country are confined to the weft of England; and while the manufacturers lofe time in complaints againft imaginary or exaggerated fmuggling of fheep and fine wool from hence, they feem to pafs over the principal caufes of the decline of their manufacture: firft, the migration of it to the Weft Riding of Yorkfhire, where, within a fhort time, fabrics of Spanifh and fine wools have begun to flourifh. And, fecondly, the ufe of Manchefter goods in many articles wherein fuperfine woollens were formerly ufed.

SILK

SILK MANUFACTURE.

We now come to one of thofe manufactures relative to which, notwithſtanding
the aſſumed principle, that Iriſh cannot
rival Britiſh manufactures, it may be difficult to make an arrangement ſatisfactory to
both countries, or which will ſuit the reſpec-
tive intereſts of each. Under this deſcrip-
tion may be included all manufactures, the
materials of which do not pay the ſame duties on import into the two countries: and
here it ſhould be explained, that when the
term, " equal duties" is uſed, it would be a
partial conſtruction to refer merely to the
duty now paid on the importation of the manufacture from Britain into Ireland, or from
Ireland into Britain. The duties on the materials ought to be taken into the conſidera-
tion; for example;

s. d.

Thoſe on the import of raw ſilk into
Britain from all foreign countries
are on the great pound of 24 oz.   4 · 6

On

                                                    s. d.

On thrown filk from the fame the
   pound of 16 oz.   -   -   7   6

On raw filk into Ireland from foreign
   countries, the great pound of 24
   ounces,   -   -   1   0

On thrown filk into Ireland from foreign countries, pound of 16 oz.   2   0½

On raw filk from Britain in Ireland
   only, 10½d.   -   -
There is a charge undrawback in   1   9
   Britain of 10½d.   -   -

On thrown filk from Britain in Ireland, 1s. 9d.   2   7
Charge undrawback in Britain, 10d.

         markable that notwithſtanding raw
fi   hrough Britain into Ireland, is
l   9d. per pound, and thrown filk
         les commiſſion and carriage more
         imported from foreign parts into
      d, yet very nearly the whole of her
     ortation of filk is from Britain, which is
   be accounted for principally by a credit
the found here which ſhe could not ſo eaſily
obtain from Italy. It ſhould be the policy
of Britain to allow filk to go from hence
without any charge on it.

The filk manufactures of Ireland are by
no means to be defpifed; nor has fhe reafon
to defpond, if they were much inferior to
what they are. It did not appear probable
twenty-five years ago, that Paifley, in Scotland, could ever arrive at any formidable
competition with Spitalfields. At that time
the former had no filk manufacture, but
now fhe makes gauzes to the yearly value of
near 400,000l. and Spitalfields makes little
indeed. Hence it appears, that a rich country in poffeffion of a manufacture, of fkill,
and of induftry, cannot always maintain
herfelf againft a poor country. Happily under the union of England and Scotland, the
migration of the gauze manufactory from
Spitalfields to Paifley is not to be lamented.
Paifley affords her gauzes cheaper than any
part of the world, and furnifhes all Europe,
and even France with them.

Many of the filk manufactures of Ireland
are excellent; her white damafks and her
luteftrings are very good; her filk pocket-
handkerchiefs are, at leaft, as good as any ;
her mixtures of filk are beautiful; her colours excel thofe of England; her tabinets
and poplins are well known and admired
every where.

It

It is computed that there are 1500 filk manufacturers in Dublin. From the following account of raw and thrown filk imported at two different periods, it appears, that the manufactures of filk in Ireland are very confiderably increafed, though not equal to her confumption, for the importation of manufactured filk has alfo increafed confiderably. Non-importation agreements have probably had little effect; if the importation of the following year did not make full amends, a private introduction of the article had fupplied what was wanting.

It will not be an eafy matter to prevent the fmuggling of filks into Britain from Ireland, and if the importation fhould be allowed fubject to equal duties; to avoid paying thofe duties, manufactures of filk would never be entered in the Britifh ports, but would be concealed and introduced among linens or articles not liable to duties. Without unfolding every piece of linen the detection would be difficult.

The quantity of filk imported into Ireland on an average of three years, ending 25th March, 1773:

B b 2   Ribbands

		lbs.	oz.
Ribbands	—— ——	557	$15\frac{1}{4}$
Manufactured filk	——	15,786	$7\frac{2}{4}$
Raw filk	——	41,793	$21\frac{1}{2}$
Thrown, dyed	——	96	14
Ditto, undyed	——	44,650	$13\frac{1}{2}$

The quantity of filk imported * into Ireland, on an average of three years, ending 25th March, 1783:

		lbs.	oz.
Ribbands	——	1,864	0
Manufactured filk	—	22,626	$3\frac{1}{2}$
Raw	—— ——	51,029	1
Thrown, dyed	——	273	$4\frac{2}{3}$
Ditto, undyed	——	63,496	$13\frac{1}{3}$

No exportations of filks, or mixtures of filks, till the year 1781, appear in the Cuftom-houfe books.

* Five years average quantity of raw and thrown filk imported into England, viz. 1779, 80, 81, 82, and 83, with the amount of duties thereon :

	lbs.	s. d.	l.	s. d.
Upon the great pound of 24 oz.	599,563	at 4 6	134,901	16 6
Organzine, :6 oz.	428,199	at 7 4	157,006	6 0
			291,908	2 6

An

An account of filk, and mixtures of filk and worfted, exported from Ireland for three years:

1781.

		lbs.	oz.
Ribbands	— —	13	8
Manufactured filk	—	430	3 :
Thrown, dyed	—	25	0

1782.

		lbs.	oz.
Ribbands	— —	19	4
Manufactured filk	—	370	3

1783.

		lbs.	oz.
Ribbands	— —	514	14
Manufactured filk	—	3,329	9
Thrown, dyed	—	309	0
Manufactured, mixed	—	2,064	12

The principal importation of manufactured filks into Ireland from Britain, are gauzes, ribbands, alamodes; fatins, plain and figured; perfians, farcenets, brocades of all kinds, and feveral other articles. The quantity of manufactured filk that came from other countries has been very trifling.

MANU-

MANUFACTURE of COTTON.

This manufacture can hardly be said to have been above four or five years in Ireland, yet it seems already to have taken root, and to be well established. It is computed that near 30,000 people * are employed in it. If it be true, its progress indeed has been rapid; but it cannot be supposed that the fabrics of Manchester are already materially rivalled, except it should be in the home consumption of Ireland. It is said in that country, that although the English manufacture, where cotton alone is used, be not only better and cheaper than that of Ireland, yet the Irish mixtures of cotton and linen are better and cheaper than the English. It may be doubted, whether it is now the case, it probably will be; there is great reason to believe that the cotton manufacture is well fixed in Ireland, and it is to be hoped, superior to untoward accidents, or such circumstances as sometimes overset newly-established fabrics. The bounty of Parliament has been

* The number of persons employed in the counties of Lancashire, Cheshire, Derbyshire, Nottinghamshire, and Leicestershire, in the manufacture of cotton, is estimated at 500,000, including women and children.

liberally

liberally extended to encourage and fupport this manufacture ; it has confequently been eftablifhed in different and diftant parts of the kingdom *. The principal eftablifh-ment of this manufacture is at the new town called Profperous, in the county of Kildare, on the borders of the bog of Allen, now a confiderable place, but where there was on-ly one fmall cottage four years ago. It is well built ; and the whole eftablifhment feems much better regulated than could have been expected in fo fhort a time †. It is to the activity,

* One perfon in Dublin within three years made 95 carding machines, 394 fpinning jennies for 70 threads each, and above 50 fpinning jennies for wool.

† The price of labour at Profperous is from 8d. to 14d., average 10d. A great number of women and children are employed : women 6d. per day or more, children from 1d. to 3d. per day. A good man fpin-ner at the jennies will earn from 6s. to 12s. per week, women from 4s. 6d. to 9s. The weavers do not earn more than the fpinners. The work people about the bleach green have 6s. or 7s. per week. The printers gain about a guinea, and at tafk work about a guinea and a half per week. The number of inhabitants are already about 3000. There are five different out-fac-tories. A great number of people are employed in the counties of Meath and Wicklow, where there are fpinning jennies and carding machines. It is debt which generally induces Englifhmen to go to Ireland to work at thefe fabrics ; and they are generally not of the

activity, zeal and fpirit of Captain Brooke, that the country owes this foundation, fo judicioufly placed at a diftance from a great town, and alfo the works near Celbridge: Balbrigen in the county of Dublin having the advantage of an intelligent and active landlord, has already a very confiderable manufacture of cotton; the principal buildings are on a large fcale, well executed, and feemingly well adapted, and the machinery in general very good. The activity of individuals affifted by Parliament has eftablifhed confiderable works in feveral parts of the kingdom *.

If the cotton manufacture fhould continue to make the progrefs it has done lately in England, it bids fair to be the principal ma-

the moft fober and fteady kind ; but they teach or inftruct. Their diffolutenefs or unfteadinefs prevents their remaining long there.

* The pleafure of feeing children advantageoufly employed in thefe works, was greatly diminifhed by learning that part of them work all night, even fo young as five or fix years old, and the wages fo low *as fix pence per week*, and from that price to thirteen pence per week, in fome places. The machinery moves fmoother, if kept conftantly at work ; it therefore goes day and night, and confequently requires conftant attendance.

nufacture

nufacture of the country. It will bear a great extension. Scotland, whofe intelligent and fteady people are fo well difpofed to manufactures, has, within two years, made an aftonifhing progrefs in it, particularly in the muflins. There are already five cotton mills erected in Scotland; and, in the city of Glafgow alone, above 1000 looms have been fet up in the laft year in the muflin branch. The late tax, however, upon cotton goods, is likely to prove very hurtful, and, indeed, nothing can be fo impolitic as that fyftem which feizes upon infant manufactures, and wrefts them from the hands of the induftrious †.

The

‡ The Britifh fuftian trade, labours under the following difficulties, and difadvantages in refpect to Ireland—ift. by an old duty of 10 per cent. on importation into Ireland; then by a bounty of 5 *l.* per cent. lately given by the Irifh Parliament on home confumption; by another bounty of 5 *l.* per cent. given by the Linen Board likewife on home confumption, which expires on the ift of January 1785, but may be renewed—By freight, infurances, and expences about 2½ per cent. more—By the late Englifh tax, which on the average is upon the grofs amount 3 *l.* per cent., and though drawn back on exportation. yet the goods exported will ftill be loaded with 8 *l.* per cent., owing to the effect of the tax. Befides which, the Irifh Linen Board gives great encourage-

C c   ment

The field for this manufacture is fo large, that the competition of different countries is not likely immediately to check the extenfion of it, in thofe which now poffefs the fabric: at all events Ireland will have her fhare. The manufacture is as fuitable to her as to any country. The cotton wool may, in general, be obtained nearly at the fame price in Ireland, in Britain, and in

ment to the Irifh manufacturer, by fupplying him with looms; and the Irifh Parliament gives alfo a bounty of 8¼ l. per cent. on exportation, fo that Britain will meet Ireland in future at a foreign market at a difadvantage of 16¼ l. per cent. from our tax, and their bounty; and in Ireland to the difadvantage of 26 l. per cent. befides the bounty given by the Linen Board. A duty was impofed laft feffion in Ireland of 1 s. per yard on all printed callicoes imported from Great Britain. The duty impofed in Great Britain is eftimated at about 6¼ l. per cent., and though allowed to be drawn back on exportation, in general it cannot be obtained, becaufe the marks put on by the Excifemen are frequently defaced in bleaching. The export of Britifh printed goods alfo muft in general fuffer from the great introduction of Eaft India goods. Eaft India white callicoes can be exported from 40 to 50 per cent. lower than Britifh callicoes. There are 60,000 pieces of Eaft India printed goods now on fale, which ufually fell from 80 to 100 per cent. lower than Britifh printed goods. Fuftians and printed goods are the principal objects of the Manchefter manufactures.

France;

France; and fo far the competition will be
fair; but the burdens of Britain give Ireland an advantage; and the cheapnefs of
linen yarn in the latter gives a confiderable fuperiority. It is the warp of all the
lower priced and many of the middle priced fuftians. In checks made at Manchefter ⅞ of the material is linen yarn, which
is wholly Irifh. Manchefter alone imports from Ireland worfted bay and linen
yarn to the amount in value on an average
of the four laft years, of 212,610*l.* 15 *s.* o *d.*
The Irifh manufacturer has the advantage
of a halfpenny per pound duty on the export of linen yarn from Ireland. The price
of cotton in Ireland was lately about 18d.
Englifh, which is about an halfpenny dearer than it was in France; but at prefent
cotton is dearer in France than in Britain *;
the

---

* A book of French patterns of cotton manufactures exhibits a great variety, and looks neat, when oppofed to a book of Englifh patterns; yet there is a
great difference in the workmanfhip in favour of the
latter. France however is taking every ftep to rival
and furpafs our cotton manufactures: it was therefore not the happieft moment for taxing them. The
French have got our fpinning machines for cotton,
and if they have as much of the fpirit of manufacture and of fteadinefs, they will be able, from the

the value of the labour, however, is fo
much greater than that of the raw material,

lower price of labour, to underfell us. Rouen was
on the verge of ruin from the fuperiority of the
Manchefter goods, but now begins to revive again.
The Swifs printed cottons are at prefent much in
vogue, and are cheaper than ours, though not fo
handfome in general. Two mills on Arkwright's
plan are now erecting in the neighbourhood of Rouen :
they have already moft of his machinery; and left capital fhould be wanting, government fupplies to a great
amount ; and Mr. Holker, whofe abilities this country fo foolifhly loft, is at the head of the manufacture,
with a confiderable penfion from the 'Court of Ver-
failles. Spinning machines are alfo fet up in the
neighbourhood of Lyons, where the people are rich
and induftrious. The late taxes on cotton manufactures add to the evil, and muft, if perfevered in,
with the other taxes on manufactures in the end ruin
the trade of this country. They ought to be all removed and laid on any thing elfe rather than upon the
fruits of induftry. No man will ftruggle to reduce
the price of his manufacture, when he knows that as
foon as he has done it, the price will be enhanced again
by a tax ; nor will ingenious men bear the thoughts of
an Excifeman prying into all his works. All means
are ufed to prevent the exportation of cotton from
France ; yet it is now higher at Bourdeaux than in
England, from the prodigious confumption of that article in their manufactures. It is now three half-
pence per pound dearer in France. Common or
middling French cotton, which at prefent in England
fells at 16 d. per pound, is at 17 d. and St. Domingo
cotton 1f⅔d.

Demerara

rial, that the difference of price is of no great confequence, even in the velverets or heavieft goods.

And this brings to our recollection the fuperiority of the cotton over the filk and other manufactures, in which the raw material is the principal part of the expence. Every manufacture is valuable in proportion to the price of the finifhed work, when compared to the price of the raw material, or in proportion to the increafed value of property created by the labour of a given number of people *. It is preferable to

purfue

Demerara cotton in England is at 21½d. per pound, Grenada cotton at 15¼d. beft Grenada and picked cotton fell at 19½d. but the price of cotton fluctuates more than moft articles. The ftaple of Demerara is the longeft and beft, and is adapted for muflins and fine goods. Eaft-India cotton, if it were permitted, and could be afforded, that is, if the freight was not too high, would be of the greateft advantage to our manufacturers, and enable them to equal the cotton manufactures of the Eaft. It is fome fatisfaction to know, that the white goods of France are, and ever will be, much inferior to ours in point of colour; owing, as is fuppofed, to the difference of water and air. As yet, the French fpin 50 hanks at the higheft to the pound; we exceed 100 by means of our machinery.

* A dyed velveret, one of the moft important articles, paffes, from the raw material to a finifhed ftate,

through

purfue this principle by a lefs advance of capital than by a larger ; which reafoning will
apply and hold good in all places, but poffibly in none more than in Ireland, which
country is fuppofed to ftand much in need
of capital. The following example may
help to prove the fuperior advantage of the
cotton.

Thrown filk *, of 16 ounces to the pound,
given to be dyed, produces 11 ounces when
fit for the loom, and cleared of gum, &c.
and is worth 40 fhillings. It will produce
(fuppofe exactly) 9 yards of luteftring,
which, at 6s. per yard, amounts to 54s.
or fourteen fhillings advance, from the firft
coft ; and allowing to the mercer only 6s. for
his profits, there will remain 8s. or one fifth,
for the manufacturer, or national profit ; if
Ireland imports annually 100,000 lbs. of raw

through the following different proceffes, viz. Batting,
picking, wafhing, drying, carding, roving, fhebbing,
fpinning, winding, doubling, twifting, re-winding,
warping, pin-winding, weaving, cutting, fcowering,
ending, fingeing, rubbing, bleaching, dying and making up.   Thefe 23 operations are almoft always performed in Lancafhire, by fo many different claffes of
artifts.   Indeed it is not unufual for feveral of them
to be again fubdivided into two or more parts, and to
be ftill performed by diftinct people.

_* The greater part of the filk imported into Ireland
is not raw.

filk,

filk, and fuppofing the profits on the other branches of this manufacture to yield an equal benefit, the amount on the whole will be 40,000l. viz. 8s. per lb. on 100,000 lbs. of filk ; and to do this, the nation employs a capital of 200,000l. and, in addition to this, the Dublin Society give 2000l. in bounties to affift the export of this manufacture.

Now if 200,000l. capital ftock, aided by 2000l. in bounties, produce only 40,000l. the calculation will ftand as follows: 200,000l. at 5 per cent. intereft, is worth 10,000l. (a year, on an average, for the manufacturing and fale will be neceffary) to which add 2000l., the bounty ——— 12,000l. and, confequently there will be } left only the net fum of } 28,000l. national profit for the fupport of manufacturers.

But fuppofing the whole to be exported, which is implied by the bounties being taken into the calculation, then the mercer's profit of 6s. on each pound weight of the materials is to be taken into the eftimate, which amounting to 30,000l., will make the grofs fum 58,000l.

The manufacture of cotton is every way preferable; 200,000l. will purchafe two million

lion of pounds weight of the beft cotton
in its raw ftate. If every pound of cotton
wrought into ftockings, fuftians, dimities,
muflins, velverets, &c. &c. produces, on an
average, fix fhillings and eight pence value
in manufacture, which is but a low eftimate,
the amount will be 666,666l. 13s. 4d. fterl.
or 456,666l. 13s. 4d. national profit, deducting, as above, 10,000l. for intereft, which
in the other inftance produces but 30,000l.
and adding the mercer's profit only 60,000l.
from which 2000l. the bounties muft be de-
ducted, leaving 58,000l. net. But the merchants profits on the exportation of the
cotton manufactures, fuppofing one half
only of them exported, will far overbalance
the profits of the filk mercer, and give the
preference to the cotton manufacture beyond all comparifon. The cotton requires
more labour, it employs more people, which
is one great national object. But the difference of labour is perhaps not fo great as may
at firft be fuppofed; the carding and fpinning of two millions of pounds of cotton,
even by the aid of machines, will require
more manual labour than the throwing and
preparing of 100,000 weight of raw filk;
the 100.000 lb. of filk is fuppofed to produce 900,000 yards of luteftring, or other
goods

goods equivalent: the two million pounds of cotton muſt make at leaſt three million yards of cloth or of ſtockings, and other goods equivalent; the labour, on this ſuppoſition, will be as three to one, in the weaving: the dying and the dreſſing, hardly in the ſame proportion; probably not more than two to one: but ſetting the profits of the merchant who exports only the one half of the manufactures produced from two million pounds of cotton, that is, 466,666l. 13s. 4d., againſt that of the ſilk mercer who exports the whole of the ſilk amounting to but 40,000l., ſtill there is left in favour of the cotton manufacture, from the ſame capital, a balance of 428,666l. 13s. 4d.

It ſhould be obſerved, that the raw cotton in the above calculation is valued at 2s. per lb., a price much higher than the general average from ſeven or ten years paſt, even including the years of the laſt war, which do not exceed from 17 to 18d. per lb. for fine cotton, at moſt. 200,000l. will (calculating the raw cotton at 18d. per lb., a fair eſtimate) purchaſe 2,666,666 lb., which will increaſe the balance in favour of the cotton manufacture 222,222l., and

D d   beſides

befides employ a greater proportionable number of people.

An account of cotton wool, cotton yarn, muflins, and manufactures and mixtures of cotton imported into Ireland, on an average of three years, ending the 25th of March, 1773:

Cotton wool,	cwt. qrs. lb.	2550 3 2¼
Cotton yarn,	lb.	2226²⁄₃
Muflins,	yards	194987¼
Cravats,	yards	122
Callicoe, ftained,	yards	3999
Fuftians,	ends	9618
Manufactures and		
mixtures of cotton, value		18278l. 16s. 2d.

An account of cotton wool, cotton yarn, &c. &c. &c. imported into Ireland, on an average of three years, ending the 25th March, 1783:

Cotton wool,	cwt. qrs. lb.	3236 1 18
Cotton yarn	lb.	5405½
Muflins,	yards	55151
Callicoes { ftained,	yards	1541½
{ white,	yards	547⅓
Fuftians,	yards	15012⅔
Manufactures and		
mixtures of cotton, value		103119l. 8s. 5½d.

An account of the export of cotton yarn, manufactures and mixtures of cotton, from Ireland, during the three following years, none being exported before 1781:

Cotton yarn. lb.	Manuf. and mixt. of cotton. value.	Fuftians. yards.
1781 239	157 7 0	1108
1782 8798	414 7 6	——
1783 2436	1418 1 0	24384

And in 1784 the exportation to America alone of cotton yarn was 800lb. manufactures and mixtures of cotton, in value 8019 *l.* 18 *s.* 2 *d.* Fuftians 47,237 yards.

IRON, and MANUFACTURES of IRON and STEEL.

The ufeful and neceffary manufacture of iron being capable, perhaps, of higher improvement and greater extenfion than any other, and being of the utmoft national importance in every point of view, undoubtedly deferves a volume; nor would it be an eafy matter to point out all its advantages and all its importance. And yet that moft effential bufinefs, the making of iron in Great Britain, has been in a great degree refcued within a few years almoft from ruin, by the ingenuity and fpirit of a few men, who deferve, at leaft, as well of their country as any of its moft favourite patriots.

The fcarcity and price of wood have rendered it impoffible to make a quantity of iron, either to enter into competition with

foreign

foreign markets, or even sufficient for home consumption and manufactures; but the improvements in making good bar iron with pit coal*, the great aid given to labour, and the expences saved by the improved steam engines, afford a reasonable hope, that in time, if no extraordinary checks should intervene, enough will be made in Britain to supply these kingdoms with that necessary article, whereby between five and 600,000 l. annually, now paid to foreign countries at their ports of exportation, exclusive of the freight and other great expences, would be saved to the nation.

---

* Some kind of coals (and generally the worst) answer the purpose of making coak much better than others.—There are sorts of coal which, when coaked, are not sufficiently cleansed of their sulphur and impurities to make a kind or malleable pig iron fit for the forges. It has not yet appeared whether the Irish coal is proper for making coak.—This opportunity may be taken of observing how ruinous the coal tax would have been to the making of iron in Britain. The quantity consumed in that business is prodigious; one company alone in Shropshire uses 500 tons of coal daily.—It was the intention to have thrown up many of those great works if the tax had been laid. In such a case the whole rents of the townships would not have supported the poor; and then it may be remarked, that the late tax upon bricks should not have extended to those used in mines or manufacture works.

This

This might feem enough to recommend it to the attention and care of the public and of the legiflature; but it would not be merely a faving of a certain fum. The employment given to fo great a number of men fhould not be forgotten, and in a manufacture which, on inquiry, will be found as beneficial as any, formed with materials dug out of the earth, not applicable to any other purpofe, confequently not interfering with any manufacture, but affifting many, nor caufing any change that may take off from other produce. When land is converted from tillage to pafture, or from wood to either tillage or pafture, there is a lofs of certain articles; but in the cafe of iron, in the making of which, ore, limeftone, and coal are ufed, there is none. It fhould be added, that no manufacturers pay more in excifes than thofe employed in this branch; and fuppofing 50,000 tons to be imported, and that one man can make a ton in a year, that he pays, in excifes of all kinds, upwards of 6l. annually, (which are computed to be the cafe,) there would be an increafe of excife, at leaft, to the amount of 300,000l., which would more than doubly pay the lofs to the revenue that would arife from the non-importation of 50,000 tons of foreign iron.

We

We are apt to confider iron and bar iron
as a raw material * ; in the latter ftate it is
a manu-

* The author, in his Obfervations on the Commerce of the American States, fell into the fame error,
and his remarks relative to the duty on import of foreign iron were founded on the ftate of the manufacture
of iron in Great Britain about 15 years ago, previous
to the late improvements. He finds that the making
of iron is a greater trade than his former information
had led him to believe ; and as it may be faid to be in
an infant ftate, and undoubtedly is increafing rapidly,
it would be dangerous to give it any check at prefent :
at leaft one third of the quantity of iron imported may
be fuppofed to be for inferior purpofes of manufacture,
and for which Britifh iron made with pit-coal may
be fubftituted. The improvements made within a
few years juftify the hopes of approaching the better
forts, if the fpirited exertions now making, are not difcouraged by the new fyftems. It is believed, that if
the duty on the import of foreign iron was removed,
many great iron works would be immediately difcontinued, which now employ fuch numbers of men in
the manner the moft advantageous to the country,
and, at leaft, fave 200,000l. which otherwife muft be
fent out of this country ; but being fpent and circu-
lated among the induftrious, a confiderable part muft
by them be ultimately paid to the national fupport in
the excife on the various articles confumed by them.
Works would be neglected, which within a few years
have coft immenfe fums, but would become ufelefs and
of no value, to the ruin of thofe men, who with great
fpirit have invefted their fortunes in them, under the
faith and expectation that the duties on foreign iron
would

a manufacture far advanced, and in a mid-
way ftage from the ore to perfection. We
ſhould

would continue. Theſe are weighty confiderations;
at the fame time it ſhould be repeated, there is a probability, that in a few years, by the exertions of feveral
very ingenious men now engaged in the bufinefs, that
we may be able fully to ſtock the market at home,
which is neceſſary to put this country on a footing
with foreign countries, and then we may gradually
lower the duty, or rather the duty will ceaſe of courfe,
as it will not anfwer to bring in iron, when it can be
made in fufficient quantities, and as cheap at home.

This much may be fairly advanced, that from the
improvements that have been made, particularly from
the capital improvement of coak bar iron by Meſſrs.
Wright and Jeſſon, which is the method now generally practiſed, that kind of iron has been much improved in its quality; and the quantity made is greatly increaſed, and likely to be more ſo; for as nearly
the fame number of furnaces are kept up as were during the war, and few cannon are now making, the
immenfe quantity of caſt iron which was annually ab-
forbed by theſe inſtruments, will be now converted
into bar iron, and many of the cannon themfelves will
be literally turned into plough ſhares, hoops, and nails
—Were the duty to be taken off foreign iron at this cri-
tical conjunction, all this trade might fall to the ground.

The fubftitution of ſteam engines in place of water
mills to work the furnaces and forges, has much increaſed the powers of manufacturing bar iron. By
whom ſteam engines were firſt applied to raife water
for the wheels of furnaces is not known to the author;
but Mr. Wilkinfon was the firſt who applied them directly

fhould obferve that the great confumption of iron is in the grofs articles and not in thofe which require the greateft degree of manufacture. Iron has this peculiar recommendation above almoft all other manufactures, that in every ftage of it, its value is fimply the product of labour, which labour is not hazardous to the lives, or prejudicial to the health of thofe employed, but, on the contrary, has been remarkably wholefome.

From 50 to 60,000 tons of pig iron, and between 20 and 30,000 tons of bar iron are made in Britain, and the annual demand for the latter is from 70 to 80,000 tons, of

rectly to blow the furnace without the intervention of a water wheel; and Meffrs. Boulton and Watts were the firft that applied fteam engines to work forge mills directly without the intervention of water wheels: they have erected feveral for that purpofe, and there are one or two on the common conftruction applied to the fame ufe, which they perform in an inferior manner, and at a greater expence of fuel—Meffrs. Boulton and Watts have alfo made feveral engines for turning mills of other forts, and are now making many more. The advantages of their engines confift in their faving twothirds of the fuel ufed to do the fame work by common fire engines, in their being more manageable, and better conftructed in every refpect.

which

which between 50 and 60,000 are imported, the value of which is fo much money paid for foreign labour. It is computed, that Great Britain makes, at leaft, 10,000 tons of iron more than fhe did a few years ago, which at 16l. per ton, the prefent average price, amounts to 160,000l.; and this quantity is likely to be much more than doubled in a very fhort period. If the demand is only 70,000 tons, the manufacturing of the whole within the country will employ 70,000 labourers, and valuing the iron only at 15l. per ton, will produce an annual profit of more than a million to the nation. But if the making of iron is not encouraged and extended, the fum that now goes from this country for that article will be increafed. The price of Ruffia iron rifes very rapidly; 5 per cent. in 1784, and as great a rife is expected in 1785. Ruffia has found a vent by the Black Sea; and fome fabrics, particularly that of Toula, which formerly fent much to England, now fend none.

The price muft increafe alfo from the im-menfe deftruction of the woods by the iron works, by the flownefs of the growth of woods, and the neglect of them in Siberia, where are the principal iron works. It

E e

is furprifing, indeed, that Ruffia can afford
iron fo cheap as fhe does.   The Abbé
D'Auteroche reports, that on the fpot, in
Siberia, iron is eftimated at lefs than 30s.
Englifh, per ton.   It is all conveyed an
aftonifhing diftance by inland carriage, yet
it is afforded at Peterfburgh at about 8s. per
cwt.   The beft fable iron comes from
Neucanfkoi in Siberia ; it is carried by land
to the Tchufchauwaia, which falls into the
Kama, and that into the Wolga below the
city of Kafan; it then afcends the Wolga,
and is brought by the Ladoga canal to
Peterfburgh.   With the decreafe of vaffal-
age and increafe of civilization, the price
of labour alfo will rife in Ruffia.   The prefent low price of iron in Ruffia is partly
accounted for by this circumftance, that
the Emprefs grants a diftrict with the
peafantry on it, and the perfon to whom it
is granted not paying for the latter, as is
ufual in other countries where negroes are
employed, the price of their labour is
merely the expence of keeping them.

An inquiry into thefe circumftances is neceffary, when not only the prefent but the
probable future ftate of the iron trade
fhould be examined.   The object is of the
utmoft

utmoft confequence, efpecially to Britain. The expediency of endeavouring, on the part of Ireland, to make iron a principal manufacture of that kingdom, and of vieing with a favourite and eftablifhed manufacture of Great Britain, may be doubted. It will be difficult to raife the manufacture in Ireland in competition with that of Britain. The capital of Ireland may be otherwife employed to advantage, particularly in manufactures fo advantageous and natural to her as leather, &c. ; but if fuch a competition fhould be thought an object for the mutual advantage of the two countries ; on an arrangement, it will be deemed fair and reafonable that the manufactures of each fhould be exported to all parts charged with fimilar or equivalent duties, and that this only can be judged an equal fettlement.

There is no article in which it will be more difficult to arrange with Ireland than on that of iron ; and in confequence of the revolutions which have taken place in America and Ireland, thofe interefted in the iron trade of this kingdom are alarmed; they think it is become matter of very ferious confideration, how far that branch of ma-

nufacture

nufacture may or is likely to be affected by its new rival fifter, Ireland.

They affert that Ireland will not obferve the fpirit of her compact, if fhe does not put the fame duty on the export of iron wares to the American ftates, to which fhe had agreed when they were dependent on England. It may be proper to ftate, that when Ireland, in 1778, obtained a free trade to the Britifh colonies, fhe undertook, by the act of her own Parliament, to equalize the duties, that the Irifh manufacturers fhould not be able to fupply the colonies on better terms than the Englifh in their refpective branches.

The reprefentatives of the iron trade in England agreed, that Ireland fhould have a participation in their branch of trade, on payment of equal duties with themfelves, the duty on bar iron being at that time very different in the two kingdoms.

It was firft propofed to impofe on all foreign bar iron imported into Ireland the fame duties as were then paid in England on the fame articles, but this propofal was declined. The only other method of equalizing

zing was, by impofing a duty on iron wares and iron exported from Ireland, as fhould fend them to market charged with duties equal to the Englifh. The following calculations for the average on which the par of duty was calculated, were fatisfactory to both parties at that time, and were deemed fair between the two countries. The gentleman who negociated for Ireland, declared himfelf perfectly fatisfied therewith, and that he was honourably treated by the iron trade of England. A claufe was immediately added to the act of Parliament then in agitation, impofing a duty of 2l. 10s. on all bar iron; and 3l. 3s. 11d. on all iron wares exported from Ireland to the Britifh colonies in the Weft Indies, and on the coaft of Africa, grounded on thefe calculations:

Calculation made in 1778, for equalizing the duty on a ton of bar iron between England and Ireland.

A ton of bar iron pays duty on importation into England 2l. 8s. 6d.* and draws back nothing on re-

* There is an addition to the duty on importation of bar iron into Britain fince 1778, as will be more particularly mentioned hereafter.

export

	£.	s.	d.
export to America or the Britiſh Weſt Indies † - -	2	8	6
A ton of bar iron into Ireland pays 10s. Iriſh duty ‡, of which it draws back 7s. 6d. on re-exportation, duty remaining is 2s. 6d. Iriſh - -	0	2	4
Difference in favour of Ireland, Engliſh money - -	2	6	2
Add, to make this Iriſh money	0	3	10
Duty to be impoſed on every ton of bar iron exported from Ireland	2	10	0

Calculation for equalizing the duty on a ton of iron wares between England and Ireland, made in 1778.

30 cwt. of bar iron is, on an average, eſtimated to produce one ton of manufactured iron wares.

---

† On exportation to Ireland or ſettlements in Africa, the whole is drawn-back except the old ſubſidy. The ſame is now allowed to America and the plantations, on bar iron, but not on wrought iron.

‡ The ſame duty is payable on importation of iron into Ireland from all parts.

30 cwt. of bar iron into Great Britain, at 2l. 8s. 6d. pays   3   12   9
30 cwt. ditto into Ireland, at 10s.
per ton Irish, or 9s. 2d. English
money, pays   -   -   0   13   9

Difference in favour of Ireland, in .
English money   -   2   19   0
Add, to make this Irish money   0   4   11

Duty to be imposed on a ton of
iron wares when exported from
Ireland   -   -   3   3   11

An act in conformity to this calculation was
soon after passed in the Irish House of Commons, and the duties above are now in force
in Ireland.

A memorial from Ireland is now before
the Ministry, complaining of the duty imposed on a ton of iron wares, as being taken
on an unfair average, and intimating that a
ton of split iron, or iron hoops, do not require so great a quantity of bar to produce
a ton of manufacture; it is true that those
two articles, and those *two* only, do not require much more than 21 cwt. of bar to
produce a ton; but it is argued, that there

is

is an immenfe variety of bright iron and
fteel wares, of which a ton cannot be manufactured from 30cwt. 40cwt. or even
50 cwt. of bar iron; even in the article of
fmall nails, 30 cwt. of bar produces only
21 cwt. 3 q. 11 lb. of manufacture. With
the approbation of both parties, the average was made on one average only, to
avoid a variety of calculations for different
articles.

It feems proper here to obferve, that the
duty on a ton of bar iron into England is
increafed, fince 1778, 7s. 7d. per ton; fo
that the true equalizing duty on Ireland
fhould now be 3l. 16s. 3d. and not 3l. 3s.
11d. The latter duty, which is now in force
in Ireland, is the difference of duty on
25 cwt. only of bar to a ton of iron wares;
an average fo much too low, that Britain
thinks fhe has now a right to complain as
the injured country in this particular.

It would have been better, and more
equal to the different manufactures of iron
in Ireland, if two averages had been taken,
one on nails, hoops, and other heavy articles; and another on the lighter and bright-
er articles of iron and fteel wares, in which
the

the wafte of the material is abundantly more confiderable; and then 25 cwt. perhaps would have been an equitable calculation for the grofs, and 40 or 45 cwt. for the fmaller and bright wares, which might have prevented the objection on the part of Ireland againft the inequality of the average.

Ireland farther fays, that the duty of 3 l. 3 s. 11 d. on her wares is too much, becaufe England makes a large quantity of iron, and confequently a great proportion of her wares go out free of duty. England confumes more than double the quantity of iron for *internal* ufes than fhe makes; it cannot therefore be juftly faid that any iron wares go out of England free of the duty paid on bar iron imported, and as Ireland can now import iron from Ruffia confiderably cheaper than it can be imported into England, Ireland is therefore fupplied for its internal ufes on better terms.

The Iron mafters of Great Britain ftrenuoufly affert there will be nothing like equality or reciprocity, unlefs both countries pay the fame duty on the importation of foreign bar iron; and that that duty fhould not be lower than it now is in England,

F f

land, viz. 2 l. 16 s. 1 d. per ton Englifh,
which is equal to 3 l. os. 9 d. Irifh, as a reduction of that duty would tend to defeat its
operation in favour of Britifh iron works,
which deferve and require at this juncture
every fupport and encouragement from the
country. Even fuch an equalization would
leave a great advantage to Ireland, as her
manufactures do not pay the number of excifes which are paid in Britain. If iron ore
fhould be wanting in Ireland, the beft is to
be had from Lancafhire and Cumberland,
and may go as ballaft to oak bark, and be
delivered in Ireland on cheaper terms than
to the makers of iron in moft parts of Britain, where this kind of ore is ufed. The
tranfportation to the eaftern coaft of Ireland
will not coft one half of what is now paid
by the iron makers at Chepftow, and in the
Ports of the Severn, where great quantities of it are fent, and through Hull to Ro-
theram, and other inland works; and in
Scotland it is ufed at a ftill greater expence;
and if pit coal and peat or turf fhould be
wanting in Ireland *, that article may be
had

---

* As to the article coals, there is plenty in fome
parts of Ireland, and probably in time they may be got
at as low a price as in England. The iron ore, the
lime

had as cheap on her eaftern coaft from Britain as in feveral parts of the latter, and much cheaper than in London, where many branches of the iron manufacture are carried on to a great extent, viz. hoops, rods, anchors, fhip bolts, &c. It is well known that coals are above 50 per cent dearer in the Thames than in the Liffey.

While Ireland had woods, fhe had alfo many iron works; but when the former were cut down and deftroyed, there was of courfe nearly an end of the latter; the improvements in making iron have encouraged her to revive them; fome fteam engines are now erecting, and fhe is rapidly increafing her manufactures of iron; and as the true means of benefiting the country would be by encouraging the making of the iron, which fhe can ufe in her manufactures, the only method of eftablifhing that

lime ftone (the ore is generally to be found where there is coal) and coal will be found in the fame neighbourhood, and with the help of fteam engines and navigations (no country is better fitted for the latter than Ireland) iron works may be eftablifhed wherever thofe articles can be found. Peat has been ufed in England in iron works, altho' to no great extent; but furnaces are now erecting in Ireland on land abounding with iron ore and coal.

work

work will be by laying the heavy duty * on
foreign iron imported, which will operate
as a bounty in favour of her iron works.
Till that is done, it cannot be expected any
quantity of iron will be made there; at prefent nothing can be expected, except an
emigration of Englifh capitals to be employed in Ireland to vend foreign labour in the
form of rod iron, hoops, fheets, and heavy
articles, to the prejudice of both kingdoms.

The labour of converting a ton of iron,
value 14l. in Ireland, into hoops, rods, &c.
will not exceed 20s., and is the whole of
the profit on this capital †; which iron, if
made in the country, the whole would be
a national profit, being fimply the produce
of fo much labour. In fhort, there can be
no doubt that the national object fhould be
to make the iron at home, and thereby fave
fo much, and employ a great number of

* Since the additional duties of two 5 per cents, and
the difcounts (have been taken off) which makes near
8s. per ton, the Englifh iron works have increafed rapidly, and feveral thoufand tons of bar iron have been
made more than were made when the duty was lefs.

† By rolling and flitting, iron is very little advanced from the bar; the labour is not fo much as ten
fhillings per ton.

people;

people; and it was thus that so much trea-
sure, formerly unknown to Britain, has
been drawn from the earth. The only
other satisfactory mode of equalization and
reciprocity, will be by laying duties on exportation of iron manufactures from Ireland to all parts, equal to the charges with
which they go from Britain, and this, it is
said, would be confonant to the spirit of the
compact, and in return for the participation
of the plantation trade.

Those concerned in the iron trade add,
that if neither of these take place, Ireland
only paying 10s. where Britain pays 56s.
she must underfell the latter in her commerce with the American States, the great
mart for British iron wares *, and also on
the

* The following calculation is also given, to prove
the advantage Ireland would have :

Calculation for iron hoops.

	£.	s.
A ton of Ruffia iron, fit for hoops, cost, in 1784, into London, nearly	14	10
Waste of metal and charge of rolling,	3	10
Cost of a ton of hoops in London, ———	18	0

Diffe-

the continent of Europe, particularly Portugal, which takes moſt iron hoops *, and ſo
materially in heavy iron wares, that ſhe
muſt very rapidly ſupplaint Britain in that
branch of trade, unleſs the export of the

	£.	s.
Brought forward, - -	18	0
Difference of duty on a ton of bar iron in } favour of Ireland,	2	7
Coſt of a ton of hoops in Dublin, —	15	13

Difference in favour of Ireland, about 15l.
per cent.

Calculation of ſplit iron.

A ton of Ruſſia bar iron fit for rod iron, } coſt into London, in 1784, about 14l. }	14	0
Waſte of metal and charge of ſlitting, -	1	10
Coſt of a ton of rod iron in London,	15	10
Difference of duty in favour of Ireland, -	2	7
Coſt of a ton of rod iron at Dublin —	13	3

Difference in favour of Ireland between 15 and 20l.
per cent.

N. B. Theſe calculations are made, on an average,
for Engliſh ports ; and the compariſon is made on a
ſuppoſition that coals are at the ſame price in the Iriſh
ports. But the difference in the Thames and in the
Liffey has been already mentioned.

* America and Portugal took two thirds of the whole
export of iron wares.

manu-

manufacture is protected by a bounty which muft exceed the duty on the import of bar iron, as 30 cwt. of the latter will, on an average, make lefs than 22 cwt. of wrought iron, and confequently the bounty fhould be near a third more than the duty; and they farther add, that they hope, if their equitable defire is refufed, and farther meafures fhould be neceffary, that the legiflature will moreover protect them, by other regulations which may be fuggefted. They declare alfo, that unlefs they are protected by the legiflature, they muft defert the works, which have coft millions, and migrate with their capitals to Ireland; the lofs to the nation, they fay, it is unneceffary for them to ftate.

It has been obferved, that equality and reciprocity require that Ireland fhould lay the fame duties on the importation of the materials of manufacture * as are paid in Britain, or that they fhall be equalized on the export of the manufactures to all parts. The firft will be objected to, on the part of Ireland, as charging her confumption

* It will ftill remain, in the opinion of many, to be examined, what compenfation fhould alfo be made for excife, window lights, &c. &c.

heavily

heavily and unneceffarily; and it is objectionable on the part of this country, unlefs the duties are drawn back on exportation to Britain, and laid on importation into Britain from Ireland : otherwife Ireland
will receive the duties or revenue arifing on
the confumption of Britain, which the latter
now enjoys.   The fecond method of equalizing, viz. by laying the fame duties on
the export of the manufacture to all parts,
will, alfo, probably be objected to by Ireland,
becaufe fhe is already in poffeffion of the advantage of fending out many articles to all
countries, except the Britifh plantations,
charged with lefs duties than the fame articles going from Britain ; and Britain will
object to this mode of equalizing, becaufe
it will be eafily evaded.   It has not been,
and it will not be, the policy of Ireland to
enforce a very exact obfervance of fuch
cautions as may be adopted : Britain would
fubmit her manufactures, her trade and
commercial laws, to the fidelity of the Cuftom-houfe officers of Ireland in many refpects.—In fhort, it is impoffible for her to
be fecured permanently in the regulations
that may be made ; but when her trade is
once gone in confequence of her arrangements, and fhe finds herfelf difapppointed,
the

the recovery of that trade, is not probable.
It has been already obferved, that equalization in general would benefit Ireland and
prejudice Britain lefs than is imagined: this
muft be always underftood under an arrangement in every refpect reciprocal; and
if Ireland really means fuch, the more the
fubject is examined, the lefs favourable fhe
will find fuch an arrangement*; and that
the whole fyftem is likely to be productive
of much more embarraffment and ill temper than advantage to both countries.

Unlefs iron manufactures go to the American States from Ireland, charged with the
fame duties and burdens as from Britain, it
is obvious, that Ireland muft in time have
the whole of this trade: and unlefs Britain
obtains this equilization, fhe fubmits not
to prefent but to certain future competition,
without the leaft return.

It has been generally fuppofed that Ireland has great difadvantages in working iron

---

* In an equal arrangement of manufactures, Ireland muft expect to give a bounty on the export of
Britifh linens, in the fame manner as it is given in Britain on the export of Irifh linens from thence.

mines, when compared with Great Britain; but the reafon does not appear*, unlefs it fhould arife from want of capital; in general it may be obferved, that the private capitals of Englifh manufacturers at prefent combat the purfe of Ireland, in the hands of a bountiful and liberal parliament. But if Englifhmen will employ their capitals in Ruffia, why fhould they not employ them in Ireland†? Some Englifhmen, with Englifh

---

* It has been already obferved that the price of Britifh coal on the eaft coaft of Ireland, is lower than it is in many parts, where manufactures of iron are carried on in Britain. It is remarkable, that as the latter affects to encourage the fpreading of manufactures, fo partial and impolitic a tax as that on coals carried coaftways, fhould be adopted. It is about five times as much as the duty on coals exported to Ireland. The duty on coals carried coaftways from one port of Great Britain to another is 5s. 4¾d. per Winchefter chaldron. The duty on coals exported from Great Britain to Ireland, is 1s. 1⅕d. per chaldron. The duty on coals imported into the port of London 8s. 7d. per chaldron. The duty on coals exported to foreign countries in Britifh bottoms, 8s. 0¼d. per chaldron. The duty on coals exported in foreign bottoms, 14s. 4 d. per chaldron.

† The extravagancies, the uncommon proceedings of Ireland, and her unfettled ftate, may reafonably prevent it at this time; and her frequent threats of an abfentee tax do not feem very judicious or well calculated to promote migration to Ireland.

Men

lifh capitals, are erecting large works in Ruffia for rolling, flitting, tinning plates, &c.

If the great improvements in making iron fhould not enable Britain and Ireland, in time, principally to fupply themfeives with that article, it is evident they muft be furpaffed in the manufactures of it. At pre-

Men will not truft their property in a country where fuch an arbitrary and impatient difpofition is fhewn, or lay it out where it can be liable to fuch difadvantage and reftraints. The author being himfelf in the predicament of an abfentee, fhould not have made this obfervation, if he fuppofed the tax likely to take place, or that the change of property from one country to the other would be very difadvantageous, at a time when eftates in England fell at 23 years purchafe, and under ; but indeed if fuch a tax could effectually be eftablifhed in Ireland, the price of land would probably fall to ten years purchafe. No abfentee, however, would keep land there longer than he could poffibly avoid it. Ireland would feel a fcarcity of money, much greater than fhe has ever experienced. As fhe may fometimes want money, it is not quite prudent to talk of fuch meafures. Englifhmen are not very fond of lending money to Ireland ; and they will be much lefs fo, when they recollect the fame reafon exifts for taxing the money of an abfentee on mortgage, as the land of an abfentee ; there is this difference, indeed, that the mortgagee draws more money in proportion, and a clearer and larger income, from the country than the proprietor of an eftate.

G g 2

fent

fent Britain alone pays above fix hundred thoufand pounds yearly for that article to foreign countries. The following account of expences on a ton of iron from Ruffia, fhews the difference in carrying on the manufacture in the two countries. No lefs than 5l. 4s. 2d. the ton.

	£.	s.	d.
Commiffion, lighterage, Ruffia, cuftom, and all other Ruffia charges, - -	0	13	10
Ruffian duty on export, -	0	9	0
* The Sound duties - -	0	2	8
Two-third port charges, -	0	1	6
Freight and infurance, about -	0	19	0
Landing, cuftom-houfe charges duty to the Ruffia Company in London, &c. &c.	0	3	0
Duty in Britain, —	2	16	1
	5	4	3

* This Sound duty fometimes amounts from 50l. to 100l. ; and more, on a fingle fhip's cargo. It is an extraordinary inftance to what nations will fubmit through habit ; but, confidering the rifing power of Ruffia, it may not long laft.

The

The duties on importation into Ireland from Britain, are,

On unwrought iron, 10s. per ton.
On hoops, 4s. 1d. per cwt.
On iron, ore, and cinders, 5$\frac{14}{16}$ per ton.

Ireland makes little bar iron; her importation of iron increafed near a third in ten years, which proves the increafe of her manufactures and of her confumption, as her importations of wrought iron have in general increafed, and not inconfiderably; but ftill the latter are not great when compared with her confumption.

On an average of three years, ending 25th March, 1773, iron imported into Ireland,

	Cwt.	qrs.	lbs.
From the Eaft Country -	74,683	3	25$\frac{1}{2}$
From Britain - -	44,352	1	4$\frac{1}{2}$
Total	119,036	1	2

Ditto

Ditto of iron, on an average of three years, ending 25th March, 1783 :

	Cwt.	qrs.	lbs.
From the Eaſt Country*	98,488	1	9½
From Britain -	74,730	0	4⅖
Total	173,218	1	14

Export from Ireland of iron and iron ware for the ſame years.

		Ironmongers' ware. Value.				Iron. Tons. Cwt.	
1771	—	29	4	9	—	9	0
1772	—	10	5	6	—	4	2
1773	—	22	13	10	—	2	4

	Hardware. Value.			Ironmongers' ware. Value.			Wrought iron. Cwt. q. ℔.			Iron. Tons. Cwt.	
1781	16	3	0	253	6	3	25	0	0	0	0
1782	22	11	4	2	19	0	75	3	7	0	0
1783	2:3	9	6	85	3	9	359	2	0	8	1

Imports into Ireland for the year ending 25th March, 1783, of iron and iron ware.

Hardware, value - -   21,773   2   10½

---

* The import into Ireland from St. Peterſburgh alone, in 1784, was 2514 tons, or 50,280 cwt.

Iron,

Iron, cwt. q. lb.	-	-	164,187	1	0
Knives, No.	-	-	579,833	0	0
Mermits, No.	-	-	9,797	0	0
Pots, No.	-	-	748	0	0
Razors, No.	-	-	14,865	0	0
Sciffars, grofe, dozens	-	757	9	0
Scythes, dozens	-	-	4,089	0	0
Small parcels, value	-	24,473	17	5½
Iron ore, tons	-	-	323	0	0

Almoft the whole of the above articles were imported from Britain, except iron, which came from feveral countries in the following quantities:

	Cwt.	q.	lb.
From England - -	61,943	2	0
Scotland - -	3,144	1	0
Guernfey - -	40	3	7
Jerfey - -	136	2	14
Sweden - -	83,489	3	14
Ruffia - -	12,873	1	21
Denmark and Norway	1,152	0	14
Eaft Country - -	63	0	0
Germany - -	525	0	0
Flanders - -	728	2	14
New York - -	90	0	0

GLASS

GLASS MANUFACTURE.

Since the heavy duty was laid, a few years ago, on glafs in Britain, Ireland has made an extraordinary progrefs in that manufacture —fhe had little of it before; but nine glafs houfes have now fuddenly arifen in Ireland. The extention of the trade of that country muft alfo be confidered as a fpur to this manufacture, although fhe did very little towards her own fupply before. She ftill imports in large quantities; but fhe muft foon have almoft the whole of this trade to the Britifh fettlements and the American States. The Britifh tax is laid in a pernicious manner on the metal; the wafte and blemifhed part are taxed and retaxed without end; and bad ware will be fent out to avoid the lofs. Many glafs houfes at Stourbridge and at Liverpool, &c. have been given up lately; the number in London is greatly reduced, and our exportation to the Continent, it is faid, is now principally confined to articles of a high price, which form but a fmall part of the manufacture. The French, alfo, have decoyed away many of the beft workmen, and have thereby improved their own manufacture of glafs.

The

The table glafs made in Ireland is very handfome, and apparently as good as any made in England; at the fame time the beft drinking glaffes are three or four fhillings per dozen cheaper than Englifh. The general-increafed confumption in Ireland appears, from the importation of moft articles, (except drinking glaffes,) in nearly the fame quantities, notwithftanding fo confiderable a quantity is now made in the country.

Her export of glafs begins to be confiderable, as appears from the following account; but in the laft year, ending 25th March, 1784, it was greatly increafed,—for fhe fent to America alone 532 dozen of bottles, and 20,736 drinking glaffes. This, however, may be confidered as an effort on the firft opening of trade with the American States; and it may be doubted whether a fpeculation of fo much rifque will fpeedily be repeated to the fame extent *. The greater part of the drinking glaffes fhe exported in the year ending 25th March, 1783, went to Portugal.

* Yet a principal houfe in Dublin has received orders from New York that would employ it two years.

H h   Account

Account of glaſs imported into Ireland, on an average of three years, ending 25th March 1773.

Bottles,	Dozens	39,768$\frac{1}{8}$
Cafes,	No.	2,083
DainkingGlaſſes, No.		209,222
Vials,	No.	8,112
Ghſs ware,	Value	3,745l. 14s. 3d.

Account of glaſs imported into Ireland, on an average of three years, ending 25th March, 1783.

Bottles,	Dozens,	42,504$\frac{2}{7}$
Cafes,	No.	2,067$\frac{2}{7}$
Drinking Glaſſes, No.		22,248
Vials,	No.	4,524
Glaſs ware,	Value	3,675l. 11s.9$\frac{1}{2}$d.

There was no export of glaſs from Ireland before 1780; ſince that time the export has been as follows:

	Bottles. Dozen.	Drinking Glaſſes No.	Glaſs ware. Value.			Cafes. No.
			£.	s.	d.	
1781	1892	——.	35	8	10	——
1782	1738	——	172	11	0	
1783	468	9910	——	——	——	——

EARTHEN

EARTHEN WARE.

The fuccefsful rivalſhip of the Britiſh glaſs manufactory in Ireland, within a very few years, ſhews the progreſs ſhe is likely to make in a ſhort period in that of earthen ware. At prefent ſhe has no very confiderable works, except of the coarſe kinds; but as foreign countries have imitated the Engliſh manufacture, Ireland will do it to greater advantage. There are no laws to prevent the emigration of workmen to that kingdom as there are in refpect to foreign countries; on the contrary, the vicinity of Ireland, added to the fameneſs of language and laws, give great facility to emigrations when the Iriſh manufactures are in a ſtate to give employment to induſtry and ingenuity.

The great and extenſive earthen-ware works in England owe their eſtabliſhment, in their prefent fuperior ſtile, to the ability and elegant taſte of Mr. Wedgwood; he may have the fatisfaction of thinking that perhaps no one man ever gave employment to a greater number of manufacturers, or was the cauſe of a greater exportation of a

H h 2

manu-

manufacture fo varioufly advantageous to his country, exhibiting at the fame time to all parts of the world, the progrefs Britain has lately made in the beautiful as well as ufeful arts.

This manufacture maintains many thoufands of poor labouring people in feveral and diftant parts of England, in raifing the raw materials, preparing and working them. No foreign materials are employed in it; its value, therefore, confifts wholly in labour beftowed upon native produce.

The freightage it furnifhes for the coafting trade, that beft and readieft fupply for the navy, is very confiderable, and peculiarly interefting, as the raw materials are brought from Poole in Dorfetfhire, Tinmouth, and other places, by thofe veffels which are employed at the proper feafons, in the Newfoundland fifhery. Thefe materials are carried coaftwife to Liverpool and Hull, to the amount of many thoufand tons yearly, and from thence by river and canal navigation, to the Potteries in Staffordfhire. What is peculiar to this manufacture, and renders it ftill more valuable is, that the wares furnifh fome of them five or fix times,

and

and none lefs than two or three times as much tonnage as the raw materials (coals excepted, which are not brought by water) and are returned by a like circuitous navigation to all parts of the coaft of this ifland, from whence they are fhipped for foreign markets. It is a known fact, that this cheap and bulky article makes a part of the cargo of almoft every fhip that leaves our ports: nor is it lefs remarkable, as a circumftance of national concern, that the quantity exported amounts, according to fome calculations, to nine-tenths, but certainly not lefs than five-fixths of the whole produce.

But as this manufacture has rifen to its prefent magnitude and ftate of perfection within thefe very few years, little attention has hitherto been paid for preferving the channels open for its admiffion into foreign markets: it has therefore been clogged with impofts and prohibitions, more, perhaps, than any other Britifh manufacture. In Sweden, Denmark, Brandenburg, Pruffia, and Portugal, it is prohibited: in the latter kingdom, indeed, we are told that it will now be admitted, but on a duty of four times the value of the goods; and in the Auftrian Netherlands,

therlands, the duty is at prefent nearly three times the value of the goods. The King of Pruffia has lately laid a double impoft on this manufacture, one upon its going into Dantzic, and another payable on the Vif-tula, in the paffage from Dantzic to Po-land. The late edict of the Emperor *, for the prohibition of Englifh manufactures, will give the laft ftroke to our exports into his dominions: In Saxony, our wares pay a very high duty : in Spain, to which our exports have been great, an impoft has late-ly taken place, more than equal to the value of our cheaper fpecies of earthen ware: in Livonia, a duty of 30 per cent. has been added to one before of 10 per cent. and in the other dominions of the Emprefs of Ruffia, the duty is likewife 40 per cent. In Hol-land and Italy, the duties are moderate ; and the demand is accordingly very confiderable, and for our beft goods.

Some of the above-mentioned impofts and prohibitions have taken place, in confe-

* This edict has been fufpended for a few months. Adminiftration feemed perfectly ignorant of the exift-ence of fuch an edict, when the manufacturers men-tioned it a confiderable time, after it had been pub-lifhed.

quence,

quence, it is faid, of our partiality to Portugal wines, and our duties on foreign linen, and our prohibition of the lace of the Low Countries, an article which is fmuggled with fo much facility that no prohibition can prevent its importation into this country.

Since we have loft the monopoly of the American market, the manufacturers on the Continent have had an additional inducement to attempt rivalling us there; for which purpofe they have hired our workmen, and taken every other ftep in their power. The rapid improvement they have made in this manufacture fhew that they have not laboured in vain, and that nothing lefs than our utmoft exertions, accompanied with fuch affiftance as Government can afford, in preferving to us the markets that are ftill left open, and opening, where practicable, thofe which are now fhut, can enable us to retain, for any length of time, that fuperiority we are at prefent in poffeffion of; for we have no advantage over many parts of the Continent either in the goodnefs or cheapnefs of our materials, and labour (which conftitutes nearly the whole of the expence of this manufacture) is at leaft cent. per cent. againft us.

Moft

Most of these circumstances will equally affect Ireland.

Account of earthen ware imported into Ireland, on an average of three years, ending 25th March, 1773.

Value.

12,085l. 3s. 0½d

Account of earthen ware imported into Ireland, on an average of three years, ending 25th March, 1783.

Value.

17,401l. 14s.

The valuations are very unfatisfactory.

None exported.

There is not time now to obferve upon the remaining manufactures in much detail ; but a knowledge of the importations and exportations

tations of the moft material of them at different periods, with a very few remarks, will furnifh matter of obfervation to thofe who wifh to examine the fubject.

The manufacture of leather and candles have been mentioned under the article, Produce of Cattle.

STOCKINGS.

It is remarkable that the importation of a manufacture fo much in the power of Ireland as ftockings, fhould have increafed fo very confiderably in ten years. It is probable, however, that the manufacture within the country has alfo increafed, though not in proportion to the increafed confumption; and the increafed importation, when combined with other obvious circumftances, afford a fair prefumption of the progreffive improvement of the kingdom. Above 7500l. went out of the country for thread ftockings; above 3000l. for cotton; and above 2000l. for worfted, in the year ending 25th March, 1783.

Importation

Importation of ſtockings into Ireland.

	Cotton. Pairs.	Silk. Pairs.	Silk & Worſt. Pairs.	Thread. Pairs.	Woollen. Pairs.	Worſted. Pairs.
1771	12,222	547	42	18,031	1,875	9,290
1772	10,365	278	0	15,621	264	4,783
1773	8,633	296	24	16,888	118	5,422

No exportation of ſtockings from Ireland during the above period.

Importation of ſtockings into Ireland.

	Cotton. Pairs.	Silk. Pairs.	Silk and Thread. Pairs.
1781	17,338	431	24
1782	20,490	360	0
1783	23,744	1,042	192

	Silk & Worſted. Pairs.	Thread. Pairs.	Woollen. Pairs.	Worſted. Pairs.
1781	228	29,655	331	5,111
1782	348	39,717	1,617	9,617
1783	580	60,570	1,318	8,944

Exportation of ſtockings from Ireland.

	Thread. Doz.	Thread. Pairs.	Woollen. Doz.	Woollen. Pairs.	Worſted. Doz.	Worſted. Pairs.
1781	432	4	297	11	1,143	1
1782	14	0	139	0	138	3
1783	79	3	259	0	393	0

HATS

H A T S.

As the exportation of hats from Ireland exceeds the importation, it is clear that the manufacture of that article muft be very confiderable there. In the year ending 25th March, 1784, the export to America alone increafed to 11,867. Neither the Americans nor the French can make good hats in fufficient quantities, through want of rabbits wool. It is furprifing at how low a price, and in what quantities, Newcaftle under Line affords felt hats.

Account of hats imported into Ireland, on an average of three years, ending 25th March, 1773.

No. 865.

Account of hats imported into Ireland, on an average of three years, ending 25th March, 1783.

No. 2012.

Account

Account of hats exported from Ireland.

In the year 1781   -   -   No. 1404
             1782   -   -   450
             1783   -   -   3211

UPHOLSTERY.

This manufacture, which includes carpeting and blankets, is much improved and extended in Ireland ; yet the annexed account shews an increased importation in ten years ; but the consumption was still more increased. If a later average, however, is taken than that ending 1773, there is some decrease in the importation: in a few years the amount probably will be trifling ; at present it is not confiderable.

Importation into Ireland of upholstery ware for the following period :

1771	1772	1773
Value.	Value.	Value.
6198l. 19s. 2d.	4318l. 9s. 11¼d.	5739l. 11s. 9d.

No exportation of upholstery ware from Ireland during the above-mentioned period.
Impor-

Importation into Ireland of upholftery ware for the following periods :

1781	1782	1783
Value.	Value.	Value.
4805l. 13s. 1d.	8977l. 17s. 11¼d.	8289l. 2s. 10½d.

Export from Ireland of upholftery ware for ditto :

1781	1782	1783
Value.	Value.	Value.
113l. 6s. 8d.	629l. 18s. 3d.	636l. 18s. od.

POT ASHES.

Notwithftanding the fpirited encouragement which is given for the making this effential article for the linen manufacture within the kingdom, the importation has increafed one third in ten years, and it muft continue to be very great; but it proves the increafe of the linen manufacture. In the year ending 25th March, 1783, the importation from all parts amounted to
130,893 cwt. 1qr. 21lb.
Value, at 25s. per cwt., 163,616l. 15s. 11d.
A great proportion, as will appear under the head of trade with Spain, came from that country.

Account

Account of pot aſhes imported into Ireland, on an average of three years, ending 25th March, 1773.

Cwt.	q.	lb.
54,297	3	$16\frac{1}{4}$

Account of pot aſhes imported into Ireland, on an average of three years, ending 25th March, 1783.

Cwt.	q.	lb.
81,028	1	12

S O A P and C A N D L E S.

In ſoap as well as in candles, Ireland has conſiderable advantages. Since 1778, ſhe has acquired a great part of the trade to the Weſt Indies and North America in theſe articles, and ſhe is likely to have ſtill more of it. Under the article, produce of cattle, it appears that the export of candles more than doubled in a ſhort time. Ireland is benefited by the duty of 1s. 6d. per cwt. on tallow exported to Britain, to which her manufacture is not ſubject. Ireland does not pay any duty on barilla imported. Britain pays 5s. 2½d. per cwt. Ireland makes very good mould candles. Great quantities

of

of tallow are imported, and confiderable quantities of foap and candles are fmuggled into the weft of England and Wales.

An average of foap exported from Ireland, during three years, ending 1773.

Cwt.	q.	lb.
712	0	21

Do. do. exported from do. during three years, ending 1783.

Cwt.	q.	lb.
3039	0	$18\frac{1}{3}$

An average of foap imported into Ireland, during three years, ending 1773.

Cwt.	q.	lb.
418	0	$23\frac{1}{3}$

Do. do. imported into Ireland, during three years, ending 1783.

Cwt.	q.	lb.
750	1	$9\frac{1}{3}$

BOOKS,

BOOKS, PAPER, &c.

Whenever any arrangement is made between Great Britain and Ireland, it is hoped that fome attention will be paid to literary property, and that copy right will be fecured on a proper footing: the correction of the abufe which prevails at prefent fo injurious to men of genius and fcience furely deferves attention. Many books have been very well printed in Ireland; ftill a confiderable quantity muft be imported, and more than would be fuppofed from the following account — Indeed the mode of rating unbound books, viz. at 10l. per cwt. is not very fatisfactory. A great number of books are carried into Ireland without being entered.

It appears that in ten years there was no great variation in the importation of writing paper into Ireland, but the quantity of printing paper was reduced above half. Several other forts of paper are imported into Ireland, but not in quantities worth mentioning.

The late duties on paper in Britain have much enhanced the price of books, and debafed

bafed the paper on which they are printed. They are taxes on trade and learning. Ireland will underfell Britain in the article of paper.

An account of the books and paper imported into Ireland, on an average of three years, ending 25th March, 1773.

	Bound. Value.			Unbound.		
	£.	s.	d.	Cwt.	qr.	lb.
Books	183	10	1	201	0	2

	Preffing. Leaves.	Printing. Reams.	Writing. Reams.
Paper	57,168	11,295	5,077

Ditto of ditto, exported from Ireland, during three years, ending 25th of March, 1773:

	Books			Paper.
	Cwt.	qrs.	lb.	Reams.
1771	11	2	0	98
1772	7	1	0	
1773	31	3	21	

An account of books and paper imported into Ireland, on an average of three years, ending 25th March, 1783.

	Bound.			Unbound.		
	£.	s.	d.	Cwt.	qr.	lb.
Books	207	14	8½	271	1	10

K k   Preffing.

Preffing.	Printing.	Writing.
Leaves.	Reams.	Reams.
Paper 85,257	4,772	5,749

An account of books and paper exported from Ireland, during three years, ending 25th March, 1783.

		Bound.			Unbound.			Paper. Writ.	Brown.
		£. s. d.			Cwt. q. lb.			Reams.	Reams.
1781 Books	1 19 6			15	3	14		22	—
1782	- - -			55	0	14		200	—
1783	- - -			174	3	14		302	98

B E E R.

Notwithftanding the great increafe of tillage in Ireland, and the improvements in hufbandry, it is extraordinary that her importation of beer fhould increafe fo confiderably, and her exportation decreafe. There muft be fome bad management ; and until fuch matters are corrected, Ireland fhould not fuffer her attention to be taken off to competitions of much difficulty and uncertainty. The duties paid in England on malt and hops are drawn back on exportation to Ireland, and even a bounty is given on malt, when barley is under 22s. per qr. The duty on beer and ale imported

into

into Ireland is 4s. 1d. per barrel, of 32 gallons, and the charges of commiffion, freight, and infurance amounts to about 4s. per barrel. It is faid the Irifh brewer has a profit of 20 per cent. on Englifh malt ufed in Ireland, compared with the London price. In the year ending 25th March, 1783, the quantity of beer imported from England was 51,405 barrels, and 190 barrels from Scotland.

Account of beer imported and exported from Ireland, on an average of three years, ending 25th March, 1773.

Import.	Export.
Barrels.	Barrels.
45,585½	3,550

Account of beer imported into and exported from Ireland, on an average of three years, ending 25th March, 1783.

Import.	Export.
Barrels.	Barrels.
54,546½	959

A G R I C U L T U R E.

Agriculture, though laft mentioned, certainly fhould be the firft in eftimation, as it is in real confequence. Yet it too often hap-

pens

pens in moft civilized countries of Europe, that this moft effential purfuit of man is neglected, and the capital of the community being diverted to uncertain fpeculations, the country remains half tilled and half ftocked. Manufactures fhould be confidered as fecondary to agriculture : and commerce, as refulting from both.

The agriculture of Ireland, although there may be many exceptions to the general rule, is very bad. The foil, however, does its part, or rather does almoft the whole. It muft, neverthelefs be acknowledged, that a confiderable improvement in hufbandry has taken place, at leaft tillage has increafed; and within ten years Ireland has become an exporter of corn, and is likely to continue: but previous to 1776 fhe ufed to import corn, and fometimes very largely. It is the want of capital in the Irifh farmers, as much as the want of a good fyftem of hufbandry, that prevents a better cultivation of the earth, and the poverty of the tenantry of Ireland is more hurtful than the fuppofed high rents *. To ftock a well-
fized

* The rent of Ireland appears high to an Englifh-man, who does not know that five Irifh acres are equal

fized farm, and to eftablifh and purfue a good courfe of management, and of crops, requires fuch a capital, as is not to be often found among them. Confequently the farms are too large for their weak purfe, and a fmall farm becomes a neceffary evil in Ireland: but it is by no means intended to recommend the latter. The great farmer, of whom fo many ignorantly complain in England, preferves us from fcarcity or extravagant prices in fummer; his opulence anfwers the purpofe of public granaries. A good fyftem of agriculture and intelligence, and riches among farmers, are the beft granaries on which a country can depend, and neither produce expence nor abufe †. Such farmers are enabled to preferve part of their crop, and to wait the market of the enfuing fummer. The little farmer, of very fmall capital, at the fame time that he is the wretched fport of every

to eight Englifh, and that no taxes whatever fall on the land, except a contribution to the highways of the diftrict.

† The mills, which have been eftablifhed within a few years in Ireland, are *her* beft granaries. They are on a great fcale, and are in the hands of very confiderable gentlemen. They anfwer as a certain market to the farmer.

irregu-

irregularity of feafons, or of every trifling
accident, is obliged to go to market with
all his corn and all his produce, at the time
the price is loweft, and before the winter
is finifhed. A more pitiable creature does
not live, even when compared with the
loweft labourer. He exifts under an unre-
mitting fucceffion of ftruggles and anxie-
ties, ufelefs to himfelf and hurtful to the
public. For the foil in his hands is not
fufficiently cultivated or half ftocked, nor
half the produce derived from it, that
might be in the occupation of a more opulent man. The expence of cattle, hufbandry utenfils, of attendance, &c. are proportionably much greater than on one of
a moderate fize. The profit is confumed ·
by the team of neceffary cattle, on a fmall
farm, or the land is not tilled, at leaft in
due time.

It is therefore of effential confequence
to divide lands properly, and to proportion
the farm, (ftill taking care not to admit too
fmall divifions) to the ability of the tenant,
rather than to his eagernefs for poffeffing
much land; and although the tenants of an
eftate may not be according to the wifhes
of the landlord, it is neither humane nor
                                    prudent

prudent to expel them all, to introduce plaufible adventurers, who, in the end, will generally give as little fatisfaction as the native. The latter will cling to the foil, and although he may not have the means, or know the beft method of deriving the greateft profit from the land, he will almoft ftarve himfelf, to pay the rent. An intelligent landlord will find fome among the tenants, fit to be brought forward; and notwithftanding the profpect may not be very promifing, yet, by affording them due protection, with a little affiftance, it is, perhaps, the beft method that can be purfued.

The Dublin fociety, which, in every fenfe of the word, is the firft inftitution of its kind in Europe, has not only been very ferviceable as a Board of trade, manufacture, and ufeful arts, but has been particularly affiftant to the agriculture of the country. Parliament fuppprts the fociety with liberal grants, and the public has reafon to be fatisfied with the attention of the members; yet many years will pafs before a good fyftem of hufbandry can be generally eftablifhed in Ireland: that country is very much behind England in this refpect, although a good mode of tillage is very far from general

ral in the latter. It is not neceffary to enter into any detail as to the agriculture of
Ireland, efpecially as Mr. Young has lately given fo fatisfactory an account of it. In
confequence of the labours of that gentleman, the rural œconomy of England and
Ireland is well known to the inhabitants of
thefe kingdoms; it is an advantage which,
perhaps, no country before fo fully enjoyed.
Some may think their neighbourhood not
defcribed to their mind, and that time
enough has not been beftowed on each fpot;
and the attention of others will be confined
to the bufinefs of remarking, that a bufhel
too much, or an acre too little, are mentioned. But while fuch obfervers thus a-
mufe themfelves, the politician will gain the
information he wants; he will meet many
good obfervations; and after an attentive
examination of the facts which are ftated,
he will find himfelf poffeffed of a very
competent knowledge of the country.

The import and export of corn, meal,
and flour, at different periods, now remain to be compared; and this opportunity
may be taken of obferving, that the export,
fince the account was laft made up, has
been very great indeed. The demand from

Scot-

Scotland has been immenfe; and alfo for cattle; a very confiderable number of the latter came to the Northern parts of England; but the quantity that went to Scotland is faid greatly to have exceeded former exportations. The crop of corn in Ireland the laft year was fo good, as to be fully equal to the demand.

Great Britain would do well to adopt the reciprocal preference offered by the laft corn act of Ireland, which is, that each kingdom, when its prices denote a probable fcarcity, fhall refort to the other for a fupply, before fhe goes to foreigners. There is another circumftance worthy imitation in this bill, which is, that it does not admit flour into the ports of Ireland, when they are open for corn, by that means, the manufacture and advantage is referved for her own mills, and the article is alfo better, becaufe corn carries and keeps better in the ftate of grain than in flour. This judicious prohibition does not extend to ground corn or flour from Britain, but this exception is faid to have happened inadvertently, and that there is an intention of making the prohibition general.

An

An account of corn and meal imported into Ireland, on an average of three years,
ending 25th March, 1773.

Barley and Malt.		Beans and Peafe.		Oats.		Wheat.	
Quar.	Buſh.	Quar.	Buſh.	Quar.	Buſh.	Quar.	Buſh.
28,320	4⅔	1,204	0	742	4	22,824	4

Flour.			Oatmeal.	Wheat meal.
Cwt.	Qrs.	Lbs.	Barrels.	Barrels.
61,127	1	21	9,906⅔	2,457⅟₃

An account of corn and meal exported
from Ireland, on an average of three
years, ending 25th March, 1773.

Barley and Malt.		Beans and Peafe.		Oats.		Wheat.		Rye.
Qr.	Buſh.	Qr.	Buſh.	Qr.	Buſh.	Qr.	Buſh.	Qr.
3,222	4⅔	194	1½	11,478	2	1,011⅟₃	0	17

	Flour.		Oatmeal.	Groats.
Cwt.	Quar.	Lbs.	Barrels.	Barrels.
151	3	9⅟	15,787⅟₃	14⅔

An account of corn and meal imported into Ireland, on an average of three years,
ending 25th March, 1783.

Barley and Malt.		Beans and Peafe.		Oats.		Wheat.	
Quarters.	Buſh.	Quar.	Buſh.	Quar.	Buſh.	Quar.	Buſh.
38,550	4	411	2⅔	490	2⅟	649	2

Flour.

Flour.			Oatmeal.
Cwt.	Quar.	Lbs.	Brrrels.
22,208	0	25 $\frac{2}{3}$	3,466 $\frac{1}{6}$

An account of corn and meal exported from Ireland, on an average of three years, ending 25th March, 1783.

Barley and Malt.		Beans and Peafe.		Oats.		Wheat.	
Qrs.	Bufh.	Qrs.	Bufh.	Qrs.	Bufh.	Qrs.	Bufh.
9,848	2 $\frac{1}{3}$	1645	3 $\frac{1}{4}$	53,285	6 $\frac{2}{3}$	30,123	6 $\frac{2}{3}$

	Flour.		Groats.	Oatmeal.	Wheat Meal.
Cwt.	Qrs.	Lbs.	Barrels.	Barrels.	Barrels.
85,284	3	11 $\frac{2}{3}$	7 $\frac{2}{3}$	11,577 $\frac{1}{4}$	66 $\frac{2}{3}$

G E N E R A L   T R A D E.

We now come to inquire into the external commerce of Ireland. The examination of what it has been, will give a very imperfect idea of the extenfion it is capable of. It feems at prefent likely to outftrip her internal trade; and care fhould be taken that the latter, which is of the greateft confequence, be not neglected.

The

The general trade of Ireland has increafed
greatly, and it will increafe much more:
fhe has had a favourable balance* on the
whole of her commerce, during this century, according to her own Cuftom-houfe
accounts, on averages of five or ten years,
and even on the years feparately, except
the following, when the balance againft her
was,

		£.	s.	d.
In the year 1701	- -	21,902	6	3
1706	- -	71,742	18	4
1709	- -	3,719	1	7
1724	- -	12,187	1	0

But in the year of the peace, viz. the year
ending 25th March, 1783, the imports rofe
high,

		£.	s.	d.
Imports	- -	3,011,771	17	$3\frac{1}{2}$
Exports	- -	2,903,732	8	$4\frac{1}{2}$

Balance againft Ireland - 108,039   8 $10\frac{1}{2}$

* Even before the year 1750, it amounted fome years
to upwards of 400,000l. and in 1747, to 798,230l.

Yet

Yet on an average of feven years, the balance was in her favour. The extraordinary import in that year, partly happened from the effect of peace, and partly from the neceffity of compleating ftock to fupply the deficiency of imports in preceding years, particularly in 1779 and 1780, when they were very confiderably lower than ufual. The table, No. III. fhews the trade of Ireland with all parts by decennial averages, from 1700 to 1760, diftinguifhes the years from that period to the prefent.

The Effay on the Trade of Ireland, publifhed in 1729, by Mr. Dobbs, obferves, that it is probable the exports of Ireland, during the period from the Reftoration to the Revolution, did not exceed 600,000l. In the year 1681,

	£.
The exports were - - -	582,814
Imports - -	433,040
Balance in favour of Ireland	149,774

It is well known how much Ireland fuffered by the war of the Revolution; and it is not extraordinary, that in 1695, three

years

years only after peace was reftored, that there fhould be a balance againft Ireland of 95,932l.

	£.
Her exports that year were -	295,592
Imports - -	391,524

Her ftock of cattle and fheep had been neglected and deftroyed during the war, and her trade had been principally in the produce of them ; but in three years afterwards, viz. 1698,

	£.
Her exports rofe to -	996,305
Imports - -	576,863
Balance in favour of Ireland	419,442

In the following year, 1699, came on the violent reftriction of her woollen trade; and in 1700,

	£.
Her exports were -	814,745
Imports - -	792,473
Balance in favour of Ireland only - -	22,272

But

But the next year, viz. 1701, was one of the very few years in which the balance of trade was againſt Ireland ;

			£.
Exports	-	-	670,412
Imports	-	-	692,314
Balance againſt Ireland		-	22,902

It is difficult at this diſtance of time to diſ-cover whence aroſe this great alteration in her trade, unleſs it can be in part imputed to the war which began at that time *. It was partly cauſed by the reſtrictions on her wool-lens; but that could not produce near the effect we have obſerved; for the greateſt export of woollens from Ireland, viz. in 1687, did not exceed in value 70,521l. and in the year previous to the prohibition, viz. 1698, it was only 23,614l †. and at the ſame time it ſhould be remarked, that the whole

* The very ſudden and rapid increaſe in 1697 and 98 may be, in great meaſure, aſcribed to the peace of Ryſ-wick, which certainly had enlivened commerce.

† This calculation is taken from Smith's Memoirs on wool. It ſeems very low ; however if it were dou-bled, it would go but a little way in accounting for the alteration.

value

value of old and new drapery imported from England in 1698, was only 9,612l. 13s 9d. and in the year 1701 it had only rifen to 16,163l. 8s. 9d. But this will be more particularly detailed under the article, Woollen Manufacture.

It appears from Tables, No. III. and IV. how greatly the trade has increafed during this century, and in a regular progreffion, the beft proof of a well-eftablifhed commerce, except the period from 1720 to 1730, during which there is a decreafe from that of the preceding ten years, to the amount, on the average, of about 110,000l. a year. It has, in 80 years, increafed more in proportion than the trade of England, and, perhaps, if it could be afcertained, we fhould find that the external trade of Ireland is, in proportion to her capital, greater than that of England ; but Ireland is far behind as to internal trade, and until there is an improvement in that refpect, fhe cannot expect to fee her people fully employed, or in poffeffion of any general affluence.

Her

Her progrefs in the prefent æra is great
and rapid; in general her imports of manufactured goods decreafe, and her exports of
manufactures increafe. Her trade to all
parts muft advance very much—Her fpirits
are now alive to improvements, and if they
take a right turn, the country will be highly
benefited. It is probable fhe will fend more
to every country than fhe has done, particularly to America and the Weft Indies. She
will fupply herfelf with foreign and colonial commodities to a greater extent than
fhe does now; but unlefs Britain relin-
quifhes that principle of the navigation laws
which makes her the mart for thofe articles,
Ireland will not become the entrepot of
them. However interefting, it is unneceffary to repeat the arguments on that head,
or to point out the various bad confequences
that would refult from it ; nor, in truth, is
the meafure in queftion neceffary to the
profperity of Ireland. The Weft Indies and
North America take of every thing that
Ireland produces or manufactures. The
markets of the Plantations and New States
are more likely to find a demand for her
manufactures, than the well-fupplied markets of Britain.

M m   Ireland,

Ireland, very properly, confiders the laſt year's ſyſtem of taxing manufaɗures in Great Britain, as bounties in favour of her manufaɗures ; and ſo do the oppreſſed manufaɗurers of Mancheſter, Glaſgow, Paiſley, &c. many of whom, and in very reſpeɗable ſituations, have, ſince June laſt, made offers to go and eſtabliſh themſelves and their manufaɗures in Ireland. The Miniſter ſhould learn, that although duties or taxes are drawn back on exportation, they are a very great weight on trade—and among other inſtances, by the much greater capital which is neceſſarily employed, the extenſion of the manufaɗure is prevented.* The manufaɗurer cannot ſpeculate : he will not make goods till ordered. Men of ſmall capitals cannot undertake buſineſs, and an oppreſſive advantage is given to great capitals. Ireland has not theſe diſadvantages—on the contrary, her manufaɗurers poſſeſs every facility and encouragement that were ever known in any country. There is one exception, however, as to external trade, a remain of the old mode of treating cuſtoms, chiefly, as a matter of

---

* There are manufaɗurers in Lancaſhire, who pay above 40,000 l. yearly to the Excife.

revenue.

revenue. She ftill lays five per cent. on *all* exports, and ten per cent. on *all* imports, with very few exceptions.

The general import trade of Ireland is carried on at Waterford, Dublin, Belfaft, Derry, and Limerick, through which places the kingdom is principally fupplied, and Cork, in comparifon to her confiderable ftate of commerce in other refpects, has not her proportion of the import trade. The country fhe has to fupply is not confiderable in point of population. This is no fmall difadvantage to that city ; but her port and fituation will always make her a firft-rate place for trade. It is, however, to be lamented that her trade is not more fteady and equal. The difference of demand for provifions in peace and war, does not fufficiently account for the inequality, as has appeared under the article, provifion trade. The fudden Peace undoubtedly caufed a very confiderable check, from the great ftock of provifions prepared and preparing, which were thrown back upon the dealers, factors, and importers. The great quantity of government ftores on hand were to be fold, and the garrifons and iflands were filled with provifions ; but the late languid ftate of

trade

trade at Cork is perhaps much more to be imputed to the check to credit, which, and the great demand for money, poffibly now affect her more, than the pacification. There are, however, fatisfactory reafons to believe that her exertions are again beginning to have full fcope and fuccefs.

Although the balance of trade is in favour of Ireland with moft countries, it is conftant-ly againft her with Norway, Denmark, Sweden, and the Eaft Country. It is often fo in the trade with France, the import of claret exceeding the export of beef and pork to that country; and fometimes the balance is againft her with Holland and Flanders. A feparate view will be given of the trade to each country; and on every account will be proper to begin with the trade to Great Bri-tain, with which country the commerce of Ireland is very great indeed; fo much fo, that when her trade with all other countries is compared to it, it feems a mere trifle.

T A B L E. No. III.

Exports and Imports of Ireland, to and from all Parts, from 1700, to 1783 inclusive.

Average of ten years.	Exports. £.	s.	d.	Imports. £.	s.	d.
From 1700, to 1710.	553023	16	0	513657	17	2½
Ditto from 1710, to 1720.	1126670	6	11¾	852905	7	11½
Ditto from 1720, to 1730.	1019809	3	2¼	856936	6	8
Ditto from 1730, to 1740.	1190253	3	4½	885044	8	2
Ditto from 1740, to 1750.	1485110	18	3	1123373	1	8
Ditto from 1750, to 1760.	2002354	5	10¼	1594164	7	1½
1760	2139388	1	0⅞	1647592	1	3⅛
1761	2244951	17	10	1527903	2	2⅛
1762	2438926	2	0½	1914798	6	11⅝
1763	2279926	4	5	1818433	6	4
1764	2595229	5	4½	2216274	7	10⅝
1765	2492064	18	1½	2139810	7	1½
1773	2971345	15	8¾	2417613	10	1½
1774	2833055	7	7¼	2358032	4	6¾
1775	3143038	1	0¼	2508415	9	½
1776	3160748	13	5¾	2654558	2	5½
1777	3148132	1	11¾	3123928	18	1
1778	3262801	7	9¼	2836802	12	11
1779	2727114	13	4	2195935	1	7¼
1780	3012178	13	9¼	2127579	9	7½
1781	2896035	7	1	3123051	9	7
1782	3400598	10	2½	2994265	17	8
1783	2903732	8	4½	3011771	17	3½

TRADE with ENGLAND.

Perhaps a more ftriking inftance of the unfatisfactorinefs of cuftom-houfe accounts does not occur than in their ftate of the trade between England and Ireland. It is generally fuppofed that the balance has been in favour of England from 4 or 500,000l. to 1,000,000l. yearly, and that it had been always greatly in her favour; but the contrary has been the cafe, two or three years excepted. The Irifh cuftom-houfe accounts are in this matter much nearer to the truth than the Englifh. The articles are rated below the value, but not very confiderably : the difference and the deception arife from the manner of valuing Irifh linens in the ports of England. In the latter they are averaged and valued at 8d. per yard. In Ireland they are valued from 15d. to 17d. per yard, which, confidering the proportion of fine linens fent from that country, is below the real value. This at once explains the difference of the Englifh and Irifh ftate of the balance of trade between the two countries, and it is obvious how great

the

the difference muſt be when we conſider that the linens exported from Ireland generally are more than half of the whole export from that kingdom, and that they are rated in England at leſs than one half of their value. Alſo worſted and linen yarn, butter, hides, &c. which are principal exports, are rated very conſiderably lower in the Engliſh cuſtom-houſe accounts.

Thus for example, taking the year 1777: 21,181,065 yards imported into England from Ireland, are valued in the Engliſh cuſtom-houſe accounts at 706,035l. 10s.*, and in the ſame year the Iriſh cuſtom-houſe accounts value the linen exported to England at 1,387,584l. 5s. 5d†.

Accord-

* All accounts laid before Parliament by the Inſpector General, are ſaid to be made up, viz. goods exported according to their current price at home, imported according to their current price abroad—freight, therefore, is not included in theſe valuations—The gains upon freight are diſtinct and additional both upon import and export.

† No cuſtom being paid on export of linen from Ireland, there is not a minute attention to the exact quantity entered for exportation; and it is ſaid more is entered than exported; on the other hand, to ſave
a trifling

According to the cuſtom-houſe accounts given by Sir Francis Brewer in his Eſſays on trade, the average exports of Ireland to England for ſix years, ending 1681, were,

	£.
Exports - - - -	231,554
Imports from England - -	346,800
Balance in favour of England -	115,246
Of the imports from foreign parts	
about - - - -	86,000
In 1681, Ireland exported of yarn	
and manufacture to the amount of	69,000
Of which linen yarn - -	12,000
Woollen ditto - - -	3,000

which two laſt articles were manufactured to advantage in England.

About 50,000l. of the 69,000 were in frizes, much of which went to England,

a trifling duty or murage at Cheſter of 1d. or 2d. per piece, a ſmaller quantity is entered for the fair than really goes—but the quantity entered at the Cuſtom-houſe of England is ſaid to be exact; therefore by doubling the value, that is, from 8d. to 16d. per yard, perhaps we arrive neareſt the truth, which cannot be minutely aſcertained, becauſe the Cuſtom-houſe accounts of Great Britain and Ireland, cannot be exactly compared : the Britiſh are made up to Chriſtmas, the Iriſh to Lady Day.

and

and was improved by new dreffing and nap-
ping; befides thefe, there was not above
4000l. in value, of Irifh manufacture exported.

In 1695, the manufactures of Ireland
exported were in value 30,463l. of which
woollen and linen yarn amounted to 20,075l.
which exceeds the quantity of thofe articles
exported before the preceding war, (as appears in the laft article,) above 5000l.

	£.	s.	d.
In 1696, imports from Eng-			
land - - -	233,543	18	4
Imports from foreign parts	101,419	16	8
In 1697, imports from Eng-			
land - - -	290,892	16	7
Imports from foreign parts	132,290	0	0

The exports this year to England of manufactures and woollen and linen yarn,
principally the two laft, amounted to
83,807l. and were confequently advantageous to England, as fhe improved them.

	£.	s.	d.
In 1698, imports from			
England - -	385,797	1	$5\frac{1}{2}$
Imports from foreign parts	191,066	0	0

N n   This

This year the amount of manufactures
fent to England of the fame fort as before,
rofe to 155,595l.

The table No. IV. gives the trade of Ireland with Great Britain for the laft thirty-
four years; from which it appears, that the
balance in favour of Ireland has varied from
4 to 800,000l.; and there has been this balance againft Great Britain, notwithftanding the trade with that part of it called
Scotland was confiderably againft Ireland.

The following fhews the great difference
of value between the imports into Great
Britain and Ireland of the product and manufactures of each country:

Value of imports into Ireland of the
growth and manufacture of Great Britain,
average of three years ending 25th March,
1782, 1,218,704l. 18s. 5¾d.

Value of exports of the growth and manufacture of Ireland to Great Britain, average for fame years, 2,420,425l. 6s. 7¼d.

The table No. I. has fhewn how great a
proportion of the whole trade to Great Britain

tain confifted in linens and linen and woollen yarn for 10 years ending 25th March, 1783, diftinguifhing each article and year.

The table No. V. gives the quantities and value of Afiatic goods exported from Great Britain into Ireland for three years, ending 25th March, 1783, diftinguifhing each fort.

$\mathcal{L}.$

The value of the total imports from Great Britain into Ireland in 1781 - - 2,432,417
Whereof the growth, product, or manufacture of Britain - 1,486,317

Remains of foreign - - - 946,100
Whereof African, American, and Afiatic, about - - 800,000

Remains of other countries - - 146,100

The tables No. VI. and VII. give the detail of the whole trade between England and Ireland, viz. the exports and imports for the year ending 25th March, 1783, diftinguifhing each article, its quantity and value.

N n 2

value. They are principally intended to fhew the articles which form the commerce of the two countries, and the mode of valuing them in the cuftom houfe of Ireland.

The two laft are the Irifh cuftom-houfe accounts, and feem more exact and correct than fuch accounts ufually are.

The following is the Englifh cuftom-houfe account of the trade between England and Ireland for the year 1783. It has already been remarked, how extremely defective the Englifh accounts are in the valuation of imports from Ireland, and what a falfe balance confequently is given.

An account of the value of the goods and manufactures exported from England to Ireland, from 5th January, 1783, to 5th January, 1784; alfo an account of the value of the goods imported from Ireland into England in the above period.

Exported

Exported to Ireland.
Britiſh manufactures and produce.

	£.	s.	d.
London - -	84,698	4	7
Out-ports - -	914,318	9	9
	999,016	14	4
Foreign goods from London	598,722	10	10
London ditto, Out-ports	549,624	12	4
Total	2,147,363	17	6

Imported from Ireland.
Iriſh manufactures and produce.

	£.	s.	d.
London - -	687,489	6	2
Out-ports - -	811,739	7	7
	1,499,228	13	9

No.

No. IV.

An account of the value of all goods and merchandize imported from, and exported to, Great Britain, from Ireland, for the following years, ending 25th March.

	Export.			Import.		
	£.	s.	d.	£.	s.	d.
1750	1,069,364	1	$2\frac{5}{8}$	920,340	17	$0\frac{3}{4}$
1751	1,229,718	5	5	1,025,677	3	$1\frac{1}{4}$
1752	1,228,992	11	$5\frac{3}{8}$	1,106,577	17	$10\frac{3}{4}$
1753	1,142,640	2	$11\frac{1}{8}$	978,144	3	$7\frac{7}{8}$
1754	1,206,791	16	$2\frac{5}{8}$	1,122,651	14	$2\frac{3}{4}$
1755	1,312,176	2	$6\frac{1}{4}$	1,039,911	10	$4\frac{3}{4}$
1756	1,146,703	19	11	912,560	16	$4\frac{1}{2}$
1757	1,480,174	5	0	958,194	8	$5\frac{1}{2}$
1758	1,462,695	15	$3\frac{3}{8}$	1,093,001	1	$5\frac{1}{2}$
1759	1,466,437	0	$2\frac{1}{4}$	996,001	15	$11\frac{5}{8}$
1760	1,450,757	8	$6\frac{7}{8}$	1,094,752	12	$11\frac{1}{2}$
1761	1,494,499	8	$2\frac{3}{4}$	1,096,989	9	2
1762	1,649,295	4	$5\frac{1}{4}$	1,338,325	8	$9\frac{1}{2}$
1763	1,562,400	9	11	1,284,891	2	$8\frac{7}{8}$
1764	1,682,196	2	3	1,567,683	1	$1\frac{3}{4}$
1765	1,693,197	5	7	1,439,969	4	$8\frac{1}{4}$
1769	2,266,151	17	$4\frac{3}{4}$	1,776,996	1	$3\frac{1}{4}$
1770	2,408,838	12	$4\frac{3}{4}$	1,878,599	6	11
1771	2,514,039	13	4	1,806,732	15	6
1772	2,405,507	8	$1\frac{3}{4}$	1,586,623	17	$3\frac{1}{2}$
1773	2,178,664	1	$4\frac{1}{4}$	1,679,212	5	3
1774	2,117,695	11	$8\frac{1}{4}$	1,711,174	13	$7\frac{1}{4}$
1775	2,379,858	9	$8\frac{1}{4}$	1,739,543	18	$4\frac{1}{2}$
1776	2,551,211	11	$3\frac{3}{4}$	1,875,525	12	$8\frac{1}{4}$
1777	2,552,296	18	$4\frac{3}{4}$	2,233,192	7	$9\frac{1}{2}$
1778	2,718,145	18	$1\frac{3}{4}$	2,076,460	16	$2\frac{1}{2}$
1779	2,256,650	0	5	1,644,770	17	$5\frac{3}{4}$
1880	2,384,808	16	7	1,576,635	13	$5\frac{3}{4}$
1781	2,187,406	15	$0\frac{1}{4}$	2,432,417	13	10
1782	2,700,760	18	$2\frac{3}{4}$	2,277,946	10	$8\frac{1}{2}$
1783	1,989,290	6	9	2,320,455	18	$7\frac{1}{4}$

N. B. This Table is formed from the Irish custom house accounts.

An Account of Goods and Merchandize, being th(
from thence exported to the Kingdom of Ireland,
inclufive, each Year diftinguifhed with the particu
imported into Ireland during the faid three Years.

Denominations.				Quantit
Drugs	— — —	Value.		—
Groceries	Cinnamon - —	Lbs.		7323
	Cloves — —	Lbs.		1943
	Mace — —	Lbs.		1944
	Nutmegs — —	Lbs.		7176
	Pepper — —	Lbs.		53727
	Piamento — —	Lbs.		555
	Rice — —	C. q. lb.		766 0
India Silks and Stuffs	— —	Value.		—
Callico	Stained — —	Yards.		1585
	White — —	Yards.		402
Muflin	— —	Yards.		74220
Saltpetre	— —	C. q. lb.		911 3
China — Raw Silks	— —	Lbs. oz.		68429
Tea -	Bohea — —	Lbs.		122456
	Green — —	Lbs.		51712

N. B. China Ware is omitted in this Accou
with Earthen Ware from England.

No. V.

An Account of Goods and Merchandize, being the Growth, Product, or Manufacture of Asia, imported into Great Britain, and from thence exported to the Kingdom of Ireland, for three Years, from 25th of March, 1780, inclusive, to 25th of March, 1783, inclusive, each Year distinguished with the particular Value of each Commodity in each Year; and total Value of the whole Quantity imported into Ireland during the said three Years.

Denominations.			Years ending the 25th of March.						Total Value of Three Years.
			1781.		1782.		1783.		
			Quantity.	Value.	Quantity.	Value.	Quantity.	Value.	
				£. s. d.		£. s. d.		£. s. d.	£. s. d.
Drugs		Value.	—	7677 1 9½	—	10121 7 6½	—	9121 2 4	26919 11 8
Groceries	Cinnamon	Lbs.	7323	2929 6 0	221¾	89 2 0	634	252 8 0	3270 14 0
	Cloves	Lbs.	1643	971 10 0	302	281 0 0	301	280 10 0	1533 0 0
	Mace	Lbs.	1944	1820 0 0	272½	226 17 6	788	636 13 4	3503 10 10
	Nutmegs	Lbs.	7170	3588 0 0	3539	1769 10 0	5388	2694 0 0	8051 10 0
	Pepper	Lbs.	53727	3581 16 0	43401¾	2893 9 0	62719	4181 5 4	10656 10 4
	Pimento	Lbs.	555	27 15 0	5392	269 12 0	2082	104 2 0	401 9 0
	Rice	C. q. lb.	766 0 7	609 9 1½	820 1 14	738 6 9	9 3 14	8 17 9	1436 13 7½
India Silks and Stuffs		Value.	—	3 15 0	—	—	—	—	3 15 0
Callice	Stained	Yards.	1585	396 5 0	1836	459 0 0	1203	370 15 0	1156 0 0
	White	Yards.	402	80 8 0	860	172 0 0	480	96 0 0	348 8 0
Muslin		Yards.	74220½	12370 1 8	51041	9006 16 8	37272	6522 12 0	27899 10 4
Saltpetre		C. q. lb.	911 3 0	2279 7 6	889 1 14	2248 8 9	1685 1 7	4183 5 7½	8691 1 10½
China— Raw Silks		Lbs. oz.	68429 0	68429 0 0	46094 4	46094 3 4	32656 0	32656 0 0	147779 3 4
Tea	Bohea	Lbs.	1224506	121450 12 0	887767	88776 14 0	1478080	147808 0 0	350035 6 0
	Green	Lbs.	517127	155138 2 0	433248	129974 8 0	570838	171251 8 0	420803 18 0

£. 1096050 2 0½

N. B. China Ware is omitted in this Account, being confounded with Earthen Ware from England.

No. VI.

EXPORTS from IRELAND to that Part of Great Britain called ENGLAND, for the Year ending March 25, 1783; distinguishing each Article, its Quantity and Value.

Denominations.		Quantities.	Medium of the current Market Price.	Total Value.
			£. s. d.	£. s. d.
Bacon { Hams	C. Q. No.	298 0 7	at 1 10 0 per cwt	447 1 10½
{ Flitches	No.	5518	0 15 0 each	4138 10 8
Beer	Barrels	88½	0 10 0 per barrel	44 6 8
Beef { Barrels	No.	68491 1/8	1 10 0 each	102736 15 0
{ Carcasses	No.	2	4 0 0 each	8 0 0
Bottles of Glass	Dozens	8 1/7	0 18 0 per dozen	7 10 0
Board;, Barrels	C. Q. No.	45 - -	0 10 0 per cwt.	22 10 0
Books, bound and unbound	C. Q. lb.	73 3 14	2 10 0 do.	184 13 9
Bread	Do.	464 3 -	0 12 0 do.	278 17 0
Bullocks and Cows	No.	160	5 0 0 each	800 0 0
Barrels empty	No.	500	0 5 0 do.	125 0 0
Butter	C. Q. lb.	108871 3 -	2 0 0 per cwt.	217743 10 0
Candles	Do.	71 2 -	1 16 8 do.	131 1 8
Cheese	Do.	85 - 21	1 0 0 do.	85 3 9
Coaches and Coachmakers' Work	Value	40 - -		40 0 0
Copper Ore	Tons	37½	3 10 0 per ton	132 2 6
Corn { Barley	Qrs. Bush.	14758	1 12 0 per quarter	23612 16 0
{ Beans	Do.	353	1 0 0 do.	353 0 0
{ Oats	Do.	15742	0 9 9 do.	7674 4 6
{ Pease	Do.	8	1 0 0 do.	8 0 0
{ Wheat	Do.	2954	2 4 0 do.	6498 16 0

Denominations.		Quantities.	Medium of the current Market Price.	Total Value.
Feathers	C. q. lb.	45 1	at 2 0 0 per cwt.	£. s. d. 90 10 0
Fish { Herrings	Barrels	823½	0 15 0 per barrel	617 10 0
{ Ling	C. q. No.	2 2 2	3 0 0 per cwt.	7 11 2½
{ Salmon	Tons. Trs.	53¼	12 0 0 per ton	639 0 0
Flax Seed, Irish	Hhds.	42	1 10 0 per hhd.	63 0 0
Glue	C. q. lb.	746 1 14	1 13 4 per cwt.	1243 19 2
Haberdashery Ware	Value	1 14 11		1 14 11
Hair { Goats	C. q. lb.	1 7	3 0 0 per lb.	174 0 0
{ Human	Pounds.	58	1 0 0 each	642 0 0
Hogs	No.	642	1 0 0 each	642 0 0
Hog's lard	C. q. lb.	3575	1 10 0 per cwt.	5362 10 0
Horses	No.	37	6 0 0 each	222 0 0
Horns { Ox and Cows	C. q. No.	667 18	0 16 8 per cwt.	555 18 8
{ Tips	Do.	22	0 6 8 do.	7 6 8
Hides { Tanned	No.	335	1 13 4 each	558 6 8
{ Untanned	No.	50204	1 6 8 each	66938 13 4
Iron	Tons	3 1/16	16 15 0 per ton	51 1 9
Ironmongers' Ware	Value	59 - -		59 0 0
Kelp	Tons	1228	1 10 0 do.	1842 0 0
Lead Ore	Do.	1/7	2 6 8 do.	
Linen Cloth	Yards	14222707	0 1 4 per yard	948180 15 7
Meal { Flour	C. q. lb.	6146 2 -	0 15 0 per barrel	4609 17 4
{ Oats	Barrels	9	0 0 6 per thousand	4 14 6
Ox { Bones	Thousands	72	0 6 8 per barrel	24 0 0
{ Guts	Barrels	136	0 16 8 per barrel	113 6 8
Pork	Do.	40855 5/8	1 10 0 do.	61283 14 0

Denominations.		Quantities.	Medium of the current Market Price.	Total Value.
			at £. s. d.	£. s. d.
Rabbits' Furs	Lbs.	5539	0 5 0 per lb.	1384 15 0
Rape Seed	Qrs. Bush.	3283	1 12 6 per quarter	5334 17 6
Salt	Bushels	80	0 1 3 per bushel	5 0 0
Silk Manufacture				1145 0 0
Skins { Calf	Lbs. oz.	229	0 5 0 per lb.	
Goat	Doz. No.	17880 10	1 2 6 per dozen	2011 18 9
Kid	C. q. No.	37 1 20	6 0 0 per cwt.	224 14 0
Lamb	Do.	21 2	3 2 6 do.	67 3 3
Rabbit	Do.	2216 -	2 5 0 do.	4986 16 9
	Do.	77 2	1 5 6 do.	98 16 3
Sope	C. q. lb.	133 3	1 13 4 do.	223 0 0
Tallow	Do.	30040 2	2 0 0 do.	62081 0 0
Tongues	Dozens	963	0 12 0 per dozen	577 16 0
Wooden Ware	Value	70 - -		70 0 0
Wool	Sto. lb.	2063 10	0 10 0 per stone	1031 16 3
Linen Yarn	C. q. lb.	34002 3	6 0 0 per cwt.	204016 16 0
Yarn { Cotton Worsted	Pounds	2436	0 1 0 per lb.	121 16 0
Small Parcels	Sto. lb.	66418	1 1 10 per stone	99627 0 0
	Value	5916 13 -		5916 13 0

£. 1865392 14 8

No. VII.

IMPORTS into IRELAND, from that Part of Great Britain called ENGLAND, for the Year ending 25 March, 1783; distinguishing each Article, its Quantity and Value.

Denominations.		Quantities.	Medium of the current Market Price.				Total.		
			£	s.	d.		£	s.	d.
Ale	Barrels	2669 7½	at 1	0	0	per barrel	2669	7	8
Apparel	Value	254 15 10					254	15	10
Apples	Bushels	17	0	3	4	per bushel	2	11	0
Arms	Value	1039 4 7					1039	4	7
Bacon { English / Foreign	Flitches	47	0	13	4	per flitch	31	8	4
	C. q. lb.	4 1 7	2	0	0	per cwt.	8	12	6
Bark	Barrels	88417½	0	7	0	per barrel	30946	7	6
Battery	C. q. lb.	1159 0 21	7	5	0	per cwt.	8400	12	0
Beer	Barrels	51405 5¼	1	0	0	per barrel	51505	2	1
Books { Bound / Unbound	Value	126 7 10					126	7	10
	C. q. lb.	228 3 7	10	0	0	per cwt.	2238	2	6
Bullion Silver	Ounces	19540¼	0	6	8	per oz.	6513	8	1
Berries Juniper	C. q. lb.	52 1 14	2	0	0	per cwt.	105	15	
Bottles of Glass	Dozens	38755	0	1	6	per doz.	6656		
Brass Shruff	C. q. lb.	67 1	3	0	0	per cwt.	202	15	
Bricks	Thousands	223	1	10	0	per M.	334	10	0
Brimstone	C. q. lb.	686 3 14	0	16	8	per cwt.	571	13	4
Candlewick	C. q. lb.	490 2 14	3	5	0	per cwt.	1594	10	7½
Capers	Lbs.	2	0	0	8	per lb.	0	1	4
Cards, Wool	Doz. Prs.	966 2	0	8	0	per doz.	386	9	4
Chalk	C. q. lb.	2241 0 7	1	0	0	per cwt.	2241	1	3
Cheese	C. q. lb.	3627 2 21	1	10	0	do.	5440	16	10½

Denominations.			Quantities.	Medium of the current Market Price.	Total.
				£. s. d.	£. s. d.
Chocolate	—	Lbs.	12	at 0 2 6 per lb.	1 10 0
Coaches, Chaifes, &c.	—	Value	3421 15 0		3421 15 0
Coals	—	Tons	220284 5/6	0 15 0 per ton	165213 12 6
Coffee	—	C. q. lb.	482 1 14	10 0 0 per cwt.	2823 15 0
Copper Plates and Bricks	—	C. q. lb.	1450 2 7	5 0 0 do.	7253 2 8
Cordage	—	C. q. lb.	449 3 21	1 3 4 do.	524 18 6
Cork	—	C. q. lb.	22 1 0	3 10 0 do.	77 17 6
Corn ⎰ Barley and Malt	—	Qrs.	23300 3/4	1 2 0 per quarter	25630 16 6
Peans and Peafe	—	Qrs.	503 1/4	1 5 0 do.	629 13 3
Corn ⎱ Oats	—	Qrs.	856 1/2	0 15 0 do.	642 0 8
Wheat	—	Qrs.	518 1/2	2 3 4 do.	1122 6 8
Drapery ⎰ New	—	Yards	409084	0 2 6 per yard	5135 10 0
Old	—	Yards	371702 1/2	0 14 0 do.	260191 15 6
Shag	—	Yards	1182 1/4	0 4 0 do.	236 9 0
Drugs	—	Value	9120 19 10		9120 19 10
⎡ Allum	—	C. q. lb.	2571 3	0 13 0 per cwt.	1671 12 8
Annotto	—	C. q. lb.	18 1 7	0 18 0 do.	16 19 6
Argal	—	C. q. lb.	23 0 0	1 2 0 do.	25 0 0
Braziletto	—	C. q. lb.	65 1 14	0 14 0 do.	45 15 3
Cochineal	—	Lbs.	4524	1 0 0 per lb.	4524 0 0
Dying ⎨ Copperas	—	C. q. lb.	3723 2	0 6 8 per cwt.	1241 3 4
Stuffs ⎩ Fuftick	—	C. q. lb.	797 3	0 14 0 do.	558 8 6
Galls	—	Lbs.	58 1	3 0 0 do.	174 15 0
Indigo	—	C. q. lb.	48998	0 6 8 per lb.	16332 13 4
Logwood	—	C. q. lb.	2459 1 7	2 5 0 per cwt.	5533 9 0 3/4
Madder	—	C. q. lb.	200 0 21	1 5 0 do.	250 4 6 1/4
⎣ Orchall	—	C. q. lb.	318 0 0	1 2 0 do.	349 16 0

O o 2

Denominations.		Quantities.	Medium of the current Market Price. £ s. d.		Total. £. s. d.
Dying Stuffs.	Redwood — C. q. lb.	3890 0 14	at 2 0 0 per cwt.		7780 5 0
	Sanders — C. q. lb.	35 0 7	6 0 0 do.		210 0 0
	Shumack — C. q. lb.	648 3 0	0 13 4 do.		432 10 0
	Smalts — Lbs.	2508	0 0 1 per lb.		125 8 1
	Stone Blue — Lbs.	112	0 0 7 do.		3 5 4
	Weeds or Straw Weed — C. q. lb.	61 1 21	0 7 0 per cwt.		21 9 2¼
	Woad — C. q. lb.	102	0 15 0 do.		76 10 0
	Small Parcels — Value	1160 1 6			1160 1 6
Earthen Ware — Value		19433 13 5½			19433 13 5½
Elephant's Teeth — No.		389	0 5 0 each		97 5 0
Fans — No.		735	0 1 8 each		61 5 0
Fish	Anchovies — Barrels	2	0 16 0 per barrel		1 12 0
	Herrings — Barrels	1030	1 0 0 do.		1030 0 0
	Oysters — Gallons	5	0 2 0 per gallon		0 10 0
	Sturgeon — Kegs	13	0 12 0 per keg		7 16 0
Flax	Dried — C. q. lb.	7 3 21	2 0 0 per cwt.		15 17 6
	Undressed — C. q. lb	206 1 21	1 15 0 do.		3511 5 4¼
Flints — Thousands		122 4/10	0 2 6 per M.		15 6 0
Furs — Value		336 4 10			336 4 10
Fustians — Ends		5184 2¼	0 15 0 per end		5888 13 1½
Glass	Cases — No.	2183½	1 10 0 each		3274 15 0
	Drinking — No.	29032	0 0 2 each		241 18 0
	Vials — No.	4160	0 6 8 per hundred		13 17 4
	Glass Ware — Value	3883 0 3½			3883 0 3½
Gloves — Pairs		743	0 3 0 per pair		111 9 0
Grindstones — Chalders		47 7/12	0 16 9 per chalder		39 3 4

Denominations		Quantities	Medium of the current Market Price £ s. d.	Total £ s. d.
Groceries	Almonds — C. q. lb.	35 1 7	at 2 15 0 per cwt.	97 2 2¼
	Aniseeds — C. q. lb	15 0 14	1 6 8 do.	20 3 4
	Cinnamon — Lbs.	631	0 8 0 per lb.	252 8 0
	Cloves — Lbs.	561	0 10 0 do.	280 10 0
	Cocoa Nuts — Lbs.	1127	0 1 0 do.	56 7 0
	Currants — C. q. lb.	691 1 7	2 5 0 per cwt.	1555 9 0¼
	Figs — C. q. lb.	90 0 0	0 12 6 do.	56 5 0
	Ginger — C. q. lb.	190 1 21	1 10 0 do.	285 13 1½
	Hulled Barley — C. q. lb.	4 0 0	1 2 0 do.	4 8 0
	Liquorice — C. q. lb.	197 0 21	1 2 0 do.	216 18 1½
	Mace — Lbs.	788	0 16 8 per lb.	656 13 4
	Nutmegs — Lbs.	5388	0 10 0 do.	2694 0 0
	Pepper — Lbs.	62719	0 1 4 do.	4181 5 0
	Piminto — Lbs.	2082	0 1 0 do.	104 2 0
	Prunes — C. q. lb.	632 0 0	0 6 8 per cwt.	210 13 4
	Raisins — C. q. lb.	121 1 0	1 4 0 do.	145 6 0
	Rice — C. q. lb.	9 3 14	0 18 0 do.	8 17 0
	Saffron — Lbs.	80	1 10 0 per lb.	120 0 0
	Succards — Lbs.	235	0 3 0 do.	35 5 0
	Succus Liquoritiæ — Lbs.	6	0 8 0 do.	2 8 0
	Sugar { Candy — C. q. lb.	4 0 0	4 0 0 per cwt.	16 0 0
	Sugar { Loaf — C. q. lb.	9352 3 7	6 0 0 do.	56116 17 6
	Sugar { Muscovade — C. q. lb.	89124 2 14	2 5 0 do.	200530 8 1½
	Small Parcels — Value	2639 16 0		2639 16 0
Gunpowder — C. q. lb.		396 1 0	3 0 0 do.	1287 16 3
Haber- { Gold and Silver Twist. — Ounces		116	0 4 6 per ounce	26 2 0
dashery { Inkle wrought — Lbs.		13	0 5 2 per lb.	3 7 2

Denominations		Quantities	Medium of the current Market Price.	Total.
			£. s. d.	£. s. d.
Haberdashery — Laces	Gro. doz.	1017 3 0	at 0 3 6 per grofs	178 0 4½
Needles	Doz. M.	340 5 0	3 2 6 per dozen	1102 17 7½
Pins	Doz. M	332 5	0 18 0 do.	298 16 0
Thimbles	No.	178264	2 0 0 per thoufand	356 8 10
Thread { Gold and Silver	Lbs Oz.	1594 4	2 0 6 per lb.	3188 10 0
Outtnall	Lbs.	1730¼	0 5 6 do.	475 15 0
Sifters	Lbs.	74¼	0 15 0 do.	55 10 0
Whited brown	Lbs.	38	0 2 8 do.	5 1 4
Small Parcels	Value	10031 15 5½		10031 15 5½
Hair { Camel's	Lbs.	342	0 8 0 do.	136 16 0
Goat's	Lbs.	4119	0 2 6 do.	514 17 6
Hats	No.	3913	0 15 0 each	2934 15 0
Hemp, undreffed	C. q. lb.	2193 0 0	0 15 6 per cwt.	1699 11 0
Hemp Seed	Hhds.	119½	2 10 0 per hogfhead	298 15 0
Hops	C. q. lb.	11353 2 7	5 0 0 per cwt.	56767 16 3
Horfes	No.	15	10 0 0 each	150 0 0
Hardware { Iron	Value	21758 5 6½		21758 5 6½
Knives	C. q. lb.	61943 2 0	0 16 0 per cwt.	49554 16 0
Mennits	No.	579557	0 0 3 each	7244 9 9
Ironmongers' Ware { Pots	No.	8589	0 0 2 each	803 18 0
Razors	No.	748	0 5 0 do.	187 0 0
Sciffars	No.	14865	0 0 6 do.	371 12 6
Scythes	Gro. doz.	757 9	1 5 0 per grofs	947 3 9
Small Parcels	Value	4089	1 1 0 per dozen	4089 0 0
	Value	23636 16 11½		23636 16 11½
Iron Ore	Tons	323¼	0 15 0 per ton	242 5 0
Ivory, wrought	Lbs.	635¼	0 12 0 per lb.	381 3 0

Denominations.	Quantities.		Medium of the current Market Price. £. s. d.		Total. £. s. d.
Lace { Gold and Silver —	68 3	Lbs. Oz.	at 4 0 0	per lb.	272 15 0
Lace { Thread Bone —	2333	Yards	0 1 0	per yard	116 13 0
Lamp Black —	3741½	Lbs.	0 1 2	per lb.	218 5 1
Latten —	8 0 7	C. q. lb.	0 6 0	per cwt.	48 7 6
Lead { Pig	6452 1 21	C. q. lb.	0 10 6	do.	3387 10 7
Lead { Red	770 3 21	C. q lb.	4 5 6	do.	3276 9 8½
Lead { Sheet	1407 0 14	C. q. lb.	0 13 4	do.	961 3 7½
Lead { Shot	744 2 7	C. q. lb.	0 15 0	do.	458 8 5½
Lead { White	1735 3 7	C. q.lb.	1 6 8	do.	2114 8 4
Lead Ore	10 0 0		4 0 0	per ton	40 0 0
Lime, Lemon and Orange Juice	882	Gallons	0 2 0	per gallon	88 4 0
Linen { British	26189	Yards	0 3 0	per yard	3928 17 0
Linen { Buckram	335	Yards	0 4 0	do.	67 0 0
Linen { Callico, stained	1203	Yards	0 5 0	do.	300 15 0
Linen { White Callico	480	Yards	0 6 8	do.	96 0 0
Linen { Cambrick	34½	Yards	1 2 0	do.	11 10 0
Linen { Canvas	17985 1¼	Yards	0 4 0	do.	10491 6 5½
Linen { Coloured	685 3½	Yards	0 5 0	do.	1371 2 0
Linen { Damask - { Napkins	1287	Yards	0 6 0	do.	321 15 0
Linen { Damask - { Tabling	1085½	Yards	0 3 0	do.	325 13 0
Linen { Diaper { Napkins	20	Yards	0 3 4	do.	3 0 0
Linen { Diaper { Tabling	30	Yards	0 2 0	do.	5 0 0
Linen { Keating	39145	Yards	0 3 0	do.	3914 8 0
Linen { Lawns	1002¾	Yards	0 3 4	do.	150 7 6
Linen { Muslin	37192	Yards	0 3 6	do.	6608 12 0
Linseed	680 1¼	Hhds.	3 0 0	per hhd.	2040 12 0
Linen, Cotton, and Silk, Brit. Manuf.	118921 3 10	Value			118921 3 10

Denominations.			Quantities.	Medium of the current Market Price.	Total.
				£. s. d.	£. s. d.
Malt	—	No.	3233	at 0 1 4 each	215 10 8
Meal - { Flour		C. q. lb.	2903	0 12 0 per cwt.	1751 16 0
Meal - { Wheat		Barrels	52	1 6 8 per barrel	69 6 8
Millinery Ware	—	Value	6931 11 6½		6931 11 6½
Mill Stones	—	No.	60	1 5 0 each	75 0 0
Oakum	—	C. q. lb.	1024 3 14	0 12 6 per cwt.	640 10 0
Oranges and Lemons		C. q. No.	421 1 14	0 2 6 do.	52 13 11¼
Oil - { Linseed		Gallons	153½	0 2 0 per gallon	15 7 5¼
Oil - { Sevil		Gallons	4563	0 3 4 do.	760 10 0
Oil - { Sweet		Gallons	1324 1/10	0 5 0 do.	331 6 0
Oil - { Train		Gallons	16147¼	0 0 6 do.	403 13 6
Printing Stuffs	—	Value	2449 13 8		2449 13 8
{ Blue		Reams	64½	0 4 0 per ream	12 18 0
{ Brown		Bundles	309½	0 3 0 per bundle	46 7 8
{ Cap		Reams	947	0 4 4 per ream	205 3 8
Paper { Painted		Reams	35½	0 8 0 do.	11 16 8
{ Printing		Reams	1694	0 2 4 do.	197 12 8
{ Pressing		Leaves	65669	0 8 0 per hund. lea.	26267 12 0
{ Writing		Reams	2823	0 6 8 per ream	941 0 0
Pasteboard	—	No.	11750	0 8 0 per hundred	4700 0 0
Pewter	—	C. q. lb.	78 0 14	4 5 0 per cwt.	332 13 6
Pictures	—	Value	694 13 6		694 13 6
Pitch	—	Barrels	1113	0 10 0 per barrel	556 10 0
Plates of Tin		Barrels	1171 7/20	2 2 0 do.	2459 16 8
Pot Ashes	—	C. q. lb.	14836 3 7	1 5 0 per cwt.	18547 15 3
Quilts	—	No.	35	2 0 0 each	70 0 0
Ribband Silk		Lbs. oz.	1853 12	2 0 0 per lb.	3707 10 0

Denominations.		Quantities.	Medium of the current Market Price. £. s. d.	Total. £. s. d.
Rezin	C. q. lb.	166 2 14	at 0 10 0 per cwt.	83 6 3
Sadler's Ware	Value.	314 12 2		314 12 2
Salt { Foreign	Bushels	1358	0 1 6 per bushel	101 17 0
Salt { Rock	Tons	17488 7/10	0 10 6 per ton	9181 7 7
Salt { White	Bushels	629160 1/10	0 1 4 per bushel	41944 0 8
Saltpetre	C. q. lb.	3330 2 14	2 10 0 per cwt.	8326 11 3
Seeds { Clover	C. q. lb.	3264 3 21	0 18 0 do.	2938 8 10½
Seeds { Garden	Lbs.	28605	0 2 4 per lb.	3337 5 0
Silk Manufactured	Lbs. oz.	16738 2	3 0 0 do.	50214 5 6
Silk Raw	Lbs. oz.	32656 0	1 0 0 do.	32656 0 0
Silk Thrown { Dyed	Lbs. oz.	283 14	1 15 0 do.	504 2 2¼
Silk Thrown { Undyed	Lbs. oz.	50581 4	1 5 0 do.	63232 15 0
Slates	Thousands	2935 1/2	0 6 8 per thousand	745 3 4
Skins { Buck	No.	4477	0 2 6 each	559 12 6
Skins { Loft	No.	89	0 10 0 each	44 10 0
Skins { Sheep	C. q. lb.	194 1 25	2 2 0 per cwt.	407 19 10½
Skins { Turkey	No.	39	0 6 8 each	13 0 6
Snuff	Lbs.	479	0 2 6 per lb.	59 17 8¼
Sope	C. q. lb.	5 0 21	1 5 0 per cwt.	6 9 0
Sope Ashes	C. q. lb.	12 0 0	0 16 8 do.	10 0 0
Spirits { Brandy	Gallons	14191 7/10	0 2 0 per gallon	141 19 5½
Spirits { Geneva	Gallons	100530 7/10	0 2 0 do.	7540 1 1¼
Spirits { Rum	Gallons	357 1 5	0 2 6 do.	357 1 5
Stationary Ware	Value	406 1 21		507 16 11¼
Steel	C. q. lb.	23396	1 5 0 per cwt.	3119 9 4
Stockings { Cotton	Pairs	1036	0 2 8 per pair	777 0 0
Stockings { Silk	Pairs		0 15 0 do.	

P p

Denomination			Quantities	Medium of the current Market Price. £ s. d.	Total. £ s. d.
Stockings {	Silk and Cotton	Pairs	192	at 0 7 6 per pair	72 0 0
	Silk and Worsted	Pairs	580	0 7 0 do.	203 0 0
	Thread	Pairs	38377	0 2 6 do.	4797 2 6
	Woollen	Pairs	1207	0 3 0 do.	181 1 0
	Worsted	Pairs	8878	0 5 0 do.	2219 10 0
Sword Blades		Pairs	1181	0 2 0 each	118 2 0
Sword cutlers' Ware		Value	466 19 4		466 19 4
Cyder		T. H. G.	281 1 26¼	5 0 0 per ton	1406 16 0½
Tar		Barrels	983½	0 12 0 per barrel	590 2 0
Tea {	Bohea	Lbs.	147808 0	0 2 0 per lb.	147808 0 0
	Green	Lbs.	570838	0 6 0 do.	171251 8 0
Tobacco		Lbs.	1262541	0 0 6 do	31566 0 6
Tow		C. q. lb.	320 0 0	1 5 0 per cwt	400 0 0
Toys		Value	7973 7 11		7973 7 11
Twine		C. q. lb.	21 2 14	3 0 0 do.	64 17 6
Tiles		No.	54678	1 10 0 per thousand	82017 0 0
Tin		C. q. lb.	258 1 21	3 10 0 per cwt.	906 1 3
Velvet		l.b. oz.	8 0 0	3 0 0 per lb.	24 0 0
Vinegar		T. H. G.	10 3 15¾	7 15 0 per ton	83 11 10½
Upholstery Ware		Value	6314 10 3		6314 10 3
Walnuts and others		Barrels	382½	0 10 6 per barrel	200 16 3
Wax, Bee's		Lbs.	6974½	0 1 0 per lb.	348 14 6
Whalebone		C. q. lb.	5 0 21	13 0 0 per.cwt.	67 8 9
Wine {	French	T. H. G.	129 1 0	25 0 0 per ton	3231 5 0
	Port	T. H. G.	12 2 31½	24 0 0 do.	303 0 0
	Rhenish	T. H. G.	0 0 10½	24 0 0 do.	1 0 0
	Spanish	T. H. G.	1 1 21	30 0 0 do.	40 0 0

Denominations.			Quantities.	Medium of the current Market Price.	Total.
				£. s. d.	£. s. d.
Wood	Barrel Staves	C. q. No.	879 2 20	0 5 0 per hundred	219 18 6
	Canes	No.	26250	5 0 0 per thousand	131 5 0
	Casks, empty	No.	2231	0 2 6 each	278 17 6
	Clapboards	C. q. No.	0 2 0	6 5 0 per cwt.	3 2 10
	Hoops	M.	3591	2 0 0 per thousand	61 1 10
	Oars	C. q. No. Value	0 0 6	4 5 0 per hundred	0 5 3
	Planks	Value	1063 7 1		1063 7 1
	Timber	Tons, Feet	539 5	2 15 0 per ton	1482 10 6
	Wooden Ware	Value	1551 4		1551 4 0
Wire	Brass	C. q. lb.	0 3 21	6 0 0 per cwt.	5 12 6
	Iron	C. q. lb.	28 0 21	2 5 0 do.	63 7 11¼
	Latten	C. q. lb.	1317 1 21	4 0 0 do.	5269 15 0
	Steel	C. q. lb.	2 0 10	7 5 0 do.	15 2 10½
Wool	Beaver	Lbs.	1977	0 18 0 per lb.	1779 6 0
	Cotton	C. q. lb.	2611 2 7	4 0 0 per cwt.	10116 13 0
	Estridge	C. q. lb.	7 1 0	4 10 0 do.	32 12 6
	Spanish	C. q. lb.	256 0 14	4 10 0 do.	1152 11 3
Yarn	Cotton	Lbs.	4600½	0 1 6 per lb.	345 8 9
	Linen	Lbs.	1894	0 2 0 do.	189 8 6
	Mohair	Lbs.	257062½	0 3 0 do.	3855 19 6
	Worsted	Lbs.	7038¾	0 4 0 do.	140 15 6
Small Parcels		Value	13066 13 6		13066 13 6

2148785 4 7

Pp 2

TRADE

TRADE with SCOTLAND.

The tables VIII. and IX. give the detail of the whole trade between Ireland and Scotland, for the year ending 25th March, 1783, diftinguifhing each article, its quantity and value.

On an average of ten years, ending 5th January, 1778, the imports into Ireland from Scotland were, in value,

	£.
	307,115
Imports into Scotland from Ireland	148,235
Balance in favour of Scotland -	158,880

But the imports from Scotland, for the year ending 25th March, 1783, were,

	£.
	171,670
Exports to Scotland, - -	123,897
Balance in favour of Scotland,	47,773

This

This alteration arifes from the lofs Scotland has fuffered in the tobacco trade. She ufed to fend to Ireland, yearly, 3500 hogfheads, before the war, and about 1000 during the war. In the year ending 25th March, 1783, Ireland imported from Scotland 1,152,496 lb.; the quantity is now reduced to a few hundred hogfheads.

The quantity of fugars which Ireland has taken in 1784, from Scotland, is much the fame as formerly, and other Weft-India articles nearly fo.

The balance is likely to be much againft Scotland for the year 1784, in confequence of the great number of live cattle fent thither this year from Ireland, and alfo a very large quantity of corn; the great demand for cattle is probably only temporary, and arofe from the very fevere winter with which Scotland has been afflicted, and through which many cattle were ftarved. Of late years the import of corn from Ireland had greatly decreafed. Corn had been imported from the Eaft Countries, or north of Europe, and had, fince the making the canals, been conveyed by them acrofs the narrow part of the ifland to the weft of Scotland.

Notwith-

Notwithftanding Scotland is fo great a linen country, it appears that the value of the linens fhe takes from Ireland is above half of all her imports from that country. On the other hand, Ireland takes not much lefs of other forts of linens from Scotland, kenting alone amounting to 40,235l. and lawns 11,175l. in the year 1783. This fhould remove jealoufy : it fhews that different fabrics of the fame manufacture may flourifh in neighbouring countries to the advantage of both. The annexed tables of imports and exports will fuggeft many obfervations to the intelligent. Between 50 and 60 years ago, the annual exports from Ireland to Scotland were about 11,900l. above half of which was oatmeal. The imports from Scotland were 31,700 l., of which coals were above one third, tobacco 7,800 l., linen and kenting 3,500 l.

No.

No. VIII.

Exports from Ireland to Scotland for the Year ended the 25th of March, 1783.

Denominations.		Quantities.	Medium of the current Market Price.		Total Value.	
			£. s. d.		£. s. d.	
Hams	C. q. No.	327 2 14	at 1 10 0	per cwt.	491 8 9	
Beef	Barrels, No.	9617½	1 10 0	each	14425 15 0	
Ditto	Carcases, No.	3	4 0 0	each	12 0 0	
Books	C. q. lb.	18 2 0	2 10 0	per cwt.	46 5 0	
Bread	C. q. lb.	37 0 0	0 12 0	per cwt.	22 4 0	
Bullocks and Cows	No.	233	5 0 0	each	1165 0 0	
Barrels, empty	No.	41	0 5 0	each	10 5 0	
Butter	C. q. lb.	5157 3 14	2 0 0	per cwt.	10315 15 0	
Candles	C. q. lb.	1 1 0	1 16 8	per cwt.	2 5 10	
Cheese	C. q. lb.	5 0 0	1 0 0	per cwt.	5 0 0	
Barley	Qrs. Bush.	630	1 12 0	per quarter	1008 0 0	
Malt	Qrs. Bush.	30	1 3 0	per quarter	34 10 0	
Oats	Qrs. Bush.	5747	0 9 9	per quarter	2801 13 0	
Feathers	C. q. lb.	5 3 14	2 0 0	per cwt.	11 15 0	
Herrings	Barrels.	142	0 15 0	per barrel	106 10 0	
Glue	C. q. lb.	20 0 0	1 13 4	per cwt.	33 6 8	
Glass Ware	Value	11 0 0			11 0 0	

Denominations.		Quantities.	Medium of the current Market Price.				Total Value.		
			£	s.	d.		£	s.	d.
Hogs' Lard	C. q. lb.	62 0 14	1	10	0	per cwt.	93	3	9
Horses	No.	376	6	0	0	each	2256	0	0
Horns, Ox and Cows	C. q. No.	211 0 0	0	16	8	per hundred	175	16	8
Hides, tanned	No.	47	1	13	4	each	78	6	8
Ditto, untanned	No.	4585	1	6	8	each	6113	6	4
Linen Cloth	Yards	990261½	0	1	4	per yard	66017	8	0
Meal, { Flour	C. q. lb.	720 0 0	0	15	0	per cwt.	540	0	0
{ Oats	Barrels	4768	0	10	6	per barrel	2503	4	6
Ox Guts	Barrels	4	0	16	8	per barrel	4	6	8
Pork	Barrels	3553 11/12	1	10	0	per barrel	1777	17	0
Salt	Bushels	60	0	1	3	per bushel	3	15	0
Skins, Calves	Doz. No.	3992 6	1	2	6	per dozen	499	11	3
Sope	C. q. lb.	79 0 0	1	13	4	per cwt.	131	13	4
Starch	C. q. lb.	4 0 0	1	5	8	per cwt.	5	3	8
Tallow	C. q. lb.	626 2 21	2	0	0	per cwt.	1253	7	6
Tongues	Doz.	348¼	0	12	0	per dozen	208	19	0
Yarn, Linen	C. q. lb.	1798 3 10	6	0	0	per cwt.	10793	0	9
Yarn, Worsted	Sto. lb.	259 0	1	1	0	per cwt.	129	10	0
Small Parcels	Value	810 6 3	1	1	0	per stone	810	6	3

£. 123897 12 1

No. IX.

Imports from Scotland into Ireland for the Year ended the 25th of March, 1783.

Denominations.		Quantities.	Medium of the current Market Price.		Total Value.
			£. s. d.		£. s. d.
Ale —	Barrels	127 1/7	at 1 0 0	per barrel	127 6 8
Apparel —	Value	206 5 1			206 5 1
Bark —	Barrels	1003	0 7 0	per barrel	351 1 0
Beer —	Barrels	190 3/4	1 0 0	per barrel	190 5 0
Books { Bound —	Value	65 0 0			65 0 0
Books { Unbound —	C. q. lb.	61 1 0	10 0 0	per cwt.	612 5 0
Bullion, Silver —	Ounces	1	0 6 8	per oz. -	0 6 8
Bottles of Glass —	Doz.	3483 1/2	0 1 6	per doz.	261 4 6
Bricks —	Thousands	1 8/10	1 10 0	per thousand	2 12 0
Coaches, Chaises —	Value	509 0 0			509 0 0
Coals —	Tons	21047 5/9	0 15 0	per ton	15785 5 0
Barley and Malt —	Quarters	3	1 2 0	per quarter	3 6 0
Beans and Pease —	Quarters	1 1/2	1 5 0	ditto	1 17 6
Wheat —	Quarters	240	2 3 4	ditto	520 0 0
Drapery { New —	Yards	11331	0 2 6	per yard	1416 7 6
Drapery { Old —	Yards	169	0 14 0	ditto	115 6 0

Denominations.		Quantities.	Medium of the current Market Price.			Total Value.		
			£.	s.	d.	£.	s.	d.
Drugs —	Value	0 2 6				0	2	6
Dying Stuffs { Copperas —	C. q. lb.	1617 2 7	at 0	6	8 per cwt.	539	3	9
Fustick —	C. q. lb.	70 0 0	0	14	0 do.	49	0	0
Smalts —	Lbs.	68	0	13	4 do.	40	16	8
Small Parcels —	Value	1616 4 0				1616	4	0
Earthen Ware —	Do.	60 1 9				60	1	9
Fish { Cod —	C. q. No.	1 2 5	4	0	0 per hundred	6	4	0
Herrings —	Barrels	154½	1	0	0 per barrel	154	10	0
Ling —	C. q. No.	281 1 5	4	10	0 per hundred	1265	17	0
Salmon —	Tons, Trs.	10 1	12	0	0 per ton	122	0	0
Flax, undrest —	C. q. lb.	157 1 14	1	15	0 per cwt.	275	3	1½
Tusteans —	Ends	¾	0	15	0 per end	0	11	3
Glass Cases —	No.	21	1	10	0 each	31	10	0
Glass Ware —	Value	1 19 6				1	19	6
Gloves —	Pairs	36	0	3	0 per pair	5	8	0
Hulled Barley —	C. q. lb.	66 2 0	1	2	0 per cwt.	73	3	0
Loaf Sugar —	Do.	518 3 14	6	0	0 do.	3113	5	0
Sugar, Muscovado —	Do.	10115 3 14	2	5	0 do.	22758	15	0
Small Parcels —	Value	0 15 0				0	15	0

Denominations.		Quantities.	Medium of the current Market Price.	Total Value.
			£. s. d.	£. s. d.
Haberdashery { Thread { Outnal	Lbs.	10082¾	at 0 5 6 per lb.	2771 15 1½
Sifters	Do.	1217¼	0 15 0 do.	912 13 3
Whited Brown	Do.	450¼	0 2 8 do.	60 1 4
Small Parcels	Value	124 0 11		124 11 0
Hats	No.	18	0 15 0 each	13 10 0
Horses	No.	192	10 0 0 do.	1920 0 0
Hard Ware	Value	12 3 4		12 3 4
Ironmongers' Ware { Iron	C. q. lb.	3144 1 0	0 16 0 per cwt.	2515 8 0
Knives	No.	264	0 3 0 each	3 6 0
Mermits	No.	1208	0 2 0 do.	120 16 0
Small Parcels	Value	269 17 11		269 17 11
Ivory, Wrought	Lbs.	8¼	0 12 0 per lb.	4 19 0
Lead, White	C. q. lb.	5	1 6 8 per cwt.	6 13 4
Linen { British	Yards	5902¼	0 3 0 per yard	938 8 2
Cambricks	Do.	407½	0 6 8 do.	135 16 8
Canvas	Do.	7638	0 1 2 do.	440 11 0
Coloured	Do.	4925	0 4 0 do.	985 0 0
Kenting	Do.	402356½	0 2 0 do.	40235 12 0
Lawns	Do.	74507	0 3 0 do.	11175 11 0
Muslin	Do.	80	0 3 6 do.	14 0 0

2

Denominations.		Quantities.	Medium of the current Market Price.	Total Value.
			£. s. d.	*£. s. d.*
Linfeed	Hhds.	100½	at 3 0 0 per hundred	301 10 0
Linen, Cotton and Silk, British Manufactures	Value	5388 14 6		5388 14 6
Mats	No.	16	0 1 4 each	1 1 4
Meal Flour	C. q. lb.	1447 0 14	0 12 0 per cwt.	868 4 0
Millinery Ware	Value	1714 4 2		1714 4 2
Oil { Linfeed	Gallons	20	0 2 0 per gallon	2 0 0
Sweet	Do.	52	0 5 0 do.	13 0 0
Train	Do.	4666 7/10	0 0 6 do.	116 14 8
Painting Stuffs	Value	10 6 8		10 6 8
Paper { Blue	Reams	3	0 4 0 per ream	0 12 0
Printing	Do.	1010	0 2 4 do.	1017 16 0
Pitch	Barrels	10	0 10 0 per barrel	5 0 8
Plates of Tin	Do.	1/5	2 2 0 do.	0 8 4
Pot Ashes	C. q. lb.	18 2 0	1 5 0 per cwt.	23 2 6
Sadlers' Ware	Value	75 0 0		75 0 0
Salt { Foreign	Bushels	37 13	0 1 6 per bushel	278 9 6
Rock	Tons	28½	0 10 6 per ton	14 19 3
White	Bushels	3006	0 1 4 per bushel	200 8 0

Denominations.			Quantities.	Medium of the current Market Price.	Total Value.
				£ s. d.	£ s. d.
Seeds	{ Clover	C. q. lb.	369 2 21	at 0 18 0 per cwt.	332 4 4½
	{ Garden	Lbs.	798	0 2 4 per lb.	93 2 9
Silk, manufactured		Lbs. oz.	3006 12½	3 0 0 per lb.	9020 6 4
Slates		Thousands	83	0 6 8 per thousand	27 13 0
Skins	{ Loſh	No.	216	0 10 0 each	108 0 3
	{ Sheep	C. q. lb.	17 3 10	2 2 0 per cwt.	37 9 9
Snuff		Lbs.	7½	0 2 6 per lb.	0 18 1¼
Sope		C. q. lb.	442 2 21	1 5 0 per cwt.	553 7 9
Spirits, Rum		Gallons	29414¼	0 1 6 per gallon	2206 1 7
Starch		C. q. lb.	3 3 14	0 16 8 per cwt.	3 4 0
Stationary Ware		Value	0 8 0		0 8 3
Steel		C. q. lb.	203 3 0	1 5 0 do.	254 13 3
Stockings	{ Cotton	Pairs	348	1 2 8 per pair	46 8 0
	{ Silk	Do.	6	0 15 0 do.	4 10 0
	{ Thread	Do.	22233	0 2 6 do.	2779 0 0
	{ Woollen	Do.	99	0 3 0 do.	14 17 0
	{ Worſted	Do.	66	0 5 0 do.	16 10 0
Cyder		Tons. C. qr.	1	5 0 0 per ton	5 0 0
Tar		Barrels	478	0 12 0 per barrel	286 16 0
Tobacco		Lbs.	1152496	0 0 6 per lb.	28812 8 0

Denominations		Quantities	Medium of the current Market Price. £ s. d.		Total Value. £ s. d.
Toys	Value	0 18 6			0 18 6
Tin	C. q. lb.	56 3 14¼	3 10 0	per cwt.	199 1 3
Upholstery Ware	Value	1929 12 7½			1929 12 7½
Wine, Port	Tons. H. qr.	1 1 52½	24 0 0	per ton	35 0 0
Wood { Balk	C. q. No.	0 3 5	20 0 0	per hundred	16 0 3
Barrel Staves	Do.	70 3 10	0 5 0	per hundred	17 14 3
Canes	No.	10	0 5 0	do.	0 1 0
Casks, empty	No.	534	5 0 0	per thousand	66 15 0
Deals	C. q. No.	39 2 15	0 2 6	each	162 10 0
Hoops	Thousand	19	4 5 0	per hundred	0 0 3
Timber	Tons. Feet	127 5	2 0 0	per thousand	0 0 9½
Wooden Ware	Value	194 1 7	2 15 0	per ton	349 5 3
Wool, Cotton	C. q. lb.	94 0 21	4 0 0	per cwt.	194 1 7
Wire, Latten	Do.	0 3 0	4 0 0	do.	376 15 0
Yarn { Cotton	Lbs.	1904	0 1 6	per lb.	142 16 0
Linen	Lbs.	359	0 2 0	do.	35 18 0
Worsted	Lbs.	112	0 4 0	do.	22 8 0
Small Parcels	Value	639 7 1			639 7 1

£. 171670 14 7¾

TRADE with BRITISH COLONIES.

It is not eafy to fpeak with precifion as to the future trade of Ireland with the Britifh colonies; it is likely to be very confiderable, but we muft not perhaps judge from the efforts made at the latter end of a war, or from what has been done on the flurry of firft opening the trade of the colonies to Ireland, for the fhort time fince the peace. Every warehoufe and fhop of that country has been emptied of commodities, good, bad, and indifferent, particularly the two laft, for exportation; we cannot, however, acknowledge that there was much forefight, (at the time the commercial character of the nation was to be formed, and alfo the character of its manufactures,) in fending out every thing that was bad. Indeed that part which went to the American States will not be paid for, although the worft woollens and iron ware, &c. which have been fent, will be fold or exchanged with the poor Indians, at a profit of 100 per cent.

TRADE

TRADE with the BRITISH WEST INDIES.

It has been already remarked, that the Britifh Weft Indies have a demand for almoft every produce and manufacture of Ireland, and therefore the export to them may become very great, unlefs, indeed, the Minifter's very remarkable fyftem of facrificing the commercial, as well as the marine principle of the navigation laws, fhould take place. If that ruinous fyftem fhould continue to be averted, the dependence of the planters on the Britifh merchants and their connections, will be the means of bringing moft of the Weft-India produce to Great Britain ; but if the trade of the Weft-Indies is to be opened to the American States, the trade of Ireland with the Weft Indies muft almoft entirely ceafe.

The American States may furnifh moft of the provifions that Ireland does ; and as to manufactures, an immediate intercourfe will be opened for linen through North Ame-

America, with all the linen countries of Europe, and fo far as the produce of the Weft Indies can find a market in thofe countries, North America will procure it; North America may traffic therewith for a great part of what fhe would otherwife take from Great Britain or Ireland. In fhort, if it be injurious to allow a free intercourfe between the Weft Indies and all countries, and in all articles, of which there can be no doubt, the allowing it with any one foreign ftate is virtually allowing it with all, and Ireland will be under circumftances infinitely worfe than fhe was before the extenfion of her trade, becaufe great quantities of her provifions and linens then went there, which, in the event now alluded to, would not.

The quantity of fugars imported into Ireland at different periods, were as follow :

		Cwt.	q.	lb.	£.	s.	d.
1753	Candy	57	1	21			
	Loaf	1791	1	7	132,603	1	3
	Mufcovado	88,817	2	14			
	White	4287	3	21			

Of

Of the mufcovado, 52,010 cwt. and 499 cwt. of white, came in the above year from Spain and Portugal.

	Cwt.	q.	lb.	£.	s.	d.
Candy	53	3	7			
Loaf	1,018	1	7			
Mufco.	103,558	0	21			
White	3,366	1	7			

1763 { 148,921 19 5¼

Of the mufcovado in that year, 2638 cwt. came from Spain and Portugal.

	Cwt.	q.	lb.	£.	s.	d.
Candy	36	0	7			
Loaf -	10,664	1	0			
Mufco.	201,109	3	21			
White	531	0	21			

1773 { 312,143 0 0¼

	Cwt.	q.	lb.	£.	s.	d.
Candy	4	0	0			
Loaf -	9,871	2	21			
Mufco.	133,110	1	0			
White	0	0	0			

1783 { 358,750 3 9

Of the latter, all the candy was from England; of the loaf, 9352 cwt. 3q. 7lb. from England; 518 cwt. 3q. 14lb. from
Scot-

Scotland ; of mufcovado from the following places :

	Cwt.	quar.	lbs.
England -	89,124	2	14
Scotland - -	10,115	3	14
Antigua - -	12,809	3	21
Barbadoes - -	3,303	1	0
Jamaica -	4,577	1	7
Newfoundland - -	11	3	0
St. Kitt's - -	3,867	2	7
Tortola - -	5,280	1	21
Weft Indies in general -	4,019	2	0

Imports into Ireland from the Weft Indies,
in the fame year ending 25th March, 1783.

	Total quantities.		
Chocolate, lbs. - -	5		
Coffee, cwt. q. lb. -	214	2	7
Drugs, value - -	18	6	0
Cocoa nuts, lbs. -	70	0	0
Indigo, lbs. - -	166	0	0
Ginger, cwt. q. lbs. -	211	1	7
Pepper, lbs. - -	13	0	0
Piamento, lbs. - -	10,611	0	0
Saffron, lbs. - -	56$\frac{1}{2}$	0	0
Succards, lbs. - -	501$\frac{1}{2}$	0	0
Sugar, mufcovado, cwt.	33,858	0	0

R r 2   Small

Total quantities.

Small parcels of groceries, val.	3 14 8
Snuff, lbs. - -	9 0 0
Rum, gallons - -	297,038 0 0
Brandy, gallons -	2¼ 0 0
Tobacco, lbs. -	301,598 0 0
Bees wax, lbs. -	280 0 0
Barrel ftaves, cwt. q. No -	60 0 0
Planks, value -	33 15 6
Wooden ware, value -	84 10 0
Timber, tons, feet -	7 0 0
Cotton wool, cwt. q. lb.	1,092 1 7

B R I-

BRITISH NORTH AMERICAN COLONIES.

The export trade of Ireland to the remaining colonies of Great Britain, in North America, will probably be confiderable. In the year ending 25th March, 1783, fhe exported,

	To Newfoundland.	To Nova Scotia.	To Quebec.
Beer - - - - Barrels.	205	20	8
Beef or Bifcuit Barrels.	1668¾	309½	656⅞
Bread - - - C. qr. lbs.	63683 14	21	240
Butter - - C. qr. lbs.	2442 2	251 3	1805 1 14
Candles - - C. qr. lbs.	228 14	343 3 14	1217 3 0
Oats - - Qrs. bufhels.	107 4	0	0
New drapery - - Yards.	1120	11123	2800
Old drapery - - Yards.	94	984	0
Flannel - - - Yards.	0	1744	0
Gloves - - - - Pairs.	48	1014	0
Haberdafhery - Value.	10 7 1	614 16 6	0
Hats - - - - - No.	273	516	0
Drinking glaffes. - No.	0	2400	0
Tanned hides C. qr. lb.	24 24	N° 87	0
Wrought iron C. qr. lb.	2	5	0
Linen cloth - - Yards.	3958	123,534	10,383
Ditto, coloured Yards.	78½	6547	193
Flour - - - C. qr. lbs.	1721 2 14	0	6
Oatmeal - - C. qr. lbs.	1921 0 ¾	0	312
Pork - - - - Barrels.	6889½	518	1466½
Shoes - - - - - lbs.	991	690	784
Silk manufac. - lbs. oz.	0	136	0
Soap - - - C. qr. lbs.	161 2 14	107 2	266
Woollen ftockings } Doz. No.	79	42	0
Worfted Do. Doz. No.	96 2	20 6	180
Sugar, Loaf, C. q. lbs.	46 2 17	0	0

Befides apparel and other articles of no great amount.

Her

Her importations the fame year from
thofe colonies were of fmall value, and confifted of few articles.

	Newfoundland. Cwt. Qrs.	Nova Scotia.	Quebec.
Cod -	529 2	——	——
Salmon -	32 tons	——	——
Train oil -	43,743 gals.	——	——

	Cwt.	Cwt.	Qr.	No.
Barrel ftaves ————	120	430	1	25

£.   s.   d.

Total Irifh produce exported to the Britifh Plantations, on an average of 9
years ending 25th March, 1782,   281,125 10 9
Ditto exported to ditto in the year ending 25th March, 1783,   -   - 381,617 1 7.
Total imports from the Britifh Plantations on an average of 9 years, ending 25th March, 1782,   -   - 103,205 2 4
Ditto from ditto in the year ending
25th March, 1783,   - -   - 118,145 8 3

TRADE W I T H T H E AMERiCAN STATES.

Ireland as well as Great Britain having
exported goods and manufactures to the
American ftates in the years 1783 and 1784
beyond any poffibility of prefent, or probable difpofition of future payment, it is much
to be feared that the capitals of her merchants, and confequently her general trade,
. will

will greatly fuffer. Ireland with a characte-
riftic eagernefs, tranfmitted to the new ftates
every exportable article that her warehoufes
and fhops could furnifh; and it is much
wifhed, at leaft by the writer of thefe obfervations, that fhe could ftand the fhock of
her impending difappointments, as well as
Great Britain. It is alfo wifhed, that fhe
may be more circumfpect in future, and be
convinced that a gradual and fteady trade,
will in the end be more permanent, and beneficial than fudden efforts, which bear neither the advantage of fore-knowledge nor
the guidance of difcretion.

In return for manufactures, Ireland might
be advantageoufly paid in tobacco, indigo,
rice, flax feed, pot afh, and naval ftores.
But fhe will find rivals for tobacco, and fome
of the other articles, that will furpafs her.
North America has not commodities at prefent to fatisfy all her cuftomers.

The greater part of the above articles fhe
has taken from Great Britain, even fince
her ports were open for them from other
countries; and above two thirds of her importation of tobacco was from thence in the
year

year ending 25th March, 1783. Indeed the
war has not been ended long enough to
afcertain what alterations peace will make.
The writer of thefe obfervations has not yet
feen the cuftom-houfe accounts of Ireland to
a later period than 25th March, 1783.* To
give an account of the Irifh imports and exports to and from the American ftates previous to that time, will decide little as to
what is likely to be the trade after peace has
been fometime eftablifhed. However it is probable the greater part of American tobacco
will come to Great Britain, and that fhe will
continue to be the mart for that article as
well as for feveral of the others; for if a
minifter fhould unadvifedly or rafhly attempt to facrifice that part of the navigation
laws on which the commercial refpectability
and naval ftrength of this ifland depend, the
people muft and would undoubtedly interfere, and the deftructive meafure muft be
revoked. But what will that minifter deferve
of the two kingdoms, who offers and promifes
to the one, what cannot be conceded by the

* He has feen a part of the Cuftom-Houfe accompts
for the year ending 25th March, 1784, fince their fheets
were at the prefs.

other,

other, and induces between the two, the alternative either of a moſt ſevere diſappointment or of certain ruin ?

Ireland is not likely to import tobacco, rice or indigo to any conſiderable amount ; it is not her intereſt in particular, that this trade ſhould change its courſe: it is enough to ſay, that if a revolution ſhould take place in that trade, and thoſe articles ſhould ceaſe to go through the medium of Great Britain to the linen countries in the north of Europe, the linen manufacture of Ireland may ſuffer. Thoſe countries uſed to take above half the tobacco exported from Great Britain.

In the year 1773, the quantity of tobacco ſhe exported to the countries north of France amounted to   54,925,491 lbs. at 4d.
To France   -   31,750,123
To Ireland   -   6,189,773
To other countries   3,911,956

Total export   -   96,776,443

Of rice, above 6 parts in 7 of the export from Great Britain went to the linen countries ; of indigo, above half.

S s   The

The average import of tobacco into Ireland from all parts, for ten years, ending
25th March, 1783, was 4,378,551 lbs.

In the year ending 25th March 1783,
Ireland imported of tobacco,

		lbs.
From England	- -	1,262,641
Scotland	- -	1,152,496
Jerfey	- - -	56,186
Denmark and Norway	-	58,190
Flanders and Holland	-	80,303
Sweden	- - -	60,950
Weft Indies	- -	301,598
America (New York)	-	487,489
Total	- -	3,459,861

and fhe exported the fame year only 844lbs.
which were fhipped to Holland and Flanders.

The confumption probably did not fall
off fo much as appears in the ftatement;
fmuggling may have fupplied much of the
deficiency.

In the fame year 150 cwt. o qrs. 21 lbs.
of rice were imported; of which 140 cwt.
1 qr. 7 lbs. came from Portugal, the fmall
remainder

remainder from England. This is below the
ufual quantity imported by Ireland; but
her importations of this article have been
very irregular.

Indigo imported into Ireland the fame
year,

			lbs.
From England	-	-	48,998
Flanders	-	-	1,316
France	-	-	2,806$\frac{1}{2}$
Portugal	-	-	1,365
Carolina	-	-	120
Jamaica	-	-	166
New England	-	-	500
New York	-	-	4,908
Tortola	-	-	600
			60,779$\frac{1}{2}$

The Irifh demand for American flax feed
has diminifhed, and is likely to diminifh;
fhe has lately been principally fupplied with
that article from Flanders, and the feed
from thence or Holland was greedily bought
up this year (1784) in Ireland, for fowing,
at 4l. 15s. and 5l. the hogfhead of 7 bufhels,
while the American fold for 50s. or lefs.
The Parliament of Ireland and the Linen

Board

Board have turned their attention strongly
to promote the supply of Irish feed within
these four years, and the feed preserved
there, bears an equal price with the American. It is purposed to distribute this year
in premiums on the growth of flax to the
amount of 16,000l.; so that it is probable
in a few years little feed will be imported
into Ireland except to refresh the species;
and it is possible she may supply considerably to Great Britain for oil.

The consumption in Ireland, of American pot ash, even before the war, was trifling; she was principally supplied from the
East Country and Spain. The American
States are likely to produce less than they
did.

As to naval stores, it is not surprising
that the demand should be small, in a country so unaccountably inattentive to the whole
business of ship building.

For such an island, her quantity of ship-
ping is comparatively insignificant; and even
at present she does not seem to understand
the difference between building ships at
home or in America.

Her

Her demand for naval ftores cannot be great, and it will not be entirely from America. This year four fhips went from Archangel, three to Dublin and one to Belfaft, and imported 4823 barrels of tar, 2468 barrels of pitch, 484 pood of turpentine, 500 pood of hemp, 2630 pood * of iron.

As to the exports from Ireland to the American States, they will be in manufactures ; they will become confiderable hereafter, and at prefent they will be much more than the States can pay for, in money, bills, or commodities.

TRADE with PORTUGAL.

The butter alone which Ireland fent to Portugal in the year ending 25th March, 1783, paid for all imports from that country.

	£.	s.	d.
Total exports from Ireland to Portugal -	174,493	18	10

Of which 46,055 cwt. of butter, at 40s. per cwt. amounted to 92,111 l.

* The Ruffia pood is nearly equal to 36 lbs. avoirdupois weight.

Total

	£.	s.	d.
Total imports from Portugal into Ireland the fame year	92,000	8	7¾
Balance in favour of Ireland	82,493	10	2¼

Next to butter, her greateſt export to that country conſiſts of woollens, viz. in 1783:

New drapery, 366,743 yards, value 36,674l.
Old drapery, 2,660 yards, value 866l.
Flannel, 1,302 yards, at 10d. 54l. 5s.

Next to woollens are beef and pork.

13,079⅙ barrels of beef,
5,530½ ditto of pork,
2,086¼ cwt. of tallow and hog's lard,
 129 dozens of tongues,
 151 flitches of bacon,
1,612 cwt. of cheeſe,
1,463 lbs. of ſhoes,

Of fiſh ſhe ſent only

Cod, barrels,	20
Cod, cwt.	5
Hake, cwt.	475½
Herrings, barrels,	290½

Ling.

Ling, cwt.   10½
Salmon, tons,   6
Of beer, barrels,   106½

But fhe fent only of linens,

43,125 yds. of plain, at 16d. per yd. 2,875l.
19,892 ditto of coloured, at 19d. per yard,
1,616l. 4s. 6d.

In 1781 Portugal prohibited the importation of printed linens from Ireland, and
even ordered fuch parcels as were then in
the cuftom houfe to be fent out of the kingdom.

The Portuguefe make a good deal of
common linen for their own confumption,
and a coarfe kind of table linen, and their
demand for fine linen from other countries
is not confiderable.   The French white linens imported into Portugal in 1776 and
1777, amounted only to 20,000 pieces, and
the Cambrayas were not fo much.   But
the great importation is of narrow Britan-
nias, from Hamburgh, amounting in 1777,
to near 200,000 pieces.   Thefe are confumed in the Portuguefe colonies ; and the
manufacture of Britain and Ireland has
not

not yet rivalled them in cheapnefs. Irifh linens pay as 120, while French pay only as 100, &c. the Irifh being imported as olando contrafata *.

Her principal imports from Portugal are wine and falt. Imported from Portugal, year ending 25th March, 1783.

	£.	s.	d.
Wine, 1949 tons, 3 hogfheads, 42 gallons - -	46,907	17	6
Salt, 326,170 bufhels -	21,744	13	4
Oranges and lemons, } 34,507 hund. } -	4,313	9	8
Raifins, 791 cwt. - -	890	0	0
Oil { Seville, 19,252½ gallons .	3,208	15	0
{ Sweet, 468 ditto -	117	0	0
Pot afhes, 4132 cwt. -	5,165	0	0
Spirits, brandy, 7684 gallons	768	9	0
Cotton wool, 106 cwt. 1q.	425	10	0

* Veflels going on the fouthern whale fifhery might difpofe of a large quantity of coarfe linens on the coaft of South America. It is faid the Brazils pay 100 per cent. duty on every thing from Portugal.

Cork,

	£.	s.	d.
Cork, 1249 cwt. 1q.	4,372	7	6
Indigo, 1365 lbs.	455	0	0
Shumack, 1069 cwt.	712	13	4
Figs, 258½ cwt.	161	10	6
Almonds, 44 cwt.	121	10	0

It is probable that both the import and export trade to Portugal will increafe, and that in the great articles of beef, butter, and pork, Ireland will not be rivalled. Cheefe is an increafing article, becaufe it is of a better quality than formerly; but a large quantity of cheefe for exportation cannot be expected from a country that makes much butter. It is faid the import of that article from Holland into Portugal is not lefs than 50,000l. fterling annually. Herrings, hake, and other fifh, are articles of probable increafe of export to that country. The camblet trade, which was always admitted, and previous to the Methuen treaty, declines. Coating has turned out camblet, and the manufacturers fhould take to coating. It is faid Ireland affords fhags and fome fort of bays cheaper than England; that in all cloths of wool under 5s. and above 10s. the Englifh excel the world at

T t   the

the Portugal market; but that between 5s. and 10s. Ireland might have an advantage; yet the ground on which the latter is founded does not appear. Thefe cloths are 50 inches, or yard and half wide.

The cuftoms in Portugal confift of

A rogoe duty, which is 20 per cent. on the value.

Donative	-	-	4
Cancilado	-	-	3

27 per cent.

And there is a claufe in the laft ordinance of rates which directs the officer to attend to the current prices, and if they vary from the rates, to increafe the duty accordingly. Fees and port charges amount to about three per cent. more, making, in the whole, 30 per cent.

The efforts of the Portuguefe to difcourage the import of woollens from Great Britain and Ireland *, are not juftifiable;

* A New Book of Rates was formed in Portugal, February 1783, by which Britifh and Irifh goods are rated much higher than formerly.

the

the produce of wool in Portugal is by no means equal to the confumption. The export is prohibited, yet near 400,000lb. are fent to Holland, under the name of Spanifh wool re-exported. The average produce of their fheep is 2½lb. per fleece, and the whole produce is eftimated at 1,700,000lb. Several manufactures have been fet up in different parts of the country, and to encourage them, every difficulty is oppofed to the entry of foreign manufactures; this only encourages fmuggling, and confequently an evafion of duties. Contraband trade flourifhes very extenfively, and it requires the vigour and refolution of a Pombal to prevent it in that country. Moft of the manufactures are carried on at the expence of the crown, of courfe they can rarely fucceed. The fineft Englifh cloth fells there at 27s. per yard. The only import of effential confequence into Ireland from Portugal, is falt; all her other imports from thence fhe might have as well from Spain and France.

The conduct of the courts of London and Lifbon, on the fubject of refufing to admit Irifh woollens into Portugal as Britifh, is

T t 2   unworthy

unworthy of them, and avails little. It is
faid, that Portugal at the time of making the
Methuen treaty, objeded to Irifh woollens
being deemed Britifh: but it is advantageous to Portugal to admit Irifh as long as fhe
admits Britifh; competition would lower
the price to her. It has been underftood,
that the difficulty is on the part of Britain.
It is vain, however, becaufe it appears, that
above three fifths of the exports of new
drapery from Ireland, are to Portugal: of
old drapery, 2660 yards; to the Madeiras,
of the latter, 5174 yards.

It therefore not only is unneceffary, but
it would perhaps prove a rafh meafure, to
lay prohibitory duties on Portugal wine.

TRADE. with SPAIN.

It was intended to give the detail of the
trade of Ireland with each country, but it
would fwell the work too much, and in
many inflances it would be only matter of
curiofity, for the reafon already given; that
we cannot form a juft idea of what may be,
from what has been, the trade of Ireland.

Thia

This obfervation, however, does not apply to Spain fo much as to fome other countries; but as war with that kingdom had only ceafed a fmall part of the year ending 25th March 1783, the trade with it confequently could not be very confiderable. The exports to Spain that year were in value only 2210l. and 886 cwt. of hake amounted to 1329l. of that fum. The quantity of linen fent there was only 2500 yds., butter 93 cwt. and pork 200 barrels. But the imports from Spain were much more confiderable, amounting to 83,412l. The pot afhes imported were in value nearly that fum, viz. 64,973 cwt. 77,967l. The only other articles of any amount imported were 1046 cwt. of raifins, and 70 tons of wine, 24 tons of which were Portugal wines.

Previous to 1783, the Irifh cuftom-houfe accounts do not feparate the trade with Spain from that to Portugal; they appear under one head.

Whatever the trade with Spain may have been, it might become very confiderable and advantageous to both countries.—She cannot

not raife to advantage many of the ftaple
articles of Ireland; fhe might take nearly
the fame articles that Portugal takes, but in
much greater abundance. It is computed
that Spain fends to her colonies, linens to
the amount of 1,300,000l.: that fhe confumes to the amount of 1,000,000l. fterling:
and the Canaries, Portugal, the Brazils, Ma-
deira, Weftern Iflands, and coaft of Africa,
take to the value of 500,000l. exclufive of
freight, infurance, commiffion, and profit;
and all this taken from France, Flanders,
and Germany. The calculation was made
25 years ago, and was probably much un-
der-rated at the time.

But in 1773, the year of the greateft
tranquillity for trade, and feemingly as advantageous to be felected as any, the quantity of linens that went to Spain and Portugal from both Great Britain and Ireland
was as follows:

	Yards.
Britifh linens from London and out ports, - - -	4,900
Irifh linens from London and out ports, - - - -	29,371

Thefe were from 6d. to 18d. per yard, and
entitled to bounty.

The

Yards.

The quantity exported the fame
   year to Spain and Portugal from
   Ireland, was   -   -   30,511
The preceding year, viz. 1772 - 16,066

But in the year ending 25th March, 1780,
the quantity of linen exported to thofe countries from Ireland, was increafed to 157,396
yards, plain and coloured.

TRADE with FRANCE.

The principal import from France is wine,
and the principal export to that country
from Ireland is beef; but the year immediately fucceeding the peace is not the beft for
noticing the exports or imports, or for judging of the trade to that country.

Within ten years, and previous to the
war, the exports to France had in feveral
inftances declined. Thefe were the principal exports :

		1765	1766	1775	1776
Beef, Barrels	-	86047	67023	70968	69377
Bifcuit, Cwt.	-	243	183	131	128

Butter,

	1765	1766	1775	1776
Butter, Cwt.	26413	19765	25570	16940
Candles, Cwt.	2341	1398	285	476
Hides untanned, No.	12166	10211	4182	3660
Pork, Barrels	1142	1087	2544	1235
Tallow, Cwt.	2277	582	3394	3197

And the following are the principal imports into Ireland from France, the others are of no great value.

Imports	1765	1766	1775	1776
Capers, lbs.	10896	4605	3358	2584
Cork, Cwt.	1260	1501	1348	1408
Gloves, Pairs	5747	5030	12726	4176
Cambrick, Yards	64852	45922	---	---
Printing Paper Reams	25694	16557	8684	10987
Writing Paper Reams	1199	1777	128	40
Salt, Bushels	9156	3529	1930	3886
Brandy, Gallon	739864	637028	335449	386194
Wine, Tons	4941	4502	2999	2689
Oil, Gallons	795	3716	1239	293

The imports from France declined still more than the exports to that country; in general we may suppose one affected the other.

THE

The TRADE with HOLLAND
and FLANDERS

Is not feparated in the Irifh cuftom-houfe
accounts. The principal exports to thofe
countries had decreafed previous to the war:
and had been irregular.

		1765	1766	1775	1776
Beef, Barrels	-	10362	7100	6257	8830
Bifcuit, cwt.	-	207	117	32	83
Butter, cwt.	-	52251	28955	10375	15330
Candles, cwt.	-	765	526	668	578
Hides, No.	-	12040	14142	2062	1381
Hogs' Lard, cwt.		1681	360	287	665
Linen, yards	-	6432	1506	4776	3180
Pork, barrels	-	1121	1431	213	726
Tallow, cwt.	-	10513	1333	2032	816

The imports into Ireland from Holland
and Flanders are very numerous, including
a confiderable quantity of groceries, drugs,
and dying ftuffs, and the following principal
articles.

		1765	1766	1775	1776
Barley and Malt, quarters,		280	20	0	2
Wheat, ditto,	-	120	1768	115	4

Undreffed

	1765	1766	1775	1776
Undreſſed Flax, cwt.	3691	1939	182	617
Thread Outnal, lb.	6270	5523	2873	8552
Thread, Sifters, lb.	2137	1948	2573	1581
Iron, cwt. -	5824	1776	2691	1355
Cambrick, yards,	1033	45	0	0
Hamb. Linen, ells,	1605	7	19	6
Linſeed, hogſh.	6587	1777	1043	5256
Ditto Oil, gallons,	31324	16950	42947	42822
Printing Paper, } Reams, }	5962	2253	1351	1371
Writing do. do.	7783	5806	5087	4803
Garden feeds, lbs.	6833	7452	10375	8047
Snuff, lbs.	5435	9388	4005	2397
Geneva, galls.	152816	83908	119804	153430
Iron wire, cwt.	1520	913	1240	1073
Steel, cwt.	1189	1118	1295	1123
Starch, cwt.	87	91	271	442

No judgment can be formed from the exports or imports, to and from theſe countries, during war. In the year ending 25th March, 1783, we find the exports to them increaſed; Beef, barrels, 21,876; Butter, 17,911 cwt.; New Drapery, 28,633 yards; Old Drapery, 2,940 yards; Flannel, 3248 yards; Frize, 700 yards; Hides, 2,972, No.; Linen cloth, 44,953 yards; Ditto, coloured, 8,489 yards; Pork, 4,495 barrels; Woollen yarn, 440 ſtones.

As to the imports the ſame year, many had decreaſed, a few had increaſed.

The

The TRADE with the EAST COUNTRY.

This includes Denmark, Norway, Sweden, Ruſſia, the Baltic, and the country north of Holland, and the trade to theſe countries is not ſeparated in the Iriſh cuſtom-houſe accounts till 1783.

Exports from Ireland to the Eaſt Country.

	1765	1766	1775	1776
Beef, Barrels —	1700	1419	136	8830
Biſcuit, Cwt. —	248	219	69	83
Beer, Barrels —	495	394	58	2
Butter, Cwt. —	98535	64638	10877	15330
Cheeſe, Cwt. —	626	277	11	17
Malt, Qrs. - —	406	785	150	0
Hides, No. —	2699	4598	612	0
Linen, Yards —	16617	16127	8542	9013
Oatmeal, Barrels	3995	788	10	313
Pork, Ditto —	324	115	25	32
Salt, Buſhels —	2004	2332	0	0
Calves Skins, Doz.	1684	600	17	35
Soap, Cwt. —	234	119	21	13
Tallow, Cwt. —	34	278	9	0

Imports into Ireland from the Eaſt Country.

Bark,

	1765	1766	1775	1776
Bark, Barrels —	254	0	1581	1550
Cables, Cwt. —	122	93	0	0
Wheat, Qrs. —	1328	1040	26	500
Herrings, Barrels	17030	24555	23597	24339
Flax, undr. Cwt.	3048	1952	6207	2966
Gun Powd. Cwt.	409	11	22	25
Hemp, under. Cwt.	17345	8660	11415	9146
Iron, Cwt.	71888	92324	135343	109206
Linfeed Oil, Gals.	252	239	46	0
Train Oil, Gals.	9163	11764	18402	10206
Pot Afhes, Cwt.	20864	20936	19962	23991
Tar, Barrels —	2404	1580	1374	1013
Barrels Stav. Hhds.	1060	979	220	1471
Deals, Hds. —	10686	9892	11441	9035
Mafts, No. —	68	119	17	6
Plank, value —	1395	724	377	243
Timber, No. —	9770	10347	9029	7912

In general it appears that as the imports
from France, Flanders, Holland, and the
Eaft Country decreafed, the exports to thofe
countries alfo decreafed ; yet the general
export of thofe articles which ufed to go
to thofe countries, did not altogether very
materially decline. It is obfervable, however, that the impolitic export of hides had
greatly decreafed.

Before the fubjeſt of the trade of Ireland
with Europe is finifhed, it may be proper to
obferve,

obferve, that all European goods * (non enumerated) may be brought from any place
in any fhipping; and the enumerated alfo
from any place in Britifh fhips †, or of the
country. Under this conftruction of the
law, it has been the conftant practice to allow all European goods to be brought here
from Ireland in Britifh fhips, upon the fame
terms as if imported direct; except,

Firft, fuch as are prohibited to be ufed
in this kingdom, refpecting which it is obvious, if the various articles of gloves,
ftockings, laces, embroideries, filks manufactured, buttons, cambricks, fringes, wires,
velvets, mixed ftuffs, &c. &c. comprized in
our long lift of prohibitions, are to be
importable from Ireland, but interdicted to

* The 12th Charles II. chap. 18, which requires
goods to be brought directly from the *aforefaid* places
of their growth, refers only to Afia, Africa and America. The reftraint on European goods is contained
in the 8th fect. of that act, directing articles, com-
monly called enumerated, to be brought only in Britifh fhips, or in thofe of the built of the country.
Se alfo 13 and 14 Charles II. chap. 11. And 6th
George I. chap. 15.

† It fhould be always remembered that Irifh and
Plantation-built fhips are deemed Britifh.

other

other nations, the frauds to which the Britifh market would be op'en, by the introduction of foreign goods, through Ireland, would be infurmountable and infinite. The general expediency of our prohibitions, whether confidered with a view to commerce or revenue, is a diftinct confideration, and makes no part of the prefent inquiry.

Secondly, Thrown filk of Italy, Sicily, and Naples, which can only be brought directly from thofe places refpectively by fea, in fhips legally navigated.

Thirdly, Drugs (not Irifh produce) which pay treble duties if brought from thence.

Fourthly, Wine, which if brought from Ireland, is not entitled to the 12 per cent. for leakage.

Fifthly, Silk crapes or tiffanies pay an higher duty, unlefs imported directly from Italy.

Total

	£.	s.	d.
Total Irifh produce export- ed to foreign countries, on an average of nine years, ending March 25, 1782,	345,118	10	9
Ditto, exported to ditto, in the year ending March 25, 1783, —	584,222	19	3
Total imports from foreign countries, on an average of nine years, ending March 25, 1782, —	605,117	4	0
Ditto, from ditto, in the year ending March 25, 1783, — —	679,289	8	7

S H I P P I N G.

It is impoffible to get a fatisfactory account of the quantity of fhipping belonging
to Ireland. The number of fhips built there
compared with her trade, is trifling. Mr.
Dobbs, who, as already mentioned, publifhed an Effay on the trade of Ireland in
1729, mentions the tonnage employed, on
an average of feven years ending 1724, to
be 181,901. In one of thofe years it was
much higher, viz. in 1722, it amounted to
286,594 tons, belonging to the following
nations:

Englifh

Englifh - - - - - 218,299 tons.
Scotch - - - - - - 18,355
Irifh - - - - - - - 33,312
Danifh - - - - - - 11,201
Dutch - - - - - - - 2,444
French - - - - - - 2,868
Spanifh - - - - - - 115
                    ─────────
                    286,594

At prefent the Portuguefe have a confiderable fhare of the carrying trade of Ireland. Such advantages are given at St. Ubes to the fhips of that place in point of duties, that they can import falt at half price.

O B S E R V A T I O N S.

The foregoing particulars are fufficient to enable us to decide, that not only the manufactures and produce in general, but that each particular article of confequence, is in an improving and profperous, ftate and that the general trade rapidly and greatly encreafes, notwithftanding the commerce with fome European countries, had latterly decreafed. Yet it muft occur to the intelligent reader, how extremely difficult it is, to make an arrangement between the two countries,

countries, equal, reciprocal, and fatisfactory. Ireland never meant perfect equality, nor could fhe accede to fuch a propofal;
if fhe did, many advantages muft be given
up which fhe now poffeffes. However
fpecious the propofition might appear, great
objections and difficulties arife on her part.
And on the part of Britain no change in
the commercial fyftem was either neceffary
or expedient: nor can alterations of the
extent propofed take place but to the difadvantage of Great Britain and of the Britifh empire. — But if this were the proper
moment to agitate matters of fuch magnitude, furely it is incumbent on the legif-
latures of the two kingdoms to include
other queftions in their difcuffion. — If all
the referved advantages of Great Britain
are now to be given up; if the two countries can be perfuaded that there is either
juftice or policy in fuch conceffions and
changes; if no means of future favour or
negociation are to be left; there are fome
unfettled points of effential confequence,
which fhould not now be neglected; nor
fhould it be poftponed to the hour of difficulty and diftrefs to arrange and afcertain
the relative exertions and political connection of Ireland in time of war.

X x   G E N E-

R E V E N U E.

The table No. X. gives an abftract of the revenue of Ireland, with the expence of management, drawbacks, premiums, &c. for the year ending 25th March, 1784

	£.	s.	d.
The grofs amount of the hereditary revenue for that year appears to be -	659,826	4	8
Expence of management, drawbacks, &c. -	261,912	16	11
Remains neat - -	397,913	7	9
On an average of ten years, ending 25th March, 1771, the grofs amount was	638,132	6	9

But as the expence of management, drawbacks, premiums, &c. have increafed, the neat produce is lefs than it was*.

* In the non-importation year, viz. the year ending 25th March, 1780, the grofs amount of the hereditary revenue fell to 561,121l. 18s. 7d.

The

	$L.$	$s.$	$d.$

The grofs amount of the additional duties for the year ending 25th March, 1784, appears to be - - 382,352 11 11

Deducting drawbacks †, &c. 16160 0 8

Remains neat - - 366,192 11 3

The grofs amount of the additional duties, on an average of ten years, ending 25th March, 1771, - - 227,882 16 6

Neat produce of the hereditary revenue and additional duties, on an average of ten years, ending 25th March, 1771, - - 711,127 8 7

The expence, management, drawbacks, premiums, &c., on an average of ten years, ending 25th March, 1771, - - 154,887 14 9

† The expence of management of the additional duties is charged on the hereditary revenue.

X x 2   Expence

	£.	s.	d.
Expence of ditto, for the year ending 25th March, 1784, exclufive of 8,263l. 10s. 6¼d. which properly belongs to ftamp duties*, -	277,072	17	7½

* The increafe is little more than may fairly be explained.

The

The Inland Revenues of Ireland, now payable. 1783.

			Total.	Annual amount about
		s. *d.*	*l.* *s.* *d.*	£.
	Strong beer and ale, the duty of every 32 gallons			
	Hereditary	2 6		
	Additional	1 7¾	0 4 1⅛	110237
	Small beer every 32 gallons			
	Hereditary	0 6		
	Additional	0 3⅜	0 0 9⅜	
	Strong waters per gallon			
	Hereditary	0 4		
Applicable to the navigation of Lagan and levied only in Lisburn district.	Additional applicable to the loan	0 10	0 1 2	121000
	On ale the Lagan duty is per gallon —		0 0 1	
	Strong waters do.		0 0 4	1600
	Cider per gallon —		0 0 1	175
	Ale licenses throughout the kingdom, yearly		1 0 0	8500
	Spirit licences (except Dublin city, Dublin county, and all incorporated towns) not less than		3 0 0	
	Spirit licences in Dublin country, and all incorporated towns, not less than —		4 0 0	
	Spirit licences on Dublin city, not less than		5 0 0	25000
	Wine licences, common retailers —		2 0 0	
	Do. —— Tavern keepers by agreement not exceeding 10*l.* or less than 2*l.*			
	Cider licenses throughout the kingdom —		0 10 0	100
Applicable to tillage.	Carriages 4 wheeled, each person keeping one or more		1 0 0	2818
	Do. 2 wheeled, do. —		0 5 0	
	On carriages additional duty			
	4 wheeled, for the first carriage -		1 10 0	
	for every other carriage -		2 0 0	5281
	2 wheeled carriages —		0 10 0	
Appropriated to charter schools.	Pedlar's licence —			
	Foot —		1 0 0	
	One horse —		2 0 0	1200
	Two horses —		3 0 0	

			Total.			Annual amouut about
			l.	*s.*	*d.*	£.
Tillage Loan.	Cards-per pack	1ſt duty	0	0	6	2600
	Do.	2d	0	0	6	2600
	Dice the pair		0	5	0	145
	Inland wrought plate	per ounce	0	0	6	1700
	The King's Rents.					
	Quit Rents. Rents reſerved on forfeitures					
	of 1641, viz.	per acre in Ulſter	0	0	2	⎫
		Connaught	0	0	1½	⎬ 50840
		Munſter	0	0	2¾	⎪
		Leinſter	0	0	3	⎭
	Crown Rents. Rents reſerved on grants of the King's lands in inheritance, ſix eſcheated counties, diſſolved abbies (in which port corn rents may he conſidered as part)—Alſo for fairs, markets, fiſheries, ferries, &c.					14800
	Compoſition Rents. A compoſition made by Queen Elizabeth and the people of Connaught, in lieu of ceſs preſs and quarterage of ſoldiers					1000
	Forfeited Lands, ſuch part of the forfeitures of 1688, as were not diſpoſed of before 24th June, 1703					754
	Beſides forfeited lands there are ſeveral lands being part of the forfeitures of 1641, which were undiſpoſed of and not being worth the quit rent.—Afterwards in Queen Anne's time, an act paſſed to enable the chief governor and council to make leaſes of thoſe lands at ſuch rents as they could get for them.—The leaſes of thoſe ſhould be found in the council office, and auditor general's office, from which laſt office, conſtats are iſſued to the collectors to put them in charge.					
	Hearth-money. Granted for ever in Charles the IId's time, in lieu of courts of wards, each hearth		0	2	0	60000
	Stamp duties on vellum, parchment and paper					33000
	Fines and ſeizures					10000
	Caſual revenue payable by the ſheriffs into the exchequer					900

		Annual amount about
		£.
Abfentee Tax, four fhillings in the pound paid on the profits of all offices and penfions by perfons in office, and penfioners who are not refident fix months in the kingdom in each year		12000
The Pells and Poundage may alfo be confidered as a part of the revenue, being a deduction of about 3 per cent. on all payments made at the treafury, which is now applied to the public. ——		
Rents of Duncannon Fort Lands, paid into the Treafury, ———		300

By Leafe bearing date the 2d day of October 1723, the following lands in the barony of Gaultier and county of Waterford, or county of the city of Waterford were

Granted to the people of Geneva. granted to the Rev. Alexander Alcock for the Term of 69 years from the 1ft of October, 1723, at the Rent of 300*l.* and 17*l.* 18*s.* 7½*d.* the quit rent thereof.

Knockroe and Paffage	——	159
Crook	———	275
Newtown	———	266
Knocknegable	——	82
Rahins	——	94
Third part of Tatleg	——	272

Total acres 1148

By the Act of Settlement 14 and 15 Char. II. chap. 2d, fec. 202, fo much of the lands forfeited in the rebellion 1641, as fhould amount to the clear yearly value of 300*l.* were to be fet out and referved to his Majefty that the profits fhould be applied to the maintenance of Duncannon Fort.

And by patent 21ft May, 21 Char. IId, the lands above mentioned were granted to truftees for the purpofes aforefaid, and new truftees were appointed by an act 10 Wm. III. chap. 15, thefe truftees made the leafe abovementioned.

By the account of receipts and payments at the Treafury, laid before Parliament

every

	£. s. d.	£. s. d.
every feffion, it appears that three fums are brought to charge on account of thofe rents from Lady-day, 1769, to Lady-day, 1771, viz. in two years, ending Lady-day, 1771, — —	1918 8 11¾	
Another in the two years ending Lady-day, 1773, — — —	890 0 0	
Another in the two years ending Lady-day, 1779, — — —	890 0 0	
		3698 8 11
Difburfements in that period —		3505 14 9
Balance in the Treafury Lady-day, 1781, -		192 14 9

Befide there are fome lands of inheritance in the crown not granted away, the greateft part of which are the appendage of fome forts, and became the temporary emolument of the governors.—And the Phœnix Park, which being part of the priory of John of Jerufalem, fell to the crown, on the fuppreffion of the fame by Henry VIII. was afterwards enlarged by feveral purchafes, and made a deer-park by Char. IId.—In former times the pafturage was fet for 105 l. a year, for the ufe of the chief governor, but that has been difcontinued fince the year 1737, in confideration that there was not fufficient to pay the underkeepers and fervants their wages.

Wool Licences, may alfo be confidered as a part of the public revenue, they arife from a fee of 4 d. per ftone paid fince the time of Charles the fecond for a licence to export wool, this does not arife from any ftatute law, but from cuftom and perpetual acquiefcence. By an act of 3 George II. the old duty of 1 s. 3 d. on export of wool is taken off, and it is to be exported duty free; but the old cuftom of 4 d. per ftone for the licence is ftill paid; fince the extinction of that duty the 4 d. feems retained as a compenfation. Some applications have been lately made claiming a difcontinuance of that duty, on account of the recent change of trade laws.—How far there be grounds for fuch application is not decided, but it fhould feem that the advantage of the Irifh manufacture pleads in favour of the continuance of fuch payment.

NATIONAL ACCOUNT.

General ſtate of the national account of Ireland, for the year ending 25th March, 1784.

	£.	s.	d.
Charge of the civil liſt,	174,918	4	7½
Charge of the military eſtabliſhment, ordnance, &c. - -	429,686	12	10
Charges purſuant to act of Parliament, and King's letters, exceedings on concordatum, military contingencies and barracks, prize bounties to the linen manufacture, and allowances to the Commiſſioners of the Public Accounts, -	493,579	4	2
Making together, -	1,098,184	1	7½

Y y   Towards

	£.	s.	d.
Towards anfwering which, muft be applied the neat produce of the hereditary revenue for the year ending 25th March, 1784, deducting management, &c. -	397,913	7	9½
Neat produce of the additional duties for the fame year deducting for drawbacks, - -	366,192	11	3
Neat produce of the ftamp duties deducting management, &c. -	26,316	10	7½
Poundage and Pells fees,	24,138	8	6
Four fhillings in the pound on employments of abfentees, - -	16,545	5	5¼
Surplus of the loan fund after paying intereft,			
Sundry balances paid to Vice Treafurer, &c.			

Charge of the civil lift, on an average of ten years, ending 25th of March, 1771, - - 1,26,334 7 5¼

Charge

	£.	s.	d.
Charge of the military eftablifhment on the fame average,	501,563	0	3
Extraordinary charges, including Parliamentary grants on the fame average,	164,762	17	10
Total expence on the fame average,	792,660	5	5
Total expence on the preceding ten years, viz. ending 25th March, 1761	626,755	3	8

From whence it appears that the expence has increafed upwards of 470,000l. yearly, fince the year 1761, notwithftanding the charge of the military eftablifhment has decreafed.

D E B T.

State of the Funded Debt, 25th March, 1784,

	£.	s.	d.
Principal of loan debentures	927,600	0	0
————— Treafury bills	604,025	0	0
————— Bank capital	600,000	0	0
	2,131,625	0	0

Intereft

	£.	s.	d.
Intereſt on the loan deben- tures, at 4 per cent. -	43,104	0	0
Intereſt on the Treaſury bills, at 4l. 11s. 3d. per cent. -	23,930	0	0
Life annuities - -	49,843	5	0
Bank annuity -	18,000	0	0
	134,877	5	0

L O A N   D U T I E S.

	£.	s.	d.
Spirits, ſingle - -	56,757	12	0
Brandy and geneva, 2d.	32,793	19	8
Rum, 2d. - -	19,276	4	7
Spirits exceeding ſingle proof	14,796	1	9
Spirits, home made * -	59,854	5	5½
Cards, 2d. - -	2,506	4	0
	185,984	7	5½
Deduct drawbacks	765	15	9½
Neat	185,218	11	7¾
Total unfunded debt, 25th March, 1784 -	47,583	16	4

* The number of ſtills in Ireland in 1780 were 1212, groſs contents in gallons 295,127. Amount of duties only 104,258 l. 17 s. 6 d.

As

An ABSTRACT of the Hereditary Revenue and Additional Duties, for one Year, with the Expence of Management, Drawbacks, Premiums, &c. from Lady-day, 1783, to Lady-day, 1784.

HEREDITARY REVENUE.

ADDITIONAL DUTIES.

STAMP DUTIES.

SALARIES on the Revenue Establishment

PREMIUMS

DRAWBACKS ON ADDITIONAL DUTIES.

PAYMENTS made to the VICE-TREASURERS in the Year ending Lady-Day, 1784; viz.

Balances at Lady-day, 1784

Arrears at Lady-day, 1783

THOMAS BURGH,
Comptroller and Accountant-General.

As long as the debt shall not exceed its prefent amount, the taxes which it occasions
will not be materially felt. The fund which
it forms, affords to the people a convenient
and fafe opportunity of invefting their money. There is no intention however of recommending a yearly encreafe of debt. Ireland raifed money during the war more
eafily and cheaper than England, and her
funds bore a very confiderably higher price,
and were fometime above par.

OBSERVATIONS.

THE moft fuccefsful of our political writers are thofe who affert roundly that the
public interefts are irretrievably funk into
diftrefs and mifery. There is the greateft
difpofition in the people to be convinced that
fuch doctrines are juft; and they greedily
adopt maxims which feem rather formed to
prepare us for another world, than to reconcile us to that, in which we are placed.
On the other hand, it is an ungrateful, and,
in general, an unfuccefsful tafk, to endeavour to undeceive the people of Britain, or
of Ireland, to fatisfy them that their affairs
are in a good way, and that, collectively
confidered, they have ample caufe for con-
tentment, and ample means of happinefs.
An author, however, who has no preten-
tenfions to popularity, who never aimed at
it, and never will, might, on the ftrength of
the facts ftated in the foregoing pages, and
proved by authentic documents, venture to
affert, that the manufactures, the trade, the
finances, and every thing appertaining to
Ireland,

Ireland, except the minds of her people, are in a good way. He might, perhaps, go ftill farther, and affirm, that no other country ever poffeffed fo many advantages, and was fo happily circumftanced. He muft not, indeed, dare to pronounce the people happy, until they may think proper to be fo ; but thus much he will contend for, that Ireland poffeffes the *great* and *ufeful* advantages of the greateft countries ; and that fhe is gradually advancing to the attainment of every advantage acquired and maintained by Britain. Her foil is excellent, her climate favourable to agriculture and manufactures ; her people capable of whatever they pleafe to undertake ; her fituation the beft for trade ; her ports numerous and good. The principal unreafonable reftrictions on her manufactures and trade have all, in great meafure, been removed. She has obtained, in a fhort time, much more than fhe ufed to claim, much more than her moft fanguine friends expected. The kingdom in general is in the moft profperous ftate, and has, perhaps, been progreffively more fo than any country in Europe during the greater part of a century.

century. But fuch is our miferable nature, that difcontent, delufion, and extravagancies feemed to gain ground; they
have fpread over the land, under circumftances which ought to have produced the
moft oppofite effects; and no longer ago
than laft fummer, if we may give any credit
to public prints, Ireland appeared to have
neither conftitution nor government, nor
common fenfe. Aggregate or other meetings had announced that a total change was
neceffary, that the Parliaments were bad,
that they were dependent, and this fhortly
after Parliament had afferted the indepen-
dence of the legiflature, and had gained
more popular advantages for the country
than all the Parliaments of Ireland ever had
done.

The people were clamoroufly declared to
be enflaved, at the very time when they
were manifeftly fuperior to all control, either of reafon or of law. Meetings were
held for unlawful purpofes, the public papers
were filled with treafon againft the conftitution and the eftablifhed government. The
wild and baneful idea of feparation from
Great Britain was difcuffed in idle fpeeches,
without exciting either aftonifhment or indignation.

dignation. Various means were adopted to enflame, and all arts employed to perfuade that the manufactures were declining, notwithftanding the moft glaring proofs to the contrary.

It is fometimes difficult to account for popular difcontents; but, in the inftance here defcribed, it is evident that they had no foundation, and that they were fomented by men, who knew they had no chance of notice but in times of anarchy and diforder, and who, in hope of plundering the wreck, enjoy the ftorm. It is, however, fome fatisfaction to reflect, that (whatever others may do) the beginners of mifchief feldom reap any advantage from it. Ireland had obtained every thing fhe defired; a moft diftreffing circumftance to her incendiaries. Pains were taken to point out that manufactures and trade were in a ruinous ftate, and all methods but the right were recommended for affifting them: great pains were taken to make a breach with England; and for want of other food for difcontent and innovation, they ftumbled, as it happened, on parliamentary reform.

The

The times immediately fubfequent to
thofe in which Parliament had afferted even
more than the people had endeavoured to
obtain, had carried all their points, and had
proved themfelves eminently independent,
do not, to an ordinary underftanding, appear exactly to have been the feafon peculiarly eligible for deftroying the conftitution
of the Houfe of Commons, or the mode of
forming it.

The arguments for and againft a reform of
Parliament are frefh in every man's memo-
ry, and it is needlefs to repeat them; but it
may be obferved, that even if it fhould be
admitted as neceffary in England, it by no
means will follow, that it is neceffary in
Ireland. The reprefentatives of Ireland
are chofen by a much greater proportion of
the people who can be qualified to vote,
than in England. The change of property
in that country, its divided interefts, the
property and eftablifhed government being
comparatively in the hands of the few,
furely are objections to throwing the power
into the hands of the multitude. It feems
reafonable to fuppofe, that while the elec-
tion is in the hands of men of property and
confideration, the elected will fulfil the purpofe

pofe of legiflation better than thofe fent by
the multitude, which has neither property
nor judgement. How fuch a change is to
produce a fet of members lefs corrupt, does
not appear: no qualification as to property
is neceffary for a feat in the Irifh Parliament; boroughs might fend buftling attor-
nies and their clerks, or unfuccefsful fhopkeepers; they would take care to have
compenfation for trouble and expence;
counties, indeed, might fend landed men
of jovial character *.

It

* One little difficulty would occur from the intended improvement of the conftitution; the Lord
Lieutenant's Secretary, who is the minifter of the
country, might, on his arrival, find it difficult or impoffible to get into Parliament; efpecially as there are
not the fame means of vacating a feat in the Irifh as
in the Englifh Houfe of Commons; but the difficulty
might lead to the putting that office on a more reafonable footing: it might be made permanent, if a proper perfon could be found conftantly to remain there.
The falary is furely fufficient, viz. 4,500l. per ann.
exclufive of all the fees of the civil and military offices, and of houfes both in Dublin and in the country; it is more than belongs to any one office in Great
Britain. If it wants dignity, the office of Secretary
of State, which moft abfurdly is at prefent a finecure,
in Ireland, of about 1500l. per annum, might be
joined to it, and the difpofition which has been fhewn,

It has alſo been ſuggeſted, that frequent
elections might be ſalutary. Without at-
tending

no longer to make judicial offices, ſinecures, perhaps,
might aſſiſt the meaſure. A permanent Secretary would
give an influence and conſiſtence to the commence-
ment of every new viceroyalty, which rarely has been
ſeen in the annals of Iriſh government. The neceſſity of making ſudden arrangements with men before
they are known, would be prevented. There is no
neceſſity for the Secretary to conſider himſelf as obliged to go out of office on every change of Miniſters in
England. Had this plan been embraced a few years
ago, probably ſuch an arrangement might have taken
place as would have made new claims or difficulties
impoſſible, and the countries might now have been on
the beſt terms, without a poſſibility of a diſagreement
on the preſent ground. It would keep up ſomething
of a permanent adminiſtration in Ireland. The uſual
expence of a proviſion for the Secretary at the end of
the Lord Lieutenant's reign, would be ſaved by this
management, and alſo 1500l. per ann. on the death of
the preſent Secretary of State. According to the preſent ſyſtem, the Secretary goes to Ireland, knowing
about as much of the country and people as the Lord
Lieutenant; is immediately beſet by the conſiderable
men of the country, of various characters, objects,
and plans, and is obliged to decide before it is poſſible for him to know the grounds of his deciſions. If
this reſident Secretary ſhould aſſume too much, the
Viceroy would naturally cauſe his diſmiſſion. Some-
thing of this kind of eſtabliſhment ſeems particularly
proper, as it is not the cuſtom of England to know
much

tending to an uncandid and vulgar prejudice, that the Irifh nation is naturally turbulent and difpofed to diforder; it may be
afked, whether triennial or annual elections
might not be inconvenient to a manufao-
turing and commercial ftate ; the advantage
of repeated appeals to the fenfe of the multitude is not obvious to every underftanding.

However refpectable the fenfe of the people may be, yet we cannot be blind to their
inconfiftencies and delufions. It feems the
fenfe of one country that the moft eligible
government is that of a mob. It is the
fenfe of another that St. Januarius's blood
ought to become liquid on a particular day;
of another, that a great orator is inftinctive-

much of the internal circumftances of Ireland, nor
ufual for Minifters to know much more than the people. We are curious and inquifitive relative to the
ifland of Otaheite ; are well informed of its manners,
cuftoms, politics, parties, manufactures, fhipping,
&c. and accurately acquainted with the difpofitions
of Queen Oberea : but we overlook the neighbouring
ifland and the characters of its people.

ly

ly a complete ſtateſman *. It *was* the ſenſe of
the nation laſt alluded to, to preſs a bill of
excluſion againſt a prince; ſhortly after to
load him with the moſt fulſome and ſhame-
ful addreſſes, and three years after to de-
throne him. It was the ſenſe of another
nation, deſcended from Engliſhmen, almoſt
univerſally to believe in witchcraft, and
while that was their ſenſe, to put to death
multitudes of the people on that account;
neither character, nor fortune, neither ſex,
nor the miniſtry of the goſpel, neither the
innocence of youth, nor the infirmities of
age, afforded the leaſt protection. The excellent governor was *addreſſed* and *thanked*
for the many executions that had been made,
and exhorted to proceed in the laudable
work. Happily in due time the judges
themſelves were accuſed of ſorcery; and at
length the people, recovering from their infatuation, appointed a faſt, prayed to God,
and imputed the ſenſe that had appeared, to
Satan and his inſtruments: and this happened at a period of time the moſt reaſon-

---

* In this country no other proof is required of fit-
neſs for every office, than oratory; that talent ſupplies
the place of all knowledge, experience and judgment.

ing

ing and enlightened in the hiſtory of man, viz. 1692.[*]

Millions of examples equally edifying could be produced; which however might not tend to reconcile a politician to the ſcheme of recurring to the ſenſe [†] of the multitude on every occaſion; more eſpecially as this recurrence may happen reſpecting points on which it is impoſſible for them to form a true judgement, on which they are likely to be enflamed, and to become the inſtruments of malice or ambition.

It is now neceſſary to go back to the year 1778, to take notice of a phenomenon which began to appear about that time. The like never has been obſerved in any country, at leaſt where there was an eſtabliſhed government. To deſcribe it ſtrictly, it may be

---

[*] See Hutchinſon's hiſtory of Maſſachuſets: alſo the hiſtory of the European ſettlements in America.

[†] *A celebrated modern courtier* being told that the ſenſe of the people ſhould be taken on a particular occaſion, anſwered, " you may take the ſenſe, and I will take " the nonſenſe of the people, and beat you twenty to " one."

called

called an army unauthorized by the laws*, and uncontrolled by the government of the country, but it was generally known, by the name of Volunteers of Ireland. Their inftitution bore fome femblance of a connection with the executive power. Arms belonging to the ftate, and ftored under the care of the lieutenants of counties, were delivered to them, upon the alarm of foreign invafion. So far they feemed to be countenanced by government; but in a fhort time they caufed no little jealoufy and uneafinefs. The arms iffued from the public ftores were infufficient to fupply the rapid increafe of the volunteers : the reft were procured by themfelves, and the neceffary accoutrements, with a confiderable number of field pieces. It anfwered the purpofe of oppofition in both countries to fpeak highly of them, and the fupporters of government in both countries mentioned them with civility. The wonderful efforts of England in America were fomehow wafted to no purpofe of decifion. American fuccefs enflamed grievances which had been long felt in Ire-

* The fame fort of thing as fome country and other meetings endeavoured to introduce in England a very few years ago.

land.

land. Ireland, in truth, had infinitely more
caufe for complaint, and had been infinitely
more oppreffed, than America ; the latter had
never fubmitted to half the hurtful reftrictions in which the other had for many years
quietly acquiefced : but now petitions, re-
monftrances, popular refolves, and parliamentary addreffes were vigoroufly urged,
and in about four years Ireland was happily
relieved from many commercial reftraints,
which fhould have been removed long before, and gained feveral other points which
fhe thought effential to her welfare. The
volunteers preferving a degree of referve and
decency, kept at a certain diftance, but were
never entirely out of fight. They had been
ferviceable in fupporting the civil magiftrate ;
Fewer caftles, houfes, or lands, were kept by
forcible poffeffion ; fheriffs were enabled to
do their duty ; fewer rapes and other enor-
mities were committed than ufual ; and here
if the volunteers had ftopt, and we had feen
no more of them after the eftablifhment of
peace, their page in hiftory would have been
fair and refpectable : but it was natural for
them to go on. The many-headed mon-
fter now began to think it would be proper

3 A to

to reform the ſtate, and to purge the Parliament of Ireland. The ſeveral corps ſent delegates; ſometimes they appeared to be the
delegates of counties. They formed a parliament of their own; they reſolved what
they pleaſed, and of courſe, that the other
parliament was a bad one. So far every
thing went on as might be expected; but
there is another part of their conduct, which
is neither natural nor rational: ſome of the
corps, perhaps for the ſake of compleating
their numbers, and poſſibly without conſide-
ration, admitted Roman Catholics; others
perhaps enrolled them latterly for the ſake of
acquiring numbers and ſtrength, to force a
reform: but that Proteſtants ſhould allow
and encourage this, and alſo the forming of
whole corps of Roman Catholics, when all
Europe was at peace, is ſcarce to be believed, conſidering the pretenſions of the latter,
and above all, their numbers. It became
the ſyſtem of the Roman Catholics, to en-
rol as many as poſſible, and particularly
ſince the peace, laſt ſpring, laſt ſummer, and
now it is going on, though not quite ſo rapidly as was expected. There is nothing
equivocal in this. They were already half
of thoſe that latterly appeared under arms;

in

in a year or lefs, they might be ten to one, for the Proteftants were gradually quitting the fervice, and the only apology for thofe who continued fince the peace, was, that they meant to prevent the volunteer arms from falling into more dangerous hands, and to counterbalance the Roman Catholics. The latter appeared fure of their plan, and feemed already to exult.

The conduct of the Roman Catholics for a length of time, except thofe concerned in this bufinefs, had been fo refpectable, that it may feem harfh to mention any thing ad-verfe to them : but, the objection is to their numbers. If they were only one fifth, in-ftead of four fifths, of the people, the writer of thefe obfervations would be the laft man to fuggeft difficulties againft their being ad-mitted to power, and every right and advan-tage. But they are men ; they do not forget the fituation in which their anceftors have been ; they are not blind to what they might acquire. A perfeverance for upwards of two centuries, under every difcouragement, and every incitement to a change, under every feverity, and fubjected to every difadvan-tage, does not prove an indifference to the

principles

principles of their religion. Thinking as
they do, feeling as they do, a nd believing as
they do, they would not be men, if they
did not wifh a change ; nor would the Proteftants be worthy the defcription of reafonable creatures, if they did not take precau-
tions to prevent it.

Left any thing fhould be deficient to
make voluntecring objectionable, Roman
Catholics were admitted to bear arms; and
left any thing fhould be wanting to make
the plan for improving the reprefentation
extravagant and abfurd, it was propofed
that they fhould be admitted to vote at
elections : a propofal, indeed, fo ftrange,
that it might well be imagined to originate
with the enemies of reform, for the purpofe of blafting the attempt. The right of
being elected, would furely follow their being eligible; but at all events the power
would be in the electors. It is curious to
obferve one fifth, or perhaps one fixth, of
a nation in poffeffion of the power and property of the country, eager to communi-
cate that power to the remaining four fifths,
which would, in effect, entirely tranfer it
from themfelves. It did not proceed from
liberality, but from folly. To what elfe can

bc

be imputed the transferring it to fo great a majority who have claims, efpecially at this time, when a peculiar policy has eftablifhed the fyftem of reftoring forfeited eftates *? The attainders and forfeitures that followed the tranfactions of 1641, 1688, 1715, and 1745, depend on the fame principles. If power is communicated, it of courfe will be made ufe of; it is ridiculous, it is contrary to reafon and nature, to fuppofe otherwife. It is not in man to be content; thofe that have acquired the means of increafing their gains, or who think they have got nothing, if they do not get more, will not be inattentive to advantages. It is not fufficient to fay the property of the Roman Catholics is trifling†,

compared

---

* The author defires to be underftood not to object to the meafure, but to the mode.

† Although there are feveral Roman Catholic families of large eftates, the number that exceed 1000l. per ann. is fmall. It has been fuppofed, however, that they are the monied men; but if we may judge from the late fubfcription to the Bank ftock of Ireland, it does not appear fo. Of 600,000l. only 60,000l. it is faid, were fubfcribed by Roman Catholics. This is not mentioned exultingly; it is fincerely wifhed they had much more. Their money was well employed in trade and agriculture. It is obferved, that fince the power of purchafing land has been allowed to Roman Catholics,

compared with that of the Proteſtants, while the diſproportion in point of number is ſo great ; and numbers, where they think they have claims, would ſoon have property, if attainable either by fair exertions or by force. Neither this obſervation, nor that the Roman Catholics were arming, is invidiouſly intended. It is natural they ſhould endeavour to avail themſelves of every advantage that may fall in their way.

The Proteſtants, not the Roman Catholics, are the objeƈts of cenſure—The Proteſtants, who, with heedleſs infatuation, have not only ſuffered, but promoted thoſe extraordinary and dangerous proceedings, who ſeemed to have loſt all recolleƈtion of paſt apprehenſions, and all ſenſe of future danger. If the opportunity offers, why ſhould not the ſame things be attempted by the Roman Catholics in 1788, which were done in 1688 and 1641 ? If any man doubts, let him look into the proceedings of the Iriſh Parliament at thoſe periods. It is unpleaſing to point out the ſimilitude between

Catholics, few purchaſes have been made by them ; but they have had ſcarce time to call in their money, if they had been diſpoſed to lay it out on land.

the

the tranfaſtions that preceded the laſt-mentioned period and thoſe that have happened lately. There is no intention of alluding to the maſſacre of 1641, nor to ſuggeſt a probability that ſuch barbarity can ever be renewed. Though much exaggerated by Proteſtant writers, the horrors of that event cannot be palliated, however they may have fallen ſhort of the example which had been ſet on the famous feaſt of St. Bartholomew, by the *moſt civilized people* of Europe.

Perhaps we ſhall be told, that the advantage of the many, not of the few, ſhould be confidered ; that the majority ſhould govern, &c. The author will not difpute with thoſe ſentimental politicians : he thinks it ſufficient at prefent, to reaſon about things as they are, and will content himſelf with obferving, that the argument or fentiment equally goes to an Agrarian law, or any levelling principle whatever: it eſtabliſhes confuſion, in the place of order.

Theſe remarks, and the dangerous circumſtances which ſuggeſted them, would have been rendered ſuperfluous, if Ireland had uſed the moment of returning peace to form her volunteer army into a national militia,

litia, and had re-eftablifhed the falutary
principle, that it is unlawful and unconfti-
tutional for men to array without the authority of Parliament.

Allowing the volunteers all the merit they
have defervedly acquired for their readinefs
to defend their country in war, and impu-
ting whatever may be irregular to the con-
fufion that prevails in time of danger and
alarm: their continuance in arms in time
of profound peace, will deftroy former merit. Their efforts will be imputed to other
motives than thofe that actuated the firft
volunteers: an intention to change the conftitution by a military force, will be imputed
to them. If a revolution takes place, it
muft end, unlefs England fhould interfere,
in favour of the Roman Catholics, who are
at leaft four to one; even an unfuccefsful
attempt would be replete with great and
obvious mifchiefs.

At the fame time that a cordial anxiety
for the true and permanent interefts of Ireland has exhorted thefe ftrictures on the fyftem of volunteering, it is a point of juftice
to acknowledge, that the volunteer officers
were in general highly refpectable, and diftinguifhed

tinguifhed both by their public talents and private virtues; and there are ftill among them, men of the firft rank and confe-quence in the country.

The good order which prevailed in thefe corps, is not lefs extraordinary than their rife and progrefs; but it is to be imputed to the good difpofition of the generality of the members, not to the nature of their confti-tution. It feems miraculous, that no mif-chief has yet happened. The *mildnefs* of government, and the good temper of the army, have done their part. None more likely, however, to be mifled, than men collected as they have been, conceiving a high opinion of their confequence and ftrength. They are liable to be perverted, and turned to the worft purpofes; in al-moft every inftance of the kind, it has proved fo. Well-meaning men who may at one time be at their head, may, at other times, find themfelves without authority, and at length be obliged to give way to thofe, whofe bufinefs it is to inflame and pervert. The young and active, and thofe who are not in the habit of thinking, will be led from one deviation to another, till at laft they are advanced too far to go back; and

some,

fome, otherwife refpectable men, who have fomething to lofe and little to gain, will repent of their attempts, to affift themfelves at elections by volunteering, or through the medium of an affected good will towards reform. All that is hinted at, may not happen ; yet moft affuredly, fome of the politicians of Ireland are playing with moft dangerous two-edged weapons. Such meafures do not become them : fuch are the ladders on which the otherwife infignificant and vicious members of fociety, or men of defperate fituations, mount, and with contempt look down on the miferable tools, through whofe folly they were enabled to afcend.

In the mean time it is known, that French money had found its way into Ireland, even as late as laft fummer, and that American emiffaries have been employed, and that France will be ready to play her ufual game. Paffing over other confiderations, it may be obferved, that the fuccefs of her machinations would be ruinous in an extreme degree both to Proteftant and Papift. Suppofing France to fucceed fo far as to produce a rebellion or civil war ; fuch a country as Ireland could not long fubfift
the

the armies of Britain, of France, of Proteſtants, and Roman Catholics. In a ſtate
of war, that country, ſo far from being able
to ſupport even ten or twenty thouſand
foreign troops, would not be able to maintain her own people. Agriculture would
almoſt ceaſe, devaſtation would ſpeedily
overſpread, and exhauſt a tract of land ſo
inconſiderable. One party ſtrong, in the
habit of predominating, and ſupported by a
Britiſh army, would conſume one part of
the iſland; and another party, by far the
moſt numerous, ſupported by the armies of
France and Spain, would conſume the reſt.
In caſe theſe ſhould not be enough, Ger-
mans, without end, might be introduced:
inſtead of being boundleſs, like America,
and inacceſſible only on one ſide, Ireland is
of ſmall extent for two armies, and acceſſi-
ble on every ſide, and no part of the iſland
far diſtant from the ſea. The war would not
be of the generous ſort that is uſually carried
on by Britain and France; it would be a
civil war; it would become a religious war,
of all, the moſt barbarous. Ulſter might
be once more vacated, and the brave Scottiſh
clans would again find a better ſoil, and
again ſhew their martial talents on the
plains of Ireland. After that fine country

3 B 2　　　　　　　　　had

had been the fcene of war, perhaps not more than two campaigns, it would be left in a worfe fituation than Cromwell left it, on his laft vifit; for it is impoffible, confidering the ftate of things, while England in any degree exifts as a confiderable country, that an ifland fo inferior in number of inhabitants, in riches, and every thing that makes one country ftronger than another, that Ireland, fo near and liable to blockade and invafion, could, for any time, continue in an independent ftate feparate from England.

Yet fuch is faid to be the view of fome; fmall it is indeed hoped, and believed, is the number of thofe who cherifh the idea of a feparation at the expence of rupture and hoftility between the countries: a profpect not more wild than wicked; wild, from the improbability of fuccefs; wicked, becaufe what are the hopes for Ireland, if fo improbable a cafe could happen as that fhe, for a time, fhould be feparate from England? it would entail mifery on millions. That poor country, which now might be the happieft in the world, inftead of being laid wafte once only, would be the conftant theatre of war and wretchednefs, on every quarrel between Britain and France. But

in

in the other cafe, of being even once the feat
of war, when fhe has loft the flower of her
people, half her inhabitants, all her manufactures, commerce, and riches, fhe muft at
length fall into her natural fituation, deprived indeed of many bleffings fhe now enjoys.

However unpleafant, thefe are matters
highly proper, as well as neceffary, to be
ftated; and he who endeavours to unfold
the fatal confequences of meafures, the
outfide of which may appear fair, is the real
friend to a country.

Let it be underftood, however, that whatever the mafs of the people may do, the
moft confiderable, in point of rank and fortune, and the beft informed, do not purfue
either the extravagancies of volunteering or
the vifions of reform.

Indeed, many others, who at firft acted
differently, had begun to fee the ftate of the
country in a proper light. After violent fan-
cies, a little recollection fometimes occurs.
Men began to be alarmed, and to recover
their fenfes. Aggregate meetings received
mortifying checks. The fpirit and good fenfe
of the country were rouzed by the extraordinary

dinary proceedings of thofe meetings. The
arming of the Roman Catholics, although
fome corps continued to form, and are now
forming, experienced certain checks. The
government of the country fhewed a degree
of fpirit. Treafon was curbed, and, fince laft
Auguft, good order was returning, mifchief
feemed to fubfide, volunteering and reform
to decline, and many of thefe obfervations
might now have been unneceffary, if very
ferious confequences were not to be dreaded
from that combination of Mr. Wyville and
Mr. Pitt, which has been not long fince announced to the public. It is no lefs than
founding the trumpet of diforder in Ireland *.

It is a little particular, that the method of
carrying points for that country lately, was

* It has been already remarked, that fince laft fummer, aggregate meetings had been checked in Ireland ;
attempts to form a congrefs had been, in great meafure, fruftrated, and good order began to prevail ; but
fince the minifter's letter to Belfaft, and the unfortunate communication above mentioned, even thofe
who had declined, and refufed to fend reprefentatives
to an illegal meeting, affembled, and named delegates
to the anti-parliament or congrefs. The bufinefs of
reform in Ireland will probably be fufpended till the
minifter's meafure for the reform of the Englifh Houfe
of Commons is known.

through

through the *effect* of volunteers. Reform
and Volunteers, may again be the cry. Reform and Volunteers, may lead to any thing.
The encouragement is complete. However
pure the patriotifm of thofe two gentlemen
may be, their plans, at this moment, are infinitely mifchievous, in refpect to Ireland, at
leaft. The authority communicated to Mr.
Wyville, by Mr. Pitt, inflames both countries againft the ancient conftitution. It
was ill timed: the wifdom and policy of it,
are not obvious.

The firft of thofe gentlemen, a preacher of
the moft peaceable and benign doctrines, is
the great patron of reform, and was among
the firft to promote correfponding committees, and affociations or volunteering in
England. The friends, however, of the
country came forward, and alarmed the
people, pointing out the mifchief that was
threatened; nor was the tafk difficult.
Affociations and Committees had produced
fuch recent effects in America, and even in
Ireland, that the very terms were defervedly
become fufpicious.

The encouragement which volunteering
and reform derive from the Minifter having,
from

from the firft, connected himfelf with affoci-
ators and reformers, muft neceffarily be a-
larming to the real friends of Ireland, and
encouraging to all the wantonnefs of fpecu-
lators and the wickednefs of incendiaries, in
both countries. What volunteering or affociations are, muft be plain to every underftanding; but whether the other thing is, in
future, to be called Reformation, Reftoration, Revolution, or Rebellion, depends
entirely on the good or bad fuccefs of the
fyftem. And let it be obferved, that the
beft-intended reform is not apt to ftop exactly where it meant to ftop, or where it
fhould ftop.

Not a man is to be met, who confiders
the *intended* propofitions of Reform of the
Englifh Houfe of Commons otherwife than
as a mockery : not a man is to be found,
who believes there is a ferious intention of
concurring in any thing like the reform * that
is

* However difficult it is to fay what the prefent Parliament may do ; to propofe a fpecific plan of reform
that can pleafe no fet of men, feems as likely means
of evading reform, as any that can be offered. An
effential reform is not now to be expected ; for although
the

is meant by the theorifts on that fubject among the people ; and at the fame time that the people of England will be difap-pointed ; the paffions of the people of Ireland will not be calmed, or their minds com-pofed : and thus thefe countries are ever to be the fport of delufion and bad policy, and beguiled or diverted from their real interefts.

It is not the intention of the writer of thefe obfervations, to avail himfelf of the bad conduct and blunders of Adminiftra-tion, or to exhibit a picture that would bear the ftrongeft colouring. He wifhes, efpeci-ally on fuch an occafion as the prefent, to

the Minifter owes his exiftence, as fuch, to a diffolu-tion, it would not fuit him to make the experiment again ; and furely the people of England are not quite fo fimple as to be impofed upon by any little partial ap-pearance of reform, or without a diffolution taking place immediately after reform. The reform will be an acknowledgement that there has been fomething wrong in the mode of electing ; which being corrected, if there remains any pretenfion to honefty and fairnefs, of courfe the people fhould have the opportunity of chufing their reprefentatives on the improved plan, the former mode being thus reprobated. The people of England have been duped, but will they readily be made to think an addition to Parliament, a reform ?

3 C   avoid

avoid every thing, that can poffibly be imputed to party. He is interefted for the welfare of the empire: Minifters and parties
are, at the beft, but fecondary confiderations, and never would have induced him,
in any fhape, to become a writer. If an attention to matters, which, perhaps, have
been generally neglected, or, perhaps, not
generally underftood, enables him to give
information, and ufefully to reprefent the
ftate of any part of the empire; that wifh
alone could tempt him to encounter the
prejudices of fome, and to expofe himfelf
to the interefted and malignant obfervation
of others.

He may have prejudices, but they are in
favour of order and eftablifhed government;
and he had rather feel fuch as tend to fupport the conftitution and tranquillity, confequently the profperity, of the empire,
than thofe which countenance innovation,
and, in the end, diftraction; efpecially at
the time that repofe is fo neceffary both to
Great Britain and Ireland, and that they
neither require, nor can be benefited by, the
kind of changes that are attempted.

It

It is the misfortune of nations, as well as of individuals, not to be content when they are well, but to fancy they may be better. They will fubject themfelves to every difficulty, and rifque every thing that is dear to them, in purfuit of ideal advantages; neither the conftitution, nor the manufactures, nor the trade of the country, require the new fyftems that are afloat; but fhould it ever be the object of a Minifter, to amufe the people with mifchievous acquiefcences, or by facrificing the moft ferious concerns, there is danger indeed. We fhould be on our guard, examine what we are about, and not decide until we underftand.

In refpect to the two countries, whenever it is poffible, let them confider themfelves as one ; and far be from thefe times the narrow and falfe policy of Davenant *, who recommends the means of diverting the Irifh from manufactures, and hindering their population from increafe ; who fuppofes England able to fupply all foreign demands; and on

---

* Davenant had accefs to public papers, and was a party and a favourite writer, as he went with the tide in popular queftions ; but he was miferably defective in juft principles of commerce.

3 C 2   this

this miſtaken notion, concludes, that for every pound of Iriſh woollens fold, a pound of Engliſh muſt remain at home; and not content with this, he farther ſuppoſed the encouragement of the linen manufacture in Ireland would prejudice the trade of England with Hamburgh. The prodigious increaſe of exports both to Ireland and Hamburgh, ſince that time, ſufficiently confute a writer, who does not ſeem to have known, that it was neceſſary Ireland ſhould be rich, or have money or ſuch produce as we might want, before ſhe could take great quantities of Britiſh manufactures.

It ſhould be as notorious, as it is true, that every encouragement given to the induſtry of Ireland, is the advantage of Britain, and that the proſperity of the one, is the proſperity of the other.

The manufactures and trade of Ireland are in a proſperous ſtate; let her not neglect them for vain ſpeculations; let both countries recollect and avail themſelves of their many and great advantages : let them not tamper with that which is good, leſt they deſtroy it. The hint given to the Italians by by their countryman, may be worthy their attention. He was in a good ftate of health; he tampered with his conftitution to make it better, and finding he had deftroyed himfelf by his quackery, he ordered the following to be infcribed on his tomb—" Stavo " bene, ma per ftar meglio, fto qui."—" I " was well, I would be better, and here I " lie."

THE END.

To enable the reader to calculate the value of the articles mentioned in the courfe of the work, the cuftom-houfe valuations of Ireland, on export and import, are here annexed.

Medium of the prefent Market Price on Export. £. s. d.	Denominations.		Medium the prefen Mark. Pri on Import. £. s.
	Ale ———	The Barrel	1 0
	Apparel —	Value	
0 3 0	Aquavitæ ———	Gallon	
	Apples ———	Buihel	0 3
	Arms —	Value	
	Bacon { Englifh Flitches	No.	0 13
	Foreign —	C. q. lb	2 0
1 10 0	Hams —	C. q. lb.	
0 15 0	Flitches —	No.	
	Bark ———	Barrel	0 7
	Battery —	C. q. lb.	7 5
1 10 0	Beef { Barrels	No.	
4 0 0	Carcafes	No.	
	Beads of Glafs	lbs.	0 1
0 10 0	Beer ———	Barrel	1 0
2 10 0	Books { Bound —	Value	
	Unbound —	C. q. lb.	10 0
0 10 0	Boards, Barrels ———	C. q. No	
0 5 0	Barrels empty ———	No.	
0 1 6	Bottles of Glafs —	Dozen	0 1
0 12 0	Bread ———	C. q. lb.	
	Berries Juniper —	C. q. lb.	2 0
4 4 0	Brafs and Copper manufactured	Value	
	Brafs Shruff ———	C. q. lb	3 0
	Bricks	Thoufan.	1 10
2 0 0	Butter ———	C. q. lb	
5 0 0	Bullocks and Cows —	No.	
	Brimftone —	C q. lb	0 16
	Bullion { Gold —	Ounces	
	Silver —	Ounces	0 6
	Bugles ———	lb.	0 6
	Cables ———	C. q lb	1 12
	Candlewick —	C. q lb.	3 5
	Capers —	lb.	0 0
0 6 0	Cards { Flaxing ———	Dez. Pks.	
	Tow —	Doz. Pks.	0 4
	Wool —	Doz. Pks.	0 8
	Chalk ———	C. q. lb.	0 1
	Camblet { Mohair —	Yards	0 6
	Worfted —	Yards	0 2

Medium of the present Market Price on Export.			Denominations.		Medium of the present Mark. Price on Import.		
£.	s.	d.			£.	s.	d.
1	0	0	Cheefe ——— —	C. q. lb.	1	10	0
			Chocolate ——— —	lb.	0	2	6
	Value.		Coaches and Chaifes — —	Value			
			Coals ——— —	Tons	0	15	0
			Coffee ——— —	C. q. lb.	10	0	0
			Copper Plates and Bucks —	C. q. lb.	5	0	0
1	5	0	Cordage ——— —	C. q. lb	1	3	4
			Cork ——— • —	C. q. lb.	3	10	0
			Corn { Barley and Malt —	qrs.	1	2	0
			Corn { Beans and Peafe —	qrs.	1	5	0
0	9	9	Corn { Oats ——— —	qrs.	0	15	0
2	4	0	Corn { Wheat ——— —	qrs.	2	3	4
1	16	8	Candles ——— —	C. q. lb.			
3	10	0	Copper Ore ——— —	Tons			
			Cotton, Linen, and Silk Manufacture —	Value			
1	12	0	Corn { Barley ——— —	qrs.			
1	0	0	Corn { Beans ——— —	qrs.			
1	3	0	Corn { Malt ——— —	qrs.			
1	0	0	Corn { Peafe ——— —	qrs.			
0	2	0	Drapery { New — —	Yards	0	2	6
6	8	0	Drapery { Old — —	Yards	0	14	0
			Drapery { Prunella — —	Yards	0	4	0
			Drapery { Shagg — —	Yards	0	4	0
			Drugs — —	Value			
			Dying Stuffs. { Allum ——— —	C. q. lb.	0	13	0
			Anotto ——— —	C. q. lb.	0	18	0
			Argal ——— —	C. q. lb.	1	2	0
			Brazillito — —	C q. lb.	0	14	0
			Cochineal — —	lbs.	1	0	0
			Copperas — —	C. q. lb.	0	6	8
			Fuftick — —	C. q lb.	0	14	0
			Galls ——— —	C. q. lb.	3	0	0
			Indigo ——— —	lbs.	0	6	8
			Logwood — —	C. q. lb.	2	5	0
			Madder ——— —	C. q. lb	1	5	0
			Orchal ——— —	C. q. lb.	1	2	0
			Redwood — —	C. q. lb.	2	0	0
			Sanders ——— —	C. q. lb	6	0	0
			Shumack ——— —	C. q. lb.	0	13	4
			Smalts ——— —	lbs.	0	1	0
			Stone Blue ——— —	lbs.	0	0	7
			Sweet Wood —	C. q. lb.			
			Weeds, or Straw Weed —	C. q lb.	0	7	0
			Woad ——— —	C. q. lb	0	15	0
			Small Parcels —	Value			
			Earthen Ware ——— —	Value			
			Elephant's Teeth ——— —	No.	0	5	0
			Fans ——— —	No.	0	1	8

Medium of the present Market Price on Export.			Denominations.		Medium of the present Mark. Price on Import.		
£.	s.	d.			£.	s.	d.
2	0	0	Anchovies — The	Barrel	0	16	0
1	5	0	Cod —	C. q. lb.	4	0	0
			Cod —	Barrel	1	0	0
0	15	0	Herrings —	Barrel	1	0	0
3	0	0	Ling —	C. q. lb.	4	10	0
			Fish { Oysters —	Gallon	0	2	0
			Pilchards —	Hhd.			
12	0	0	Salmon —	T. qr.	12	0	0
			Stock —				
			Sturgeon —	Keg	0	12	0
1	2	0	Eels —	Barrel			
1	10	0	Hake —	C. q. lb.			
2	0	0	Feathers —	C. q. lb.			
			Flax { Dreft —	C. q. lb.	2	0	0
			Undreft —	C. q. lb.	1	15	0
			Flints —	M.	0	2	6
			Furs —	Value			
			Fustian Ends —	End	0	15	0
0	0	10	Flannel —	Yard			
1	10	0	Flax Seed —	Hhd.			
0	1	0	Fustians —	Yard			
0	1	8	Frize —	Yard			
			Cases —	No.	1	10	0
per Hd. 0	1	0	Glass { Drinking —	No.	0	0	2
			Rhenish —	Webb			
			Vials —	No. Hhd.	0	6	8
			Glass Ware —	Value			
1	13	4	Glew —	C. q. lb.	0	16	8
0	1	6	Gloves —	Pair	0	3	0
			Grindstones —	Chald.	0	16	8
			Almonds —	C. q. lb.	2	15	0
			Annifeeds —	C. q. lb.	1	6	8
			Cinnamon —	Lbs.	0	8	0
			Cloves —	Lbs.	0	10	0
			Cocoa Nuts —	Lbs.	0	1	0
			Currants —	C. q. lb.	2	5	0
			Figs —	C. q. lb.	0	12	6
			Ginger —	C. q. lb.	1	10	0
			Groceries { Hulled Barley —	C. q. lb.	1	2	0
			Liquorice —	C. q. lb.	1	2	0
			Mace —	Lbs.	0	16	8
			Nutmegs —	Lbs.	0	10	0
			Pepper —	Lbs.	0	1	4
			Piaminto —	Lbs.	0	1	0
			Prunes —	C. q. lb.	0	6	8
			Raisins —	C. q. lb.	1	4	0
			Rice —	C. q lb.	0	18	0
			Saffron —	Lbs.	1	10	0

Medium of the present Market Price on Export £. s. d.	Denominations				Medium of the present Mark. Price on Import £. s. d.
	Groceries	Succards — The		Lbs.	0 3 0
		Succus Liquoritiæ		Lbs.	0 0 8
		Sugars	Candy —	C. q. lb.	4 0 0
4 12 0			Loaf —	C. q. lb.	6 0 0
			Muscovado —	C. q. lb.	2 5 0
			White —	C. q. lb.	4 0 0
		Small Parcels —		Value	
	Gunpowder —			C. q. lb.	3 5 0
	Haberdashery.	Gold and Silver	Fringe	Oz.	0 10 0
			Twilt	Oz.	0 4 6
		Inkle	Wrought	Lbs.	0 5 2
			Unwro't	Lbs.	0 3 0
		Laces —		Gro. Doz.	0 3 6
		Needles —		Doz. Th.	3 2 6
		Pins —		Doz. M.	0 18 0
		Thimbles —		No. M.	2 0 0
		Thread	Bridges —	Lbs.	
			Black —	Lbs.	
			GoldandSilver	Lbs. oz.	2 0 0
			Outnal —	Lbs.	0 5 6
			Piecing —	Lbs.	
			Sifters —	Lbs.	0 15 0
			White brown	Lbs.	0 2 8
		Small Parcels		Value	
	Hair	Camels' —		Lbs.	0 8 0
		Goats' —		Lbs.	0 2 6
3 0 0		Human —		Lbs.	0 1 10
0 5 0	Hats —			No.	0 15 0
	Hemp	Dreft —		C. q. lb.	1 0 0
		Undreft —		C. q. lb.	0 15 6
	Hemp Seed —			Hhd.	2 10 0
	Hops —			C. q. lb.	5 0 0
6 0 0	Horses —			No.	10 0 0
	Hardware —			Value	
1 0 0	Hogs —			No.	
1 10 0	Hogs' Lard —			C. q. lb.	
0 16 8	Horns	Ox and Cows —		C. q. lb.	
0 6 8		Tips —		C. q. lb.	
1 13 4				No.	
2 16 0	Hides	Tanned —		C. q. lb.	
1 6 8		Untanned —		No.	
	Indian Silk Stuffs —			Value	
per ton.16 15 0	Ironmongers' Ware.	Iron —		C. q. lb.	0 16 0
		Knives —		No.	0 0 3
		Merinits —		No.	0 2 0
		Pots —		No.	0 5 0
		Razors —		No.	0 0 6
		Sciffars —		Gro. Doz.	1 5 0
		Scythes —		Doz.	1 0 0

3 D

Medium of the present Market Price on Export. £ s d	Denominations.		Unit	Medium of the current Mark. Price on Import. £ s d
	Ironmongers' Ware.	{ Small Parcels —	Value	
2 0 0		{ Iron, wrought —	C. q. lb.	
Value	Ironmongers' Ware —		—	
	Iron Ore ——		Tons	0 15 0
	Ivory, wrought ——		Lbs.	0 12 0
1 10 0	Kelp ——		Tons	
	Lace	{ Gold and Silver —	Lbs. Oz.	4 0 0
		{ Thread Bone ——	Yards	1 0 0
	Lamp Black ——		Lbs.	0 1 2
	Latten ——		C. q. lb.	6 0 0
	Lead	{ Pigs	C. q. lb.	0 10 6
		{ Red	C. q. lb.	1 5 0
		{ Sheets	C. q. lb.	0 13 4
		{ Shot ——	C. q. lb.	0 15 0
Tons 2 6 8		{ White —	C. q. lb.	1 6 8
	Lead Ore —		C. q. lb.	4 0 0
	Lime, Lemon, and Orange Juices —		Gallons	0 2 0
	Linen	{ British —	Yards	0 3 0
		Buckram ——	Yards	0 4 0
0 5 0		Callico { Stained —	Yards	0 5 0
		Callico { White —	Yards	0 4 0
		Cambrick —	Yards	0 6 8
0 1 7		Canvas ——	Yards	0 1 2
		Coloured —	Yards	0 4 0
		Cravats ——	Yards	
		Damask { Napkins —	Yards	0 5 0
		Damask { Tabling —	Yards	0 6 0
		Diaper { Napkins —	Yards	0 3 0
		Diaper { Tabling —	Yards	0 3 0
		French ——	Ells	0 2 0
		Hamburgh ——	Ells	0 3 0
		{ Bagg —	Ells	0 4 0
		{ Gallick —	Ells	0 5 0
		Kenting ——	Yards	0 2 0
		Lawns —	Yards	0 3 0
		Muslin —	Yards	0 3 6
0 1 4		Ticking —	Yards	0 2 4
		Plain ——	Yards	
	Linseed ——		Hhd.	3 0 0
	Linen, Cotton, and Silk, Brit. Manuf.		Value	
	Masks ——		No.	
0 15 0	Matts ——		No.	0 1 4
0 10 6	Meal	{ Flour —	C. q. lb.	0 12 0
		{ Oat —	Barrel	0 7 0
1 0 0		{ Wheat —	Barrel	1 6 8
		{ Groats —	Barrel	
	Millinery Ware —		Value	
	Mill Stones —		No.	1 5 0
0 15 0	Molasses ——		C. q. lb.	

Medium of the prefent Market Price on Export.	Denominations.		Medium of the current Mark. Price on Import.
£. s. d.			£. s. d.
	Oakum	C. q. lb.	0 12 6
	Olives	Gallon	0 2 2
	Onions	Barrel	0 10 0
	Oranges and Lemons	C. q. lb.	0 2 6
	Oils { Linfeed	Hhd.	0 2 0
	Sevil	Gall.	0 3 4
	Sweet	Gall.	0 5 0
Ton 12 0 0	Train	Gall.	0 0 6
0 6 8	Ox { Bones	M.	
0 16 8	Guts	Barrel	
	Painting Stuffs	Value	
	Paper { Blue	Ream	0 4 0
Reams 0 1 6	Brown	Bundle	0 3 0
	Cap	Ream	0 4 4
	Card	Ream	0 5 0
	Painted	Ream	0 6 8
	Printing	Ream	0 2 4
	Preffing Leaves	Hund.	0 8 0
	Whited brown	Ream	0 1 6
0 3 0	Writing	Ream	0 6 8
	Pafte Boards	No.	0 8 0
	Pewter	C. q. lb.	4 5 0
	Pictures	Value	
	Pitch	Barrel	0 10 0
	Plates of Tin	Barrel	2 2 0
	Pot Afhes	C. q. lb.	1 5 0
	Printing-letters	C. q. lb.	4 5 0
0 0 9	Plank, three Inch	Feet	
1 10 0	Pork	Barrel	
4 0 0	Pewter wrought	C. q. lb.	
	Quills	M.	0 1 8
	Quilts	No.	2 0 0
	Rape of Grape	T. hh. g	
5 0 0	Ribband { Silk	Lbs. oz.	2 0 0
	Silver	Lbs. oz	0 10 0
	Rozin	C. q. lb.	0 10 0
0 5 0	Rabbits' Fur	Lb.	
1 12 6	Rape Seed	Qr. Bufh.	
Value	Sadlers' Ware	Value	
	Salt { Foreign	Bufh.	0 1 6
0 1 3	Rock	Ton	0 10 6
	White	Bufh	0 1 4
	Salt-Petre	C. q. lb	2 10 0
	Seeds { Clover	C. q. lb.	0 18 0
	Garden	Lb.	8 2 4
5 0 0	Silk { Manufacture	Lb. oz.	3 0 0
2 10 0	Thrown { Dyed	Lb. oz.	1 15 0
	Undyed	Lb. oz.	1 5 0
	Raw	Lb. oz.	1 0 0

3 D 2

Medium of the present Market Price on Export. £. s. d.	Denominations.		Medium of the present Mark. Price on Import. £. s. d.
	Buck	No.	0 2 6
6 0 0	Goat	C. q. lb.	8 0 0
	Losh	No.	0 10 0
	Seal	No.	0 1 6
	Sheep	C. q. lb.	2 2 0
	Turkey	No.	0 6 8
2 16 0	Skins { Calf	C. q. lb	
1 2 6		Doz. No	
0 1 2	Fox	No.	
3 2 6	Kid	C. q. lb.	
2 5 0	Lamb	C. q. lb	
1 5 6	Rabbit	C. q. lb.	
0 5 2	Otter	No.	
	Slates	M.	0 6 8
	Snuff	Lb.	0 2 6
1 13 4	Sope	C. q. lb.	1 5 0
	Sope Ashes	C. q. lb.	0 16 8
	Spirits { Brandy	Gall.	0 2 0
	Geneva	Gall.	0 2 0
	Rum	Gall.	0 1 6
1 6 8	Starch	C. q. lb.	0 16 8
Value	Stationary Ware	Value	
	Steel	C. q. lb.	1 5 0
	Stockings { Cotton	Pairs	0 2 8
	Silk	Do.	0 15 0
	Silk and Cotton	Do.	0 7 6
	Silk and Worsted	Do.	0 7 6
doz. prs. 1 5 0	Thread	Do.	0 2 6
do. 1 4 0	Woollen	Do.	0 3 0
do. 2 0 0	Worsted	Do.	0 5 0
	Sword Blades	No.	0 2 0
6 0 0	Cyder	T. H. G.	5 0 0
	Sword-cutlers' Ware	Value	
0 5 0	Shoes	Lb.	
2 0 0	Silk and Worsted mixed Manuf.	Lb. Oz.	
Value	Sadlers' Ware		
	Tar	Barr.	0 12 0
	Tea { Bohea	1 b.	0 2 0
	Green	Lb.	0 6 0
	Tobacco	Lb.	0 0 6
	Tow	C q lb.	1 5 0
	Twine	C q lb.	3 0 0
	Toys	Value	
	Tiles	M.	1 10 0
	Tin	C. q. lb.	3 10 0
2 0 0	Tallow	C q lb.	
0 12 0	Tongues	Doz.	
	Velvet	Lb Oz.	3 0 0
	Vinegar	T H G.	7 15 0

Medium of the present Market Price on Export.			Denominations.			Medium of the present Mark. Price on Import.		
£.	s.	d				£.	s.	d.
	Value		Upholstery Ware	—	The	Value		
			Walnuts and others	—	—	Barr.	0 10	6
			Wax ⎰ Bees'	—	—	Lb.	0 1	0
			Candles	—	—	C. q. lb.	8 10	0
4	0	0	Wax	—	—	C. q. lb.		
			Whalebone	—	—	C. q. lb.	13 0	0
			Wine ⎰ French	—	—	T. H. G.	25 0	0
			Port	—	—	Do.	24 0	0
			Rhenish	—	—	Do.	24 0	0
			Spanish	—	—	Do.	30 0	0
	Value		Wooden Ware	—	—	Value		
			Wood ⎰ Balk	—	—	C. q. lb.	20 0	0
			Barrel Staves	—	—	C. q. lb.	0 5	0
			Canes	—	—	No. M.	5 0	0
			Casks empty	—	—	No.	0 2	6
			Clap Boards	—	—	C. q. No.	6 5	0
			Clap Holt	—	—	C. q. No.	6 5	0
			Deals	—	—	C. q. No.	4 5	0
			Hoops	—	—	M.	2 0	0
			Masts	—	—	No.	2 5	0
			Oars	—	—	C. q. No.	4 5	0
			Plank	—	—	Value		
			Spars	—	—	C. q. No.	3 5	0
			Timber	—	—	T. Feet	2 15	0
			Wainscot	—	—	C. q. No.	20 0	0
			Wool ⎰ Beaver	—	—	Lb.	0 18	0
			Cotton	—	—	C. q. lb.	4 0	0
			Estridge	—	—	C. q. lb.	4 10	0
			Spanish	—	—	C. q. lb.	4 10	0
0	10	0	Wool	—	—	St. lb.		
			Wire - ⎰ Brass	—	—	C. q. lb.	6 0	0
			Iron	—	—	C. q. lb.	2 5	0
			Latten	—	—	C. q. lb	4 0	0
			Steel	—	—	C. q. lb.	7 5	0
0	1	0	Yarn - ⎰ Cable	—	—	C. q. lb	1 12	0
			Cotton	—	—	Lb.	0 1	6
			Grogram	—	—	Lb.	0 2	0
Cwt. 6	0	0	Linen	—	—	Lb.	0 2	0
			Mohair	—	—	Lb.	0 3	0
			Sail	—	—	Lb.	0 0	6
1	10	0	Worsted	—	—	Lb.	0 4	0
0	12	0	Woollen	—	—	St. lb		
	Value		Small Parcels	—	—	Value		

www.ingramcontent.com/pod-product-compliance
Lightning Source LLC
Chambersburg PA
CBHW032314280326
41932CB00009B/803